The Poetry

of

Travelling in the United States

Caroline Gilman

LITERATURE HOUSE / GREGG PRESS

Upper Saddle River, N. J.

Republished in 1970 by
LITERATURE HOUSE
an imprint of The Gregg Press
121 Pleasant Avenue
Upper Saddle River, N. J. 07458

Standard Book Number—8398-0660-4
Library of Congress Card—71-104465

118930

Printed in United States of America

THE

POETRY OF TRAVELLING

IN THE

UNITED STATES.

BY CAROLINE GILMAN.

WITH ADDITIONAL SKETCHES,

BY A FEW FRIENDS ·

AND

A WEEK AMONG AUTOGRAPHS,

BY REV. S. GILMAN.

The Traveller delighteth in the view
Of change and choice, of sundry kind of creatures,
To mark the habits, and to note the hue
Of far-born people, and their sundry natures,
Their shapes, their speech, their gait, their looks, their features.
Breton's Longing of a Blessed Heart.

NEW-YORK:

S. COLMAN, 141 NASSAU STREET.

1838.

NEW YORK:
Printed by SCATCHERD & ADAMS.
No. 38 Gold Street.

THIS WORK

IS GRATEFULLY DEDICATED

TO THOSE INDIVIDUALS, WHOSE HOSPITALITY

MADE TRAVELLING POETICAL,

BY

C. G.

A*

PREFACE.

A WORK of the character here presented to the public carries upon its "very head and front" its own recommendation or its failure. It makes no pretensions to add much weight to the stock of literature. It will prove a sufficient satisfaction to the author, should it be found to give new interest to the valuable department of the pleasant reading of the day. The intention was to present something in the same volume which might prove attractive to both the Northern and Southern reader; to make the book particularly a gratifying and instructive companion to all classes of travellers who circulate through the land, and if it come to this, it will be a source of gratification to the writer, as it is presumed it may be to all who love that land, to find something done, in this manner, to increase a good sympathy between different portions of the country.

CONTENTS.

CONTENTS.

CONTENTS.

NOTES OF A NORTHERN EXCURSION.

NORFOLK, *April* 24, 1836.

> Once more upon the waters! yet once more!
> And the waves bound beneath me as a steed
> That knows his rider."

THE sea, however, was not unto me " like a horse that knows its rider," but rather like an old mule that kicked and jerked backward. Yet let me not say a word against the South Carolina, that bore me from Charleston. She is a " brave ship," and long may she stem the waves in security, transporting happy hearts in her ocean cradle, an emblem of the State whose name she bears. Let me not recal mere physical suffering, nor the wry looks of ladies with soiled night-caps, and the more forlorn aspect of sea-sick men with long beards; it is enough that it was a bright April day when we neared the Chesapeake. How curious are the associations connected with a name! I had been amused in early life with the term Rip Raps; and all the books and newspapers in the world could not divest me of the association of belaboured knuckles, until I saw this odd-looking fortification, and felt that I was gazing on a favorite retreat of the first officer in our country. And Point Com-

1

fort too,—old Point Comfort ; it is a very great piece of simplicity to acknowledge, but I was quite startled with the *uncomfortable* looking guns. Spring was slowly advancing, and it was pleasant to see stripes of green struggling through the discoloured grass on the banks, like a smile on a harsh countenance.

The Marine Hospital is a noble edifice externally, and I learned that it is equally well arranged in its various departments ; but two officers told me that nothing would induce them to avail themselves of its advantages. How extensively this feeling prevails with regard to such establishments ! I learned, for the first time, that there is a tax of two dollars levied on every individual who arrives in this country, whether native or foreigner, for the maintenance of the United States' Navy Hospitals.

Norfolk appeared to me to have been underrated in its appearance ;—however it may be, I enjoyed the good fare at a well-attended hotel, walked in business streets that looked busy, and in retired streets where the hand of taste had not been idle. A beautiful flower, now pressed in my Bible, was gathered for me by a fair hand in a choice greenhouse on Sunday, and I found a noble temple in which to offer up my grateful thanks to God for guiding me thus far. I must stop to give merited praise to the crowded congregation in Bishop Mead's church, for the *oneness* with which they joined in the forms of the Liturgy. They knelt together, rose together, and their voices ascended in religious harmony from the pews with the fine choir above. No individual looked as if the service was for others and not for him.

A polite acquaintance conducted us, on Saturday afternoon, to the Navy Yard and Dry Dock at Gosport. After crossing the ferry we entered Portsmouth, and a little cluster of houses on the right, called *Charleston*, stirred up associations that might well claim a rivalry, insignificant as was the spot, with the noble work of art we were to contemplate.

WASHINGTON, D. C.

I enjoyed beyond description our excursion up the Potomac in the fine steam-boat Columbia. A fresh, pure breeze threw new life into my frame: friends, as agreeable as kind, beguiled the way; and the sun, bright and clear, shone above without exhausting me. The captain of the Columbia has been sailing up and down the river forty years. When asked if his sleepless nights did not injure his health, his reply was, that he became *sick* if he did not keep awake *four* nights in the week, and was actually made so once by sleeping every night for a fortnight.

The shad and herring fisheries produce an animated effect at this season of the year on the Potomac. Nets are thrown out all along for many miles; and the fishermen's huts, with their curling smoke, scattered along the shore, and their skiffs, apparently reposing on the waters, give a

picturesque effect to the scene. Our captain informed us that some of the nets are three miles long ; in
this case the fishermen have to take advantage of
the tide to aid them in drawing them in. The season of fishing lasts but six weeks.

And now Mount Vernon appeared. I had had
dreams, or thoughts like dreams, of this scene from
childhood. My earliest idea was, of a high mountain set apart, where I fancied Washington to have
stood, taller and larger than other men, dictating to
the country. Older fancies came, and I have thrown
the light of imagination round the spot, while his
figure in the front ground grew bright in the contemplation. The place was actually before me now,
and my heart thrilled with the consciousness that he
had stood there, that there his dust reposed, that
there were nurtured those thoughts which made me
politically what I am. I am not given to tears, but
they started to my eyes. I put the world behind
me as a vain thing, and was *alone* with Washington.

We reached the city. I would rather, for my
own taste, have seen the capitol divested of the
dome ; but it is an imposing building, and the more
I look upon it, the more I enjoy its beautiful proportions and its emerald terraces.

And now it is midnight, and I am here. It is
only five days since we bade farewell to Charleston.
A serenade of French horns is sounding before our
residence. I know not how many fair hands are
drawing aside their curtains, for one is as much a

stranger to one's next neighbor in these large establishments as in a crowded city.

I should have said that we passed the evening at the
rooms of one of the members of the House. It was
really amusing to hear the announcement of names
from all quarters of the Union. If any thing can
remove prejudices, it is coming here and seeing this
variety. But prejudice is a tough old knot, and
will not be removed half the time without killing
root and branch too. Here are persons whom I
have not seen for years, with the same little tricks,
graceful or otherwise, of manner: one plays with
his fingers, another rubs his thigh, another feels his
chin, just as he did twenty years ago, and keeps
his likes and dislikes in the same proportion; he is
the same man, too, perhaps, for good and for evil.

Thanks, indeed, for my good fortune. Mr. Clay
speaks to-morrow on the Land Bill. I can scarcely
think of sleep when this prospect is before me—such
a realization of my wishes—indeed, thus has it been
with me since my last final struggle to quit for a
while my quiet home. Blue skies have looked
down, kind hands have been extended, kind hearts
opened, and now in the field of mind I am likely to
reap a rich harvest.

One feels, on leaving the quiet South, passing rapidly on, and entering Washington while Congress
is in session, as if inhaling gas. Any one of the
attractions here would be great singly, but when one
combines the imposing view of the public buildings,
refined and various society, where the play of so-
1*

cial feelings softens the glow of powerful intellect, and the debates, where mind follows mind like wave upon wave, now showing the light foam of dancing billows, now rushing and sparkling like a gathered sea, and swallowing up the less powerful waters; all these things coming suddenly on a retired individual, are for a few days bewildering.

The galleries were crowded to hear Mr. Clay's speech—(many suppose his last.) The Land Bill is a hackneyed theme, and Mr. Clay was oppressed by indisposition; but still I saw the power beneath, with which he has wielded, and will, under other circumstances, still wield the lever of human sympathies. He spoke three hours. There is something as sublime as melancholy to me in the decline of a statesman; and the thought, that a mind which has ruled so many minds should lie by like a severed branch, would be only melancholy, if the doctrine of immortality did not come in and tell of its probable triumphant change hereafter, when the knee shall not tremble, nor the hand be raised to the moist and dizzy brow, nor the voice grow tremulous with age or care. The mind of this great man did not seem to me to be faded. There is the shadow of an eclipse rather over his heart than his intellect, which will, *must* burst forth again and again.

A visit to Washington is certainly imperfect without an introduction to the President. Nothing can be more striking than the gentleness and courtesy of his manner to ladies and youth, contrasted with his energetic will. He pronounced, at our visit, a tender and beautiful eulogium on his late pastor in this city, as being " one of those good trees which were known by their fruits."

The Congressional burying-ground is an interesting place, though not so picturesque as such a spot should be. The monument to Gerry, former Vice-President, is rich ; but there is a *setness* about the long line of tombs of the senators and representatives rather chilling to the eye which associates poetry with the grave. It has been mentioned to me as a favorite idea with some of the members of Congress to make Mount Vernon the Congressional burying-ground ; to erect the great Washington monument there, and remove those which have been raised on the present site. This would indeed be worthy of the noble plans which have already been accomplished in the capitol and its grounds. Whether, however, there is not something more touching in the lonely burial-place of our country's idol, even if its waving trees and natural flowers are not better suited to those deep musings which absorb him who comes to pay his tribute to that shrine, it is difficult to say.

Many laborers are at work on the Congressional burial-ground in this city ; but every thing looks stiff, as if the unconscious occupants there were really placed for show.

> Tomb nods to tomb, each marble has its brother,
> And every monument reflects the other.

In a drive this morning with Colonel —— and his

lady, we saw a solitary grave in the woods; and its
contrast to the studied character of the Congressional burying-ground led my thoughts into the following train:—

THE CONGRESSIONAL BURYING-GROUND,
AND THE WOODLAND GRAVE.

The pomp of death was there,—
The lettered urn, the classic marble rose,
And coldly, in magnificent repose,
Stood out the column fair.

The hand of art was seen
Throwing the wild flowers from the gravelled walk;—
The sweet wild flowers,—that hold their quiet talk
Upon the uncultured green.

And now, perchance, a bird
Hiding amid the trained and scattered trees,
Sent forth his carol on the scentless breeze,—
But they were few I heard.

Did my heart's pulses beat?
And did mine eye o'erflow with sudden tears,
Such as gush up 'mid memories of years,
When humbler graves we meet?

A *humbler* grave I met,
On the Potomac's leafy banks, when May,
Weaving spring flowers, stood out in colors gay,
With her young coronet.

A lonely, nameless grave,
Stretching its length beneath th' o'erarching trees,
Which told a plaintive story, as the breeze
Came their new buds to wave.

But the lone turf was green
As that which gathers o'er more honored forms;
Nor with more harshness had the wintry storms
    Swept o'er that woodland scene.

The flower and springing blade
Looked upward with their young and shining eyes,
And met the sunlight of the happy skies,
    And that low turf arrayed.

And unchecked birds sang out
The chorus of their spring-time jubilee ;—
And gentle happiness it was to me,
    To list their music-shout.

And to that stranger-grave
The tribute of enkindling thoughts, the free
And unbought power of natural sympathy,
    Passing, I sadly gave.

And a religious spell
On that lone mound, by man deserted, rose,—
A conscious presence from on high; which glows
    Not where the worldly dwell,

*　　*　　*　　*　　*　　*

I was surprised to find myself as much interested
in the House as in the Senate. The play of features
is more diversified, the range of passion wider. In
the midst of some eloquent and powerful passages of
Colonel Bell of Tennessee, I saw a lad enter, and
present a bunch of hyacinths to an old gentleman, a
member. If his thoughts did not wander to some
far-off spot, where flowers were tended by young and
loving hands, I know not the language of eyes ; but
while I was romancing, another lad entered, and pour-

ed biscuit enough for a family-supply into the table-drawer of another member, and my speculations were changed.

I am never weary of looking at the capitol, in all its various external and internal arrangements. I give myself eye, ear, and soul even to the most inconsequential debates, and when certain men do rise, I feel such a thrill rush through my heart as makes me feel that enthusiasm belongs not to youth only.

I have considered myself fortunate in hearing a debate mostly from western men, in the senate, on the subject of removing obstructions in the Mississippi; not that there was much eloquence—indeed, the subject did not call for it—but that I witnessed developements of the state feeling, which seems to be growing throughout our country. Oh, that western giant! how it is striding along—all sinew, and nerve, and impulse, like its own rushing river, bearing down obstacles, and treading with its great foot on things heretofore held immoveable.

Washington is not, as I expected, a good place for removing mere state feelings. *My constituents!* the very phrase carries with it a host of local sympathies, perhaps prejudices. I see other great men beside C——— and P——— in the senate, but how is it that when they rise I feel as if the reputation of a father or brother was at stake? I meet in society gentlemen of brilliant minds, and sound thought, and polished manners; but how is it that the Southern delegates seem to me clothed with double interest? The secret is all in state feeling.

I am sorry for this, sorry for the clanship which prevails, for it seems to me that at Washington the Union only, and its great interests, should fill our thoughts ; but thus it is ; and I am carried away by the stream, and a word against Carolina is a personal offence to me.

Amid the clanship, however, there is a general and beautiful courtesy, which in private leads to the happiest results ; a pleasant jest is the very hardest weapon used, and that sparingly. The extreme Northern and Southern members are on terms of the most agreeable intercourse.

A singular, and to me affecting contrast to the general tone and contents of the public buildings here, is presented by the exhibition of the Indian portraits and costumes in the War Department, and the display of mechanical art in the patent office.* It speaks a language of such power, that if one had time to think in Washington, it would afford musing for the day ; but one is hurried away—a debate is to be heard, where some speaker is to move or try to move the nation ; or a party for Mount Vernon are going to steal from this busy scene, and grow pensive over the tomb of Washington, or Georgetown is to be visited, with its institutions ; the Jesuits' college, curious from its calm contrast to this hurrying spot, and the Nunnery, where young voices are tuned to harmony in a quiet so deep that even the ripple of the world's waters is not heard ;

This valuable building has been destroyed by fire.

or mere fashion calls us, with its imperative voice, to look at some new shrine ; or etiquette, still more imperiously forces us from what we *would*, to what we *must* do.

MAY.

The May Day Ball. Nature will not be crushed even at Washington, or rather Carusi, in his brilliant saloon, erected her banner last evening. But Nature *was* crushed, poor thing, at Carusi's, who, with all his art, could not control the immense concourse which pressed to see the Queen of May and her Floras as they passed in procession up the hall. Many a mother's heart leaped as the thought of her absent ones rushed upon her memory while looking on those young flower-crowned brows.

I was glad that I could not hear a word of the addresses, though I stood close to the Queen ; I was glad that the fair crowner, when she unpinned the wreath from her pretty blue cushion that was handed her by a little cupid-boy, clapped the pin in her mouth, though it had not the effect of Demosthenes' pebbles ; I was glad of all this, because it showed that, though the society is necessarily very artificial here, these young creatures were still natural beings. Had the pretty crowner deliberately replaced her pins in the cushion, and spoken oratorically, I should not have loved her half so well. The May day ball gives an interesting view of Washington. Every lady in the city is invited, and every gentleman may attend by purchasing a ticket for a small sum. What a mixture of emotions are swelling in such a crowd! I met a friend of my youth unexpectedly. She kissed me with sudden impulse, and there was a struggle with her tears. An Indian passed us—not perhaps,

"A man without a tear,"

for he was dressed in the costume of civilization, except a brilliant belt of bead-work, that told us what he had been.

"The stoic of the woods"

had become a Washington beau.

Almost the first small sleeves that have been seen in America for seven years appeared at Carusi's, on the person of a Virginia lady, who has been to France. What a sensation! There was half a shudder among the company as they felt the immense sacks on their arms, contrasted with those new sleeves without one relieving plait, tight—tight as a suit of armour, from the shoulder to the elbow. A pair of black mits were on the arm, which rendered the novelty more striking from the contrast in colour, the dress being white.

Both Houses have adjourned to-day on account of the death of Gov. Manning, one of our representatives. This adjournment gives one an opportunity for long and delicious conversations with various visitors. How delightfully the great men here pour out their social and home feelings, if I may use the term. Being really at home themselves, they give a peculiar charm to a stranger's intercourse.

2

I am alternately attracted by the deep running stream of political thought in one, the playful, fanciful sallies of another, and the calm, dignified, affectionate manners of others from different quarters of our country.

I attend the debates, I flatter myself, with right views ; not with an eager curiosity to hear this or that man, a desire perhaps subdued by private intercourse, which furnishes a richer knowledge of characters and minds ; not with a nervous anxiety about any particular question ; but, gazing on the great stream of things, I watch, with almost equal interest, the leaf that is floating down the tide, and the mighty bark laden with thought and power. The Houses are like a vast map, on which, though there be small as well as large cities laid down, they are inhabited by human beings, who belong to the whole family of our country, and the spot which now seems insignificant may be destined, in the many commercial and political changes to which we are incident, to be "a great people." Such, too, may be the varied destinies of the minds and the topics brought together here.

To a feminine glance, the Navy Yard at Washington is more attractive than at Gosport, from its neat and tasteful arrangement. There is something in visiting a great war-vessel that fills my mind for a long time. It is a perfect poem, from its first giant arrangement on the stocks, until it is sent forth to its intended work of destruction, a miniature floating world. The Columbia, now fitting out at the Washington Navy Yard, and carrying fifty-four guns, is less in dimensions and power than the Virginia at Norfolk or the Pennsylvania at Philadelphia. I was glad of an opportunity of visiting her with an experienced and intelligent officer. She is finished but not furnished, and the eye therefore is not deceived by attractive decorations, but takes in her immense capacity, in all its apparent simplicity, but actually consummate art. The armoury in the yard is as prettily arranged as a lady's boudoir, and it presents a curious association of thought to see such deadly weapons of destruction a matter of tasteful exhibition.

All the iron work for the United States' Navy is made in this yard. The steam apparatus is wonderfully simple and beautiful. I watched the operation of moulding the red-hot iron with those huge trap-hammers; and as my head was full of Congress at the time, I likened the heated and flashing iron to the members, excited in debate, when down comes upon them, in some powerful mind, a trap-hammer of legislation, and shivers and moulds them at its will.

There are a few trophies here of considerable interest; two brass cannon, taken at Tripoli, on the grounds; a lion, the figure-head from the Macedonia in the armoury, and others which I forget.

Mr. Clay and Mr. Walker of Mississippi have had some sparring. Mr. Clay was excited, and in ten minutes showed more of character, and withering satirical power than in his whole speech on the Land Bill. I could scarcely realize that he was the calm speaker who dwelt so long on argumentative illustrations and numerical details. The shake of his arm was like Jupiter's ; and the repetition of some single word, for which he has long been distinguished, was singularly effective.

To-day I attended a religious service at the capitol. The waves of the world had rolled off; even the echo of a stormy debate of the preceding day on the frontier appropriation bill had died away, and we were left, amid that beautiful hall, with its lofty pillars and arching dome, to commune with the Deity. The congregation sat in the seats of the members. Many persons remark that their attention is distracted by the associations of the place ; but to me, who have yet a lingering touch of enthusiasm, the solemnity was rather enhanced by them. I felt what the Sabbath is ; how it comes in like some messenger of love, throwing a curtain over sleeping care, or lighting up a torch to animate our future way. Mr. Higby, the officiating chaplain, is an earnest, dignified speaker. " Now is the day of our salvation," was his theme ; and he is not answerable, if we who heard him did not look far down into our own hearts, and avail ourselves of the " accepted time." The service of the Episcopal Church was read. A distinguished senator from the south-west appeared to be intently studying his prayer-book until the service commenced, and afterwards joined loudly in the responses. His air was extremely devotional. I should judge him to be a real lover of the Liturgy.

I have seen nothing more curious than the contrast in appearance between certain two prominent aspirants for the Presidential chair. They look as if they belonged to different worlds. The one, with his floating gray hair claims the epithet venerable,—perhaps neither of the candidates would be satisfied with that term.

This evening an Indian came to an officer at our lodgings on business. We clustered round him. He was a Chief of the Chippewa tribe from Michigan, dressed in a rich and becoming costume, with broad silver belts round his arms and wrists, large, glittering silver ear-rings, and scarlet trimmings. He has recently returned from England. He went out with six of his tribe, and three died of the small-pox, among them his wife and nephew. He told us that she was buried in London, and that a grave-stone with her name was there. He came to Washington to negotiate about the lands of his tribe. Some of our party asked if he was going to move westward. " Cut head off first," was his reply ; and he laughed so long and loud, that it was painful to hear him.

The chief topic of interest in the senate to-day was the memorial from Philadelphia, requesting Congress to acknowledge, at as early a period as possible, the independence of Texas ; and this brought out a varied play of character in the ardent Preston, the dignified Webster, Judge Porter of Louisiana with his keen and happy humour, Mr. *** with his old combination of set words and high-flown figures, and Mr. Buchanan and Mr. Shepley, with less striking characteristics, but still all marked.

2*

In the House was a discussion of the Exploring Expedition, in which Reynolds has been so long interested. I consider myself happy in having heard Mr. Phillips of Massachusetts, in a lucid and elegant speech, in which he dwelt with great eloquence on the character of the merchant.

MOUNT VERNON.

THE fashionable world of Washington were rolling off to the race-course on the 10th of May, when we started for Mount Vernon. The sky was clear, and nature in her happiest spring garments. The road from Washington to Alexandria is in good order, but the scenery not particularly attractive. I think the distance is nine miles. No one wishes to linger at Alexandria, except he should meet, as we did, an old resident who can defend warmly what is defensible, and show the few interesting objects to be seen ; indeed, it is a curious step from Alexandria to Mount Vernon ; the one teeming with the most worldly associations, and the other sacred to the highest feelings of our nature.

The road to Mount Vernon from Alexandria is intolerably bad, and no one probably passes it without thinking *before he arrives,* that he has paid too dear for his whistle ; but once place your foot on that mount, and if a spark of sensibility is within you, it begins to kindle ; and as you tread on the walks which Washington planned, as you gaze on the waters of the Potomac, where his eye often reposed, as you note the green-house where his noble

mind loved to rest with nature after its toils, as you
see the books in his library, (that spot which brings
one mind so near to another,) and remember that his
hand turned the pages of that history for information, or that Bible for comfort, as you see the christ-
ening bowl over which his name was probably pronounced, and his young spirit dedicated to God, and
then turn to the spot where rest his remains, and
fancy that spirit matured, glorified, a partner of angels, a glow, such as is only known in a few precious
golden moments of existence, is felt rushing over
your soul, touching an electric chain from the far
past to the endless future.

And yet sadness follows, for decay is on that spot ;
the summer house is a ruin, and the rest of the establishment would be, did not some members of the
family, at a considerable sacrifice of time and expense, reside there a few months of the year, to preserve it from the depredations of *visiters* and natural
decay. The soil is too unproductive to render the
place an object of pecuniary consideration.

The dwelling-house had originally four small rooms
on a floor, but General Washington added a dining
hall of handsome dimensions and finish. Too much
of the old furniture is removed ; it would have been
in good taste to have allowed at least one room to
remain as it was at his death. I wish Congress
would superintend the spot, and by requests and re-
wards get back as much as possible of what was
once there.

I have conversed with several of the Washington

statesmen about Mount Vernon. One seemed to think it might be bought if the family did not *ask too much for it*, and be kept as a kind of national show, and support itself! One was for having it the Congressional burying-ground, with the proposed monument towering on its heights. One thought it should remain in the family of Washington while the name lasts, and that Congress should make an appropriation for its preservation, and appoint keepers to superintend it, but most of them shake their heads, and think that nothing can be done *just now*. Oh, what a burning indignation will be felt by and by against this generation, when that summer-house which Washington erected, does totter to the ground, when that green-house no longer presents a relic of his taste, when those walks where his feet trod are covered with the wild grass, and the walls which sheltered him, decay and fall.

Any stranger can visit the ground :—to see the dwelling-house, you must send in a card, and a letter of introduction of course is necesary for an admission to the family. Nothing could be more courteous than our reception ; and the gentle, and graceful, and dignified lady who presides there, mingles happily in our associations with the memory of him who has sanctified the scene.

*   *   *   *   *

Washington private parties are like all others. Delightful conversation is interrupted by delightful music, and delightful music drowned by delightful conversation, so that neither can be enjoyed ; just as

one begins to feel the mental pulse of a great man,
another is brought to be introduced ; just as you are
scanning the pretty face of a belle, or the stronger
features of a blue, the throng drives and sunders you ;
now and then a roar of laughter from some quarter
tells you that a joke is going on, which you are too
far off to hear, and as you see the ice-cream just
within your reach, it is whirled away : when the Babel sounds are at their height, you wonder why you
have nothing to say, and on looking round find many
just as idle starers :—you begin to think of home,
and a rocking-chair, and repose, and so good-night
and away.

But the charm of Washington is its small parties ;
there mind pours itself out in its beautiful and strong
varieties.　No lassitude is felt, for the ever-flowing
wave of novelty brings its daily supplies, refreshing
and adding to the soil of thought.　I may sometimes have been disappointed at the Capitol, sometimes in mixed society, but never in social intercourse ; and it is worth a pilgrimage to hear the
rich, dispassionate flow of talk in ***, whose elegant
mind misfortune has touched but not broken ; the
varied, illustrative, classical, playful strain of ***,
whose heart is on his lips, but whose heart never so
far precedes his head as not to show you how *long*
that is ; with the deep reflecting views of ***, who
forces you to think, and who seems to have an intellectual diving-bell, with which he looks clearly
at objects not even seen by the common eye.　Then
there is our Irish senator, the Congressional Demo-

critus, whose jests in private are sunbeams, but
in the senate chamber are to his opponents sunbeams radiating from steel—these, and many more,
infuse a life into conversation untouched in variety
elsewhere.   I am absolutely jealous at a large
Washington party, of the intellectual waste ; not so
in small circles, where mind acts directly on mind,
and every thought is treasured.

BALTIMORE.

Washington is behind us—its beautiful Capitol,
on which the eye lingers in unsated admiration, has
faded away ; as we leave it the heart is· full—the
mind is full.   Great and elevating scenes, farewell ;
new and tender friends, farewell ; a stranger has
fed on your thousand flowers, and has borne away
the hive of memory, overflowing with honied stores !

As we entered the rail-road car, an old man took
his seat in front of us, dressed in homespun, with a
miserable hat, sun-burnt face, a *chaw* of tobacco in
his mouth, and two soiled bundles in his hand.   I
shrank instinctively from the contact, and dreaded two
hours' intercourse with such a low-looking creature ;
it even occurred to me that there ought to be a separate car for well and ill-dressed people.   After a
while he took out an old leather pocket-book, and
among a few other loose papers, unfolded one which
had the seal and signature of Lewis Cass ; and as
my eye ran over the plain printing, I perceived that
it was the pension certificate of Edward Dennis of
Maryland, *a revolutionary soldier.*   What a change

came over him! There was the difference to me in his countenance of Moses when he ascended and descended the mount—a glory was around him!

The old man turned the paper over and over, read it and re-read it. He wanted sympathy.

" This is worth a long journey," said he at length, showing it to a passenger near him ; " four hundred dollars down, and eighty dollars a-year, for a man seventy-eight years old ;" and he took out the bills from the pocket-book, and a large handful of General Jackson's shiners from his waistcoat.

I longed to give him my purse to put his money in, but was ashamed ; my hand was on it, but I drew it back ; it will look too sentimental, I thought.

" Why have you not applied for a pension before ?" said the passenger to whom he had showed the bond.

The old man smiled. " Because I didn't want it. You wouldn't have had me ask for it 'till I wanted it, would ye ?"

A gentleman, whose name, if I dared to give it, would lend a new interest to this little narrative, a New England man, but one who takes a deep interest in the South, was reading. I whispered to him the character of our fellow-traveller, and he laid down his book.

After a while the old man took it up and read, without glasses, two or three pages with apparent interest.

" How much might you have given for this book ?" said he to the owner.

" I shall think it a cheap purchase," was the reply, " if an old soldier of the Revolution will accept
it ;" and taking out his pencil, he wrote—

" *Presented to Edward Dennis, a soldier of the
Revolution, by one who is now reaping the fruits of
his bravery.*"

The old man smiled as he received the book,
turned it, looked at its cover, then within ; and taking the pencil from the hand of the giver, wrote in
fair characters the name which he saw on the first
leaf. But after all he could not realise that it was
a gift, and, as his pockets were overflowing, he took
out a dollar.

" No, no, my good friend," said the giver, " put
it up ;" and in a lower voice added, " don't you show
your money to any body again but your wife."

" No more I wont," said the old man understand-
ingly.

Repeatedly, during the excursion, he gave the
book, inside and outside, the same long, pleased look
with which he had received it.

We reached Baltimore on its noble rail-road,
when one, whose elegant and varied conversation
had made two hours seem as moments, and the old
soldier, with his treasure, went on their opposite
ways.

One cannot but be struck, coming from the South,
with the appearance of the bricks in this noble and
growing city. The texture is as fine and smooth as
plaster of Paris, and the colour has peculiar freshness. The prevailing idea of English travellers be-

gins to strike me of how *new* every thing looks. The square on which the Washington Monument is erected, will be an ornament of which the Baltimoreans may be proud. The fountains should be an object of imitation in our more Southern cities; the very sound is refreshing; and I loved to see the thirsty and weary go down the marble steps and enjoy the common though priceless blessing of a draught of water. The fountain in Calvert street is picturesque. Over it is a temple of classic proportions, and behind it a grassy spot, shaded with trees, where children find a cool retreat. At one of the markets, and perhaps at others, is a fountain perpetually flowing, which, though not particularly ornamental, has a pure and cooling aspect, and is particularly useful in that location.

I attended Vespers at St. Mary's Chapel, which is connected with the College. The building is small, but exquisitely proportioned in the Gothic style. The Cathedral may be to others more gorgeous and imposing, but give me St. Mary's Chapel. We entered as the last glories of the setting sun, shining through the Gothic windows, revealed its fair proportions. Several young girls went one by one to confession, while a priest dressed the altar with natural flowers. Then rose the Vesper hymn. Beautiful temple! the differing forms which guide my spiritual worship, did not prevent me from joining in the hymn which rose to the Deity in that sunset hour, beneath thy arch.

The Cathedral did not satisfy me. My imagina-

3

tion is too busy with its fancies of the gorgeousness
of European churches. The very word Cathedral
brings thoughts to my mind that America cannot
realize. The Independent Church, on the contrary,
from the usual simplicity of that denomination, surprised me by its elaborate workmanship. Yet the
Cathedral is really magnificent to an eye accustomed to the plain churches of America. The decorations are rich, and the dimensions imposing. I was
somewhat disappointed in the pictures; only one of
them equalled my expectations, though I say this with
no pretensions high to connoisseurship. I know
more than one friend in Charleston who would have
given anything for the beautiful natural tulips that decorated the altars. The temptation was strong to
have stolen and sent them a bunch or two, and to
make one's confession afterward.

The ruins occasioned by the mob are still visible
here, a sad degrading relic of human passion. When
we count up our blessings further South, let our ex-
emption from this evil never be forgotten.

A rainy day has given me an opportunity of
looking over a well-filled private library. I do not
own the old British poets, and therefore seize on
them when an opportunity occurs. I cannot re-
frain from copying the following lines from Byrom,
a poet born in 1691, and commending them equally to
the sedentary occupant of a rocking-chair, the busy
housewife, or the curious traveller. They speak of
truth and duty to all, and I would advise the young to
commit them to memory.

ARMELLE NICHOLAS'S ACCOUNT OF HERSELF.

(Selected from the Poems of John Byrom.)

To the God of my love, in the morning, said she,
Like a child to its parent when waking I flee;
With a longing to serve him, and please him, I rise,
And before him kneel down, as if seen by his eyes:
I resign myself up to his absolute will,
Which I beg that in me he would always fulfil;
That the prayers of the day, by whomever preferred,
For the good of each soul, may be also thus heard.

If obliged to attend to some household affair,
I have scarce so much time as to say the Lord's prayer.
This gives me no trouble; my dutiful part
Is obedience to him, whom I have at my heart,
As well at my work, as retiring to pray,
And his love does not suffer in mine a decay;
He has taught me himself, that a work which I do
For his sake, is a prayer very real and true.

I dress in his presence, and learn to confess
That his provident kindness supplies me with dress;
In the midst of all outward employment I find
A conversing with him of an intimate kind:
How sweet is the labour! his loving regard
So supporting one's mind, that it thinks nothing hard;
While the limbs are at work, in the seeking to please
So belov'd a companion the mind is at ease.

In his presence I eat, and I drink, and reflect
How food of his gift is the growing effect;
How his love to my soul is so great, and so good,
Just as if it were fed with his own flesh and blood;
What a virtue this feeder—his meat and his drink—
Has to kindle one's heart, I must leave you to think;
He alone can express it, no language of mine,
Were my life spent in speaking, could ever define.

When, perhaps by bad usage, or weariness prest,
I myself am too apt to be fretful at best,
Love shows me, forthwith, how I ought to take heed
Not to nurse the least anger by word or by deed;
And he sets such a watch at the door of my lips,
That of hasty cross words there is nothing that slips;
Such irregular passions as seek to surprise,
Are crushed and are conquered as soon as they rise.

Or if e'er I give place to a humour so bad,
My mind has no rest till forgiveness be had ;
I confess all my faults, as if he had not known,
And my peace is renewed by a goodness his own,
In a manner so free, as if after my sin,
More strongly confirmed than before it had been ;
By a mercy so tender my heart is reclaimed,
And the more to love him by its failing inflamed.

Sometimes I perceive that he hideth his face,
And I seem like a person deprived of his grace,
Then I say—'Tis no matter, altho' thou conceal
Thyself as thou pleasest, I'll keep to my zeal ;
I'll love thee, and serve thee, however this rod
May be sent to chastise, for I know thou art God,
And with more circumspection I stand upon guard,
Till of such a great blessing no longer debarred.

But suff'ring so deep having taught me to try
What I am in my self-hood, I learn to rely
More firmly on him who was pleased to endure
The severest extremes, to make way for our cure:
To conform to his pattern, as love shall see fit,
My faith in the Saviour resolves to submit;
For no more than myself (if the word may go free)
Can live without him, can he help loving me.

Well assured of his goodness, I pass the whole day,
And my work, hard or easy, is felt as a play ;

I am thankful in feelings, but pleasure or smart,
It is rather himself that I love in my heart.
When they urge me to mirth, I think, O ! were it known,
How I meet the best company when I'm alone!
To my dear fellow-creatures, what ties me each hour,
Is the love of my God to the best of my power.

At the hour of night when I go to my rest,
I repose on his love like a child at the breast;
And a sweet peaceful silence invites me to keep
Contemplating him, to my dropping asleep:
Many times a good thought, by its gentle delight,
Has withheld me from sleep a good part of the night,
In adoring his love, that continues to share
To a poor wretched creature, so special a care.

This, after my heart was converted at last,
Is the life I have led for these twenty years past :
My love is not changed, and my innermost peace,
Tho' it ever seemed full, has gone on to increase.
'Tis an infinite love that has filled me, and fed
My still rising hunger to eat of its bread,
So satisfied still, as if such an excess
Could have nothing more added than what I possess.

No one should leave Baltimore without a tribute to Page's admirable hotel; next to the private, domestic kindness which fell to our happy share, I should commemorate Page's.

As I parted from Baltimore, I felt a desire to know more of the place, and of the intelligent minds that direct its growing powers.

PHILADELPHIA.

There is nothing particularly interesting in the
route to Philadelphia ; one passes along in the luxurious ease of steam travelling, scarcely sensible on
the level way of any transition.   One interesting human object attracted me in the boat,—a Quaker lady
of the old school.   Her cheerful and intelligent look
and conversation, her peculiar attire, and, more than
all, her benevolent smile, drew my attention.   By
a curious likeness, however, this Quakeress of sixty
years, in her drab silk and close hat, was associated
in my mind with the belle at Washington—their
sleeves and mits were cut in precisely the same manner ; thus fashion turns round the wheel, and causes
extremes to meet.

I missed the lofty forest trees of South Carolina
in Maryland and Delaware, and there is on the mail
route, at present, no well-stored farms or attractive
country-seats to supply the deficiency.   There is an
air of sterility in the soil, and no clustering vine or
waving moss conceals it with its graceful drapery.

Pennsylvania was attained.   I cast, in passing, an
enthusiastic glance at the waters of the Susquehanna,
and dreams of Wyoming, and snatches of Campbell's
exquisite poem, rushed across my thoughts.

The pictures along the way gradually brightened,
the beautiful city of friends appeared.   It was no
mere *name.*   The welcome hand of friendship *was* extended as we stept on its busy wharves.

My first curiosity, when I enter a new city, is to
see what supports and characterises it.   At Wash-

ington, I looked for statesmen; at Alexandria I
sought not, my olfactory nerves at once pronounced
fish to be the great commercial lever; at Baltimore,
I visited the Roman Catholic institutions; when I
go to Lynn, in Massachusetts, I shall ask for shoes
—at Wethersfield, Connecticut, I shall feel bound,
though I abhor them, to taste onions; of course, at
Philadelphia my first inquiry was for Quakers and
Schuylkill water.

And delightful it was to me to see the Quakers.
I involuntarily changed my Southern gait to a
shorter and trimmer step, I squared my shoulders,
and kept my countenance straight forward; I did
more, I looked into my heart, and asked if that was
pure; I laid closer over it the folds of humility; I
brushed away the dust of worldliness, I sheathed the
weapons of carnal passions, and put on spiritual garments. And in the same spirit, after a draught of
pure water, rendered more delicious by the ice of the
Schuylkill, I visited Fair Mount,* and rejoiced like
another Undine in its waterfalls and fountains, and
felt how the river was like God's spirit, spreading
somewhere at first in unattainable beauty, then carried through the dark channels of human life, seemingly lost until man inquires and strives for it, and
then breaking out in new modifications, pouring its
blessings on all who ask, and they are glad.

* At this spot is the reservoir which furnishes all the inhabitants of the city with water in the second stories of their buildings

I am most grateful for beauty in all its forms. Had I been carried blindfold to the machinery at Fair Mount, and then permitted to behold it alone, I should have been agreeably excited by its singular combination of simplicity and power; its wheels would have rolled on awhile in my memory, I should have paid the usual tribute of wonder to man's ingenuity, and have dreamt of those iron arms that seem so human in their operations ; but now that I have gazed on the placid river, marked the shaded green of its beautiful borders, seen the sculptured images awaking graceful associations, stood by the clear basin and felt a longing like youth to rush in and stand under its showery fountain, heard the roar of the giant Art contending with and counteracting the giant Nature, climbed the precipitous eminence, and watched the setting sun throwing his golden smile on all, this leaves a deeper stamp—the stamp of the beautiful ; and as I feel now the cool elements on my hands, or taste its freshness, I am carried back to that scene on the Schuylkill.

My knowledge of Wm. Penn is just awakened ; to be sure I have seen him in geographies and histories, or rather, I have seen a coat with stiff skirts and a broad-brimmed hat ; but now the spirit of Wm. Penn is around and above me, not divested, I confess, of the hat and coat ; he is still a Quaker, but colossal, and the skirts of his drab garment sweep over this great city.

The Philadelphians are now ornamenting public squares laid out by him, so distant from the original seat of business, that none but his prophetic mind could have dared to stretch so far : and yet population has reached them, and in a year or two their shade will refresh and beautify the bustling scene.

I cannot but regret the deficiency of public walks in Charleston.   Is it not possible, before the spirit of utility (if utility has a spirit) claims every thing for her own in our fair city, to appropriate in various parts of it some spots to verdure and shade, where our children can revel amidst glimpses of nature, instead of struggling through King-Street for sugar-plums and ice-creams ?   Our City Square, perfect as it is, is limited, and too public.   We want our Battery enlarged, shaded, and decorated.   It has all the elements of natural beauty.   The avenue from Broad Street might be rendered picturesque, and a lot appropriated there for a public square.   Mazyckboro' affords points of great attraction, but a stroke from the stiff skirt of Wm. Penn has just touched my fingers, and reminds me that I am a humble, inquiring traveller, and not a dictator at home.*

Water is a delicious element, but man wants something else ; so I went to the Mint, to see that which cannot, however, always command the precious element.   This is a perfectly Philadelphian building, so chaste and elegant.   I felt at first, when I saw the steam machines spitting out their gold and silver

---

* These suggestions have been already anticipated by the City Council of Charleston, who are adopting measures to have them sooner or later realized.

coins, somewhat of the same elasticity and glee that I did at the exploits of the Water Goddess at Fair Mount. Creation is the charm, whether it be of an atom or a mountain.

But one turns moralist very rapidly over bushels of silver and gold which one cannot touch. Divers forgotten texts of the Psalmist came to my memory, and I walked down the steps, as Colderige says "an altered man."

On the banks of the river is a garden called Lemon Hill, which the proprietor has loaned for charitable purposes for a year. It is fancifully arranged, though going to decay; a cavern,—a grotto,—summer houses,—seats formed in trees, &c. lend an agreeable variety to the scene. A carved *modern* Cerberus, which is a dog with one head instead of fifty or three, guards the cave; within the grotto is a cool spring; the arbors are gay with flowers, the walks smooth and shady; the views from the mansion picturesque; and when one has done with reverie, or sentiment, or abuse, or whatever may be the calling of his *intellectual* nature, his outer man may be refreshed with ice-creams and cakes, in rooms comfortably arranged, small ones for the few to pour out their social communings, or more capacious ones for the many to gaze and speculate. If the traveller should be asked to dine in the city, and half forgetting the good cheer, be carried away by high and exciting discussion with some full fraught minds, and wish to come down gently to his common level, let him go with a friend to the sparkling beauties of

Fair Mount, or the retirement of Lemon Garden, and come home cooled and refreshed to his Mocha or Souchong.

I had an odd sensation in visiting the Pennsylvania Hospital, that Pool of Bethesda, where Charity stands to heal the suffering, and where the unfortunate subjects of insanity are treated with so much humanity, skill, and success. I fancied that every body was crazy. The sober and polite gentleman who superintends the medical library, the respectable and willing attendant who showed us the building, and the visiters fresh from the every-day affairs of Chesnut-Street, or the Exchange, were objects of suspicion to me. I half shrank when they approached me. I am not aware whether this is a common feeling.

The patients are wisely kept from observation; a few of the gentle and happy only go at large. A passing glance is enough to tell the inquirer that all must be right in this institution, as far as human sagacity can plan, and that the poor victims of the sad infliction of insanity are every way more comfortable than when subjected to the irregular habits of home. I was allowed to look into the room of a Frenchman, whose sole comfort is in reading and writing. He has a collection of favorite books, and thrusts his writings upon us.

As we were going through the kitchen, the neatness of which is remarkable, my attention was arrested by a smiling looking personage, who was boasting that he had just crossed the Red Sea with the Israelites; as we passed him, he took off his hat,

and said, bowing profoundly, "the ladies were allowed to go over first."

The insane are to be moved to a building devoted
exclusively to them.   Every thing is as exact and
neat in the apartments of the sick, as if affection
had trodden with gentle footsteps around the sufferers and smoothed their pillows.   I left the spot with
a full heart, and felt that I had been to the gate of
the temple which should be called Beautiful.

The scene changes now, and I am at the Deaf and
Dumb Asylum, where the "unruly member," that
riots in a Lunatic Hospital, is chained.   These are
institutions which vitally affect the human race;
the moralist may own with a sigh the inutility of
teachings which, as youth never learns but from experience, affect only individuals, and cannot reform
a world; but these practical efforts are seen and felt
throughout the constitution of society.   Five girls,
and an equal number of boys, were exercised in trans-
ferring each other's thoughts, conveyed by motions
of the hands, to the black board; the ease with which
they communicate their ideas, the accuracy of the
spelling, even the variations of expression, while all
retain the same thought, the rapidity with which
they conjugate verbs, compare adjectives, &c. &c.,
are singularly interesting; and the kindness with
which they aid each other when they detect inaccu-
racies, was not lost on one, who, like me, considers
an affectionate impulse of the heart worth all intellectual treasures.   We visited the sewing hall, which
was lined with happy faces, the girls being employed

in making various useful articles. This was presided over by a Quaker lady, whose pure and placid
expression seemed a guarantee to the happiness of
the pupils. Placed among the girls, and apparently
a pet, was a grandson of Jefferson, a boy of great
beauty and vivacity, about six years of age.

The shoe-making establishment is large, and many
boys were industriously occupied in it. Two rooms
of instruction are well provided with pictures, charts,
and different objects adapted to enlarge the knowledge of the pupils, and give accurate notions of general things ; for instance, small phials containing various kinds of grain, rice, camphor, &c. &c. Then
there were shells, minerals, a chemical apparatus, and
other things necessary for more advanced instruction.
One of the pupils made four years since a little
steam engine, which is heated by spirits of wine ;
a track is laid on the floor of two rooms, and the
Lilliputian affair—

Walks o'er the rail-way like a thing of life.

Nothing can exceed the rapture of the young
spectators as with increasing velocity it darts by
with its little hiss and splutter. I half longed to attach a car full of dolls to it ; I entered far more into the spirit of its size than into its more important
associations. Most of the floors and stairs of the
Asylum are of stone, as security against fire ; what
boards there are, are exquisitely white, and the kitchen
is, in neatness, the queen of kitchens.

But a more affecting sight to me was the Institu-

4

tion for the Blind.   There was no public exhibition, but a private visit, with an order from a superintendant, furnished us with a much more favorable view. When I think of those sightless orbs, I can hardly realize that my name, which I now see so neatly printed, together with the watch-guard round my neck, in which I can detect no false stitch, is their work.   After we entered, the teacher asked if I would like to have my name printed ; on my answering in the affirmative, he called Mary Ann !   A very pleasing looking girl of fifteen groped her way easily to the table, where the box of blocks was placed ; the letters are pricked, not colored.   While Mary Ann was forming my name, she held a kind of converse with the blocks, now jesting, now scolding if the right letter did not meet her touch, but all in a low, pleasant tone.   The name was completed without mistake in a few minutes.   A little boy spelt at my request, and Mary Ann was next called to read a chapter from one of the Gospels in raised letters. She reads rapidly, but no oratorical tone has ever fallen with such power on my ears as the words of Jesus from the lips of that blind girl.   The teacher then gave out arithmetical questions of great difficulty, which he himself worked on the black-board. Nothing could be more earnest or ambitious than the air with which they went to work to calculate, or the look of triumph assumed by those who were the quickest or the most successful.   At this period their music master came.   There was great eagerness and interest in their manner, and many a sly joke was whispered.   They began with a German chorus, each part nobly sustained, the girls remaining in one room and boys in the other.   I had been carried along by the variety and interest of the scene up to this point, not a little aided by the vivacity, even drollery. which characterized the manners of many of the girls; but now that their countenances were fixed, their sightless orbs mostly turned upward, and their voices swelling in a rich concert of praise and thanksgiving, my tears could not be restrained; fortunately the air ceased, and one of Mary Ann's slily whispered jokes restored me to self-possession.   After the German, followed several English airs, which again were succeeded by instrumental music, combining violins, clarionets, flutes, horns, bassoon, bass viol, forming in all a really grand concert.   The music being over, the girls separated, and we visited the sewing apartment, where they began to collect, going unaided to their various occupations, making rugs, straw baskets, watch-guards, bead-bags, &c. &c. As we descended to another room, we found Mary Ann at an elegant harp, which has lately been presented to the Institution by a Philadelphian.   She was very shy, but consented to give us her first tune; another young lady played on the piano-forte.

A singular thing occurred lately in the Institution, which, as it was told me, a *stranger*, without reservation, I may relate.   A young man and girl, both blind, having become attached to each other, went out of town secretly, unaccompanied, and applied to a clergyman to marry them.   The youth was very prepossessing in his appearance. and the minister was for a little while deceived. At length his suspicions being roused, he said, "You are blind." It could not be denied ; and looking beneath the young lady's bonnet, he found her in the same predicament, and of course declined uniting them. They were sent from the Institution. The capacious building which is now in progress, will probably separate the different sexes more effectually ; but Love, though blind, has never yet been prevented from finding hearts.

The Exchange is a building, imposing in size and beautiful in architecture. The ceiling is in fresco, a new embellishment in our country, but a perfect substitute for carving. I could not appreciate the business-advantages of the spot, but I prayed in my heart that the upright spirit of Wm. Penn might be nurtured in the thousands who tread that marble pavement, softening the hard hand of thrift, enlarging cunning's crafty eye, and blending the just with the essential.

I was invited by the venerable and urbane Librarian of the American Philosophical Society to visit the rooms of that Institution. Among other attractive objects, a Carolinian's attention will be arrested by the Mexican relics presented by our fellow-citizen, Joel R. Poinsett, Esq. forming as they do a conspicuous group. One of the most interesting things to me is a likeness of William Penn before he became a Quaker, dressed in the fashion of the time ; but *Franklin* is the presiding genius there.

I felt this as I sat in his chair, gazed on his mild
countenance in the various revelations of the artist,
and read his hand-writing, carrying as it does in
every line the impress of his mind. State interests
will probably preclude any great literary or scientific rallying-point from being established in our
Union; but this Society, from its central position and
its connexion with the memory of Franklin, will perhaps long lay the highest claim to that honor. At
the suggestion of a celebrated female foreigner, the
Librarian keeps a book where literary or other distinguished visiters insert their names.

Not the least attractive part of the intellectual feast
in visiting the Society's rooms is the cheerful old
age of its venerable Librarian. I confess my thoughts
often wandered from the curious and exciting objects
around me, and dwelt on one whose intellectual "sun,
or light, or moon, or stars," at this advanced period
of existence, is not darkened. Still may "the silver
cord" of his life be strong, and the "golden bowl"
unbroken. When we see such usefulness and philanthropy, we do not feel that "all is vanity."

I have attended St. Stephen's, the St. Michael's
of this city, an expression that may imply somewhat
of aristocracy mingled with piety. Here the ideal
of Episcopalianism is embodied, where *form*, in its
most perfect and approved modes, leads the worshipper to the Deity; where the carved columns give
classic grace to the temple; where the delicately
shaded light streams through the stained Gothic
windows, where is read the studied Liturgy, the re-

4*

sult of thinking minds for successive years; where the organ rises in architectural grandeur, and scientific voices are trained to praise; where fashion treads with elastic step in floating veils and glowing flowers; and the gay and the great, as well as the poor and unhappy, go to bow body and soul before the decorated shrine.

I have attended the Independent Church, where the simple and the elegant combine in architecture, where are heard reasonings, which crown the spiritual heights of man's intellectual dominion, and appeals which search the hidden depths of his nature; where the throng come to listen and to admire,—perchance to feel and resolve; and I trust, with God's blessing, to repent and improve.

And I have attended a Quaker's meeting. "Oh, when the spirit is sore fretted," says the eloquent Charles Lamb, "even tired to sickness of the janglings and nonsense-voices of the world, what a balm and solace it is to go and seat yourself, for a quiet half hour, upon some undisputed corner of a bench among the gentle Quakers! Their garb and stillness conjoined, present an uniformity, tranquil and herd-like—as in a pasture — 'forty feeding like one.' Wouldst thou be alone, and yet accompanied; solitary, yet not desolate; a unit in aggregate; a simple in composite;—come with me into a Quaker's meeting. What is the stillness of the desert compared to this place? What the uncommunicating stillness of fishes? Dost thou love silence, deep as that 'before the winds were made?' Go not out into the wilderness; descend not into the profundities of the earth; shut not up thy casements; nor pour wax into the little cells of thy ears, with little-faith'd, self-mistrusting Ulysses. Retire with me into a Quaker's Meeting."

And to a Quaker's Meeting I went, and seated myself on the straight, hard benches, and looked around on the human fixtures. There were three of us dressed like the world's people, restless, leaning on our elbows, trotting our feet, playing with our fingers. I had a mind to have slipped off my gay shawl and thrown it under the seat, and I tied my bonnet-string tighter, that I might shut out a little of the world, and look more like the forms before me, which seemed as inanimate and breathless as the twenty-four jugs containing human beings in the Arabian Nights. I might have pulled off a dozen shawls, and it would not have moved those spiritual posts, those quiet, intellectual craters. I say craters; for who knows not that passion is not crushed, but covered by that outward bearing—that the most staid Quaker must from his human conformation utter groans and tears—that the thunder is roaring and the fire raging within, though verdure and sunshine be around the mountain? And yet how different were we, the restless triad, from that " forty feeding like one !" I began to fear that we should have what Charles Lamb calls " a sermon without hands;" but a young woman took off her bonnet, rose, and facing the assembly, in a clear, musical, and most pathetic tone, addressed DEATH. As she proceeded, her voice became agitated, tears rolled down her cheeks, her frame shook with emotion, she could not proceed, but, covering her face, sat down.

I was prepared for stillness—repose—calm exhortation; but tears—passion—in a Quaker's Meeting —I should have as soon expected to have seen the halcyon fluttering on a summer's sea. After this movement, the silence again deepened like a pause in nature, when the elements have been at strife. Even we, the worldly triad, sat still, with hands folded, heads straight forward, quiet as if the body were not ; our hearts were brought in contact with spiritual things, and, as Charles Lamb again hath it, I saw the dove visibly brooding.

There was a motion. How quick is perception in such an assembly !—The same individual untied and took off her bonnet, threw herself on her knees, and prayed. The deep pathos of her voice was heard in strong supplication, with an earnestness that would not let God go ; but tears came again—choked her utterance—the words were lost in uncertain tremblings—she sat down—and we were left once more to unuttered musings.

After a while, rose another female, calm as the star of evening ; yes, just so clear and lonely as that star, walking in its (to us) quiet depth of solitude, though we know not how many eyes of light are near it— not a ripple of the world's waves was seen on her placid face. Her exhortation was to those who, having triumphed over error and seen new light, are in danger of abusing their privileges. Self-possessed and rational, she laid open her text, in its various bearings, with the precision of a prepared discourse. There was a peculiarity in her pronunciation, an additional sound to her final letters, which is sometimes heard in Methodist preaching, and which, though incorrect, rather enchained attention than excited disapprobation.

That voice has passed away—we are all passing away, and I shall never again listen to its sounds. Yet memory will often recall it in some still Quaker-like moment of existence, amid my far-off duties; and who knows but when relieved of earthly weights and prejudices, that gentle voice, even if in a future world it still shrinks from mingling in hymns of harmony, may address us in sweet exhortations on eternal realities!

It is hard for me to believe that the *voice* must die —will it not be the *voice* of those we love, which shall guide us to their distant choirs, or call us to some spot, apart even in heaven, to tell us in secret of their new joys? I can give up the eye-beam, the lip-smile, the touch; the form may moulder and depart to dust; but surely the voice will only glide away, and wait somewhere in silence to welcome us again.

While walking in Chesnut street to-day, I heard a mocking-bird in a cage pouring out its brilliant tones. It touched me to the very heart:

Bird of the South! is this a scene to waken
   Thy native notes in thrilling, gushing tone?
Thy woodland nest of love is all forsaken—
     Thy mate alone!

While stranger-throngs roll by, thy song is lending
　　Joy to the happy, soothings to the sad ?
O'er my full heart it flows with gentle blending,
　　　　And I am glad.

And *I* will sing, though dear ones, loved and loving,
　　Are left afar in my sweet nest of home,
Though from that nest, with backward yearnings moving,
　　　　Onward I roam!

And with heart-music shall my feeble aiding,
　　Still swell the note of human joy aloud;
Nor, with untrusting soul, kind heaven upbraiding,
　　　　Sigh mid the crowd.

　　　　*　　　*　　　*　　　*

I have had the rare privilege of seeing one of those links that unite us with past history—one of the few individuals, who now remain as noble specimens of our forefathers, surrounded by every association that can give us an awakening interest in the past.

Between Philadelphia and Germantown is the country-seat once owned and occupied by a secretary to William Penn. There, too, lives now, at the age of seventy-five, his grand-daughter, standing like a solitary, graceful pillar on classic ground. Every thing under her roof speaks of former days, except her warm and tender affections, which, though they shine on the memory of the dead, revolve, with a bright philanthropy around the living.

We rode up an avenue through an open lawn skirted with woods, until we reached the old brick edifice. We entered, and received from its occupant the beautiful Quaker salutation " Welcome ! I am glad to see thee, friend." She belongs to the true aristocracy of our country. She is upright in person, with a clear, intellectual eye, and a softness of manner fitted to the higher walks of society. She was dressed in a nice Quaker cap, a short chintz wrapper, and neatly folded muslin kerchief. This is her usual costume, and it would make a fine lady blush to see how mind, towering mind, throws a glory over this simple array.

I was soon seated in one of her high-backed chairs, and as I glanced at the china tiles around the wide fire-place with scripture illustrations, showing how David slew Goliah, and how the wicked Herodias danced before the king,—at the *beaufet*, filled with old china, from whose minute cups was drank, if drank at all, the stinted revolutionary draught,—at the three legged tables with their broad tops turned up against the wall—at the ponderous book-case, whose mahogany had assumed almost the hue of ebony, yet shining with the housekeeper's brightness, —and as our hostess pointed to the sofa and chairs on which Wm. Penn had sitten, the table where his secretary had written, and where ink, to which the revolutionary ink was young, still lay, looking, as she said, as if it were sometimes spattered in agitation,— as I saw the letters of Wm. Penn, and read familiar words, which bring the dead so near to the living,— when I heard her tell how, when a little girl, she climbed the fence and heard the declaration of Independence read,—while she spoke of Washington, and Pinckney, and Rutledge, and Jefferson, as companions and friends—I felt the spirit of the Past sweep on and brood over the scene.

There was a sofa, the back of which was higher than our heads, which her grandfather had boasted was sent out from England as the last fashion, and which she said was probably the kind that Cowper described as large enough for two.

The building which has impressed me the most deeply, since I saw the Capitol, is the Penitentiary of the city. As one approaches its massy walls and towers, a European association occurs to the mind, (such as reading furnishes,) which is rarely furnished in this country. The Philadelphians study external elegance in every thing; one recognises this love of the beautiful in their halls, churches, private buildings, dress; and even in their prisons, the melancholy thought of sin and punishment is softened by the idea, that every alleviation which care and cleanliness, and external attraction can bestow, is there. Philadelphia, I must acknowledge, sits like a peerless bride among her sister cities, with her white wedding garments, and the orange wreaths in her hair!

As we stood in the inner court of the Penitentiary, we saw, on all sides, the long galleries, with wards above and below, where each prisoner has a separate cell; solitary confinement being the leading feature and principle of the establishment. A very few attendants perform the duties of supervision. While we were there, dinner was being served. It was wheeled in, carefully covered to keep it warm, and delivered in bright tin pans, at each door, slightly ajar, and which was carefully shut as we passed. Over head, the same distribution was going on in the upper wards, the vehicle being a car propelled on a railway. There are two hundred and fifty beings in this noiseless region ; twenty-one only are females. No convict knows who is his neighbor, or whether he has one. Work is provided for them, which they crave eagerly, but there is no obligation for them to do it. Deprivation of employment is a punishment.

We were shown a cell just vacated by an inmate of many years' standing, as a specimen of all. It was capacious, and well lighted from above. By simply turning a spout, water, that Philadelphia blessing, could be procured at any moment ; every cell is provided with this luxury ; a flue of a stove also runs through each room. A bedstead, which turned up against the wall at pleasure, was comfortably furnished. The inmate had been taught to make shoes, and his bench remained with the tools as he left it ; among other articles of comfort and necessity, was a small looking-glass suspended from the wall. This set me busily to musing. To think of a man's watching his daily decline for twelve or twenty years in that little glass, and see the eye grow dim and the hair turn gray, and compare the laughing glance of boyhood, or the self-satisfied smile of manhood, with the withering touch of age, alone—alone !

There was a door leading outward from the cell, into a small enclosure, surrounded by a high wall,

5

where the prisoner was allowed to pass one hour daily, watched by a sentinel from above. In this solitary promenade were several plants, which the prisoner had cultivated in his walking hour. At seeing this, I again fell into thought. When we are happy, and at liberty to gather all plants, from " the cedar of Lebanon to the hyssop on the wall," how our affections cling to some one flower that graces our windows or is caressed by our fireside! How we raise its new leaves, and watch its unfolding bud, and inhale its odour! What then must be the feeling of the prisoner of years when he sees a spontaneous blade of grass or flower springing up in the barren earth by his cell!

This is indeed a *comfortable* prison : it would not require a great stretch of poetry for the suffering poor, who contemplate these things, to say

> O had we a tight little cell of our own,
> In some snugly-built prison, far off and alone!

But then the word *we* or *I* makes a prodigious difference, and therein consists the secret of the Philadelphia Penitentiary discipline.

In leaving the prison, I found I had been accustomed to expend too much of the pathetic in sympathy. Vice never before has had its claims so impartially balanced, nor has so much mercy ever been mingled with so much justice. I left the Penitentiary with a light heart, but my thoughts recurred again to the deserted cell, and were embodied in these words :—

THE RELEASED CONVICT'S CELL.

AT THE PHILADELPHIA PENITENTIARY.

Within the prison's massy walls I stood,
And all was still. Down the far galleried aisles
I gazed—upward and near; no eye was seen
No footstep heard, save a few flitting guards
Urging with vacant look their daily round ;
For in the precincts of each narrow cell,
Hands, busiest once amid licentious crowds,
Voices that shouted loudest in the throng,
Were now as calm, as erst the winds and waves,
When Jesus said, *be still.*

    I was led on
To where a convict ten slow years had dwelt
A prisoned man. Released that day, he sought
The world again. *Wide open stood his door.*
Hard by the cell, (where for brief term each day
He walked alone, to feel the blessed breeze
Play on his cheek, or see the sunbeam dawn
Like a fond mother on her erring child,)
There was a little spot of earth, that woke
Within my breast a gush of sudden tears.
His hand had tilled it, and the fresh grass grew
Rewardingly, and springing plants were there
One knows not how, lifting their gentle heads
In kind companionship to that lone man.

 Who can portray how gladly to the eye
Of that past sinner, came in beauty forth
Those springing buds, in nature's lavish love ?
Perchance they led him back, in healthful thought,
To some green spot, where, in his early years,
The wild-flower rose like him, unstained and free.

 Oh, many a thought swept o'er my busy mind,
And my heart said, God bless thee, erring one,

Now new born to the world!! May heavenly flowers
Spring up and blossom on thy purer way!
    A deep, pathetic consciousness I felt
Stirring my soul in that forsaken cell.
It seemed the nest from which had flown the bird ;
Or chrysalis, from whose dark folds had burst
Th' unfettered wing ; or grave, from whence the spirit,
Wrapp'd in earth's death-robe long, had sprung in joy.
Thus be the *door of mercy oped for me*,
And leaving far the prison-house of sin,
Thus may my spirit range.

Among the pleasant excursions around Philadelphia, is Bartram's garden, which, besides its own botanical value and romantic location, is interesting from its being the favorite spot where Wilson, the ornithologist, pursued his studies. The schoolhouse where he taught, is on the road ; and as one rides by, his innocent character and useful life press vividly on the memory. The dwelling-house at the garden is very ancient, and bears this distinct inscription on the outside, placed there by its indomitable Quaker owner, who was charged with heresy by his sect.

'TIS GOD ALONE, ALMIGHTY LORD,
    THE ONLY ONE BY ME ADORED.
                        JOHN BARTRAM, 1770.

The green-house and nurseries are rich in plants and the garden forms an irregular, and therefore an agreeable stroll. The pionies, which defy the culture of our Southern florists, are here in gorgeous bloom. My heart was made glad by the delicate scent and yellow blossom of a barberry bush on the highway. There is nothing that recalls the past more vividly than the perfume and color of a long-forgotten flower. Farewell to thee, Philadelphia! Again I say, in truth, thou sittest like a bride among thy sister cities!

NEW-YORK.

The elements were busy in their gardening operations, when I left Philadelphia in the steam-boat Trenton, and the rain poured as if Fair Mount and the river goddess of the Schuylkill were translated upwards. Fortunately, but little of interest is to be seen in this route; fortunately, too, when the elements are busy without, the social principle is active, and one has an opportunity, in the suspension of what may be called the telescopic view of things, to turn to the microscopic, and hold the glass to individuals. And I must pause to say, that up to this time I have not seen, among the passengers, one rude act or look since I entered the steam-boat at Charleston for Norfolk. One little group I may except; but to their honor be it said, they strove, as much as human nature could, to restrain the feeling of the ludicrous. They sat near the head of the stairs of the Ladies' cabin, which were slippery with the dampness of the day. As the passengers came in like Cowper's rose-bush, "dripping and drowned," there seemed to be no one to communicate this fact of slipperiness, and a considerable proportion of the company descended to the cabin in an involuntary

5*

slide on their backs. I have said that the scent and color of flowers brought back recollections of child-hood, but no less is a strong reminiscence awakened by seeing an individual slip and fall on his back down a flight of stairs. What person in childhood has not been the subject of this unexpected indigni-ty? The little group to whom I recently referred, appeared for a while to have their moral sense cloud-ed; they thought it almost Quixotic to arrest the steps of a hundred people with unsolicited advice, and at last it seemed yielded to as a kind of fate, that the cabin should be reached by this summary process.

I was able to devote a little time to the reading of Sartor Resartus, which has recently been pub-lished by subscription at Boston. It appeared ori-ginally in Fraser's Magazine, (London,) and its views have become a popular philosophy among some en-thusiastic admirers. The title implies, the Patcher Repatched; and it is professedly the philosophy of clothes, which no one can understand without read-ing, and not many with. Carlyle, the author, is one of the most exquisite writers in the Edin-burgh Review, and has been for some time ex-pected on a visit to America. One is first struck with the quaintness of the title and arrangement of Sar-tor, then attention becomes rivetted to the perfect English of the style. It is almost a poem, having, with apparent irregularity, a perfect plan in deve-loping the course of reflection in a young man, who has the usual trials of education, followed by mental and bodily afflictions. It is a work to be read with pains-taking. Whatever results readers may arrive at respecting its religious transcendentalism, no one can rise from it without feeling that he has a larger mind than when he commenced it, that he has taken a higher step in his intellectual movement, and can look down to the point from whence he started ; true, the new land may be covered with mists and shadows ; there may be an unreal rainbow and sunshine where it is not, and stars seemingly below, but which are, in fact, above ; but still it is a *new* goal. Some will pause and wonder, some return, or stand like me, calmly rubbing their eyes for new light, and ready, if truth directs, to take another flight.

The rain was still pouring when we arrived at New-York, yet the bustle of the city was scarcely checked. We passed through Broadway, and reached the fashionable residences in —— Place, where all is as quiet as exclusiveness can desire. I could scarcely believe that while we were sipping our tea, thousands of men had collected in the Park, with the intention of arresting the verdict of Judge Edwards on the strike of the Tailors. As we drove through the streets the next day, leisurely, I could see the dreadful elements of a mob at every turn in the *foreign* faces around me. The most trivial circumstance—the drawing a large block of granite, the breaking a carriage, &c., attracted a crowd with incredible quickness. This city is a striking contrast to Philadelphia. Instead of a bride in her wedding garments, New-York looks more like

" The old woman who lived in a shoe,
" Who had so many children she didn't know what to do."

The shoe of New-York, however, is of India-
rubber, and no one can visit the suburbs without feeling the great progressive impulse which its legisla-
tors have given to its wonderfully elastic powers.
Every where its avenues are stretching out their
long arms, and population is spreading over them.

After a drive about the city, in which I glanced
at the Battery, the churches, the public squares, the
new university, which stands a conspicuous monument of improved taste in building, and the wide
avenues opening on every side with a noble pro-
phecy of this immensely spreading metropolis, I
began to single out particular objects.   St. John's
Square belongs to the private residences that en-
circle it, the occupants of which keep keys of the
gates.   At this season of the year the foliage is
deep and beautiful.   The ground in which the victims of yellow fever were interred in the deadly
seasons, has been rescued from the encroachments
of the increasing population, and reserved as a public square.   How few think, as they tread this spot
with light footsteps and hearts, of the once suffering
sleepers that rest below.

Near Manhattanville, seven miles from the city,
is the New-York Lunatic Asylum.   Dr. Francis,
an eminent physician of this city, in a published
letter on the subject, says that this institution is a
proud trophy of *Mr. Eddy's* laudable perseverance,

and therefore I looked with earnestness and interest on the plain portrait of Mr. Eddy in the common parlour of the building.   And a " proud trophy" it was to adjust medical treatment and Christian kindness to the neglected and mistaken wants of lunacy ! Indeed, when we remember the brutal and unphilosophical treatment of those poor sufferers in a former period, it was like saying to darkness, " let there be light !" and there *was* light.   The sufferers felt it in the amelioration of their wild and restless pain, and their friends feel it with hearts of thankfulness as they rely on a new and judicious philanthropy.

There are two hundred and fifty lunatics in the establishment.   A salutary law allows none of them to be seen by strangers, except when introduced by the attending physician.   In all the cases I have seen, the physician is welcomed as a friend.   I found in their apartments every resource of which their situation will admit ; in one was a piano, in the hall a billiard-table, balanced seats, battledoors, &c.   They ride and walk stately.   About eighty attend religious service on Sunday, and those who wish, dance to musical instruments on Thursday afternoons.   The superintendant informed me that many of them looked forward with great interest to the dance, arrange their dresses, &c.   I was startled at first by such a singular combination of ideas, but on reflecting, I saw its admirable philosophy in obtaining for them voluntary exercise.   From the cupola I had my first view of the far-famed Hudson, or North River.

I visited also the Bellevue Hospital, which is
supported by the city. There are now twenty-two
hundred occupants! It is said that emigrants, on
landing, inquire for this institution! There is a
wonderful air of neatness over this crowded scene.
I could scarcely believe it, with such a mass. The
old women looked as if they had been scrubbed with
soap and sand as well as the floors, which were as
white as those of a Philadelphian. Bouquets of
clover and dandelion were placed on the stoves by
the side of many of these old crones. When I returned to the city, and saw some of the wretches
about the streets, I thought a change from such
filth to the stripping and washing, and clean clothing of Bellevue, might nearly kill some of them.

Every American traveller will pause with pleasure at the Academy of Design. It is well before
or after visiting the picturesque scenes of our country, to know what hands are to immortalize them,
perpetuating their beauties and wonders. We lingered till twilight in the hall, and were about departing, when it was lit up by a magic touch, with
gas, so instantaneously that I could scarcely realize it. The light was clear, and beautiful as day.

We were, of course, attracted by the productions
of our young fellow-townsman, G. W. Flagg. I
could not help recalling the time, some years since,
when I had seen a specimen of his painting handed
about a drawing-room in Charleston, while the little artist sat blushing, but conscious of his own
powers.

Hubert and Arthur is a wonderful realization of Shakspeare's description. The expression of grief and doubt in Hubert, as the young Arthur kneels in pleading sorrow before him, would seem to have been the result of the experience of years rather than the short observation of youth. The *Savoyard Musician* is spirited.

Chess is a fine personation of a perplexed player. The contracted brow of the young man seems to bear the weight of a nation upon it. His fair opponent does not satisfy me ; she is too stiff. As far as my recollection serves me, young ladies decide quickly, and then throw. themselves into an easy attitude, even in critical states of the game. Our Southern party could hardly be induced to pass the negro girl who is handing refreshments to the chess-players, and who, perceiving her young master in perplexity, is straining her eyes to find out the cause. The sketch is perfect ; and reminded us of many a sable friend at home, whose prayers, we know, are often raised for us on our distant way !

The *Nun* is to me the least attractive of Flagg's pictures. It wants the spiritual grace which is associated with our imagination of those God-dedicated beings ; but the *Match Girl* is exquisite ; the subdued look of poverty, which seems to be speculating on its next resource, is very touching ; ragged and hungry, the grace of youth bursts through the whole.

Those who wish a more extended account of the

exhibition will find one in several consecutive numbers of the New-York Mirror by a spirited and intelligent hand.

I can scarcely dwell a moment on West's Death
on the Pale Horse, since one visit is only long
enough to take in the general conception. When
I left it, I felt as if I had tasted only one sip of a
delicious goblet. I shall bear about in my memory
the great outline until I return in the fall to another
survey.

I find the insubordination of the poorer classes a
theme of constant discussion. One circumstance
may serve to illustrate the state of things in that
respect. When driving through Broadway with a
friend in her private carriage, I observed that a
ragged boy had jumped on behind. I called her attention, and asked her why she did not order him
off?

"I am afraid to," was her answer ; "the last
time I did so, I was cursed through Broadway with
the most revolting and opprobrious epithets ; and a
gentleman received the same treatment, who was
with me a short time after."

Turning to the intruder, she said, quite humbly,
"Will you be kind enough to get off?" and, much
to her surprise, the boy *consented*. Is the advantage of emigration to compensate us for the vices
and insubordination it is introducing? I hear com-
plaints respecting servants wherever I go, and I
think it must arise from their entire separation
from their friends and relations. I have in vain

looked among them to find relatives enjoying each other's leisure, and sharing each other's cares ; all are strangers to each other ; in every kitchen is the isolated American girl, or stout Irish woman, or free negro.

The vast resources of this city, what it has accomplished, and what it proposes ; its delightful location, its literature, and its charities, and, let me add, its degradation, have set me to musing, and brought out thoughts like these :

THE CITY OF NEW-YORK.

Atlantic city ! brightly art thou beaming,
  Throwing thy kindling ray o'er land and sea,
Enlightening myriads with thy far-spread gleaming,
      Home of the free !

Giant of wealth ! thine arm of mighty power
  Sweeps to thy coffers gold from distant shores ;
While on each asking hand thy Danae shower,
      Its treasures pours.

Religion's nurse ! on spire and towers still flying,
  The Christian standard floats unfurled and free ;
Never our bold forefathers' claim denying,
      Mind's liberty !

Favourite of nature ! on thy green shore dwelling,
  Bright spring-flowers bloom,—the wild birds carol gay,
And the green ocean laves thy broad pier, smiling
      In noisy play.

Haven of ships ! thy storm-tried masts are standing,
  With their tall foreheads to the meeting clouds,
A floating world—the billowy world commanding,
      With their tough shrouds.

6

Syren of pleasure! in thy halls bright glancing,
  Youth gaily springs, and prunes her buoyant wing.
Do purity and truth the mirth enhancing,
          Their chorus bring?

Oh, mighty city, to thy trust is given
  A moral influence—a Christian sway!
Souls throng thy busy streets to people heaven,—
          Let them not stray.

Atlantic cities! rouse ye all from sleeping
  Sin's deadly sleep, lest drops of grief be wrung
From Him who o'er Judea sadly weeping,
          Her death-note sung.

GOWHANNUS, LONG ISLAND.

It was not without delight that I left even the ele-
gances and refinements of the city for the natural
attractions of this beautiful scene on the bend of
Gowhannus Bay. The house of my friends stands
in a valley, with an open view of the sea on one
side, while on the other runs up a graceful hill, sur-
mounted by a summer-house, which commands the
picturesque country around. It is happiness from
this elevation to gaze on the sun as it sinks behind
the opposite hill, throwing its parting glow over the
tranquil waters, or to watch the clouds in the long
twilight brighten and brighten, and even die in glory.
Now a boat rowed by young girls shoots out from
the shore, and their merry, or sacred songs come
sounding on the pebbly beach; now laughing voices
are heard from the strawberry gatherers, who linger
on the hill, picking the fruit, betrayed by its ripe,
rosy hue, hanging in unstinted fulness from every

stem, and asking only to be gathered; then come deeper shadows on hill and ocean, and lights beam out from the many boats, whose white sails yet brighten the shaded waters, and the city shows its thousand, thousand eyes in the distance, and rockets rise sweeping up on the sky till they sparkle and are gone; and then ascends, too, the evening star, and the moon displays her young crescent, and we feel how impotent is man with his millions of hogsheads of whale oil, his tons of spermaceti, his oceans of tallow, and his countless pipes of gas. How is he nothing, and less than nothing, compared to those planets walking silently in the western sky!

FISHKILL LANDING.

It was raining when we rose on the morning of the twenty-first at 5 o'clock, and as we rode through the streets of New-York to the steam boat an hour later, they were as quiet as a village. I began to tremble for the pleasantness of our North River excursion as I stepped over the dirty wharves, and entered the damp boat, and saw the crowds hurriedly and drippingly press on board. The last bell rung, the rain was suspended, and out came the glorious sun! He scattered the clouds that had been so dense, and gave us that chastened light which is best for viewing scenery on the water. On darted The Champlain; the city was passed; the Palisades came in sight, a range of rocks from twenty to five hundred feet in height, commencing between eight or ten miles from the city. On the opposite side were beautiful residences and picturesque openings. Thirty-three miles from New-York we saw the massy walls of the Sing Sing Prison ; and as we bounded away like birds, joyous and free, I sighed that man should thus blast and forfeit his higher destiny by sin.

But man was soon forgotten in delicious nature. The Highlands came in sight, with their blue crests, nearer and nearer, until I felt the majesty of their strength ; and then from admiration came a lofty repose, a trust that he who creates and rules nature will guard and love me ; and thus thinking, I was as calm as a part of that great and beautiful whole.

Anthony's Nose appeared, heaving its great mass against the sky. I never can remember heights. The only idea I can give of its immense character is that a rose should be as big as a hogshead for Anthony's Nose to smell of, and a pinch of snuff proportioned to its capacity would set all New-York sneezing.

Then followed the usual rush to see the upper Anthony's Nose, or rather face ; and all were crying, where ? where ? there ! there ! higher ! lower ! above ! below !

> Some saw a mouth and some a nose,
> And some the outline of a chin.*

I perceived nothing but a gray rock, with its green

---

* Some saw a hand, and some an arm,
And some the waving of a gown.
                    Lay of the Last Minstrel.

drapery, but I saw better things in that majestic scene; not a bare outline, but it was as if God's image were stamped on every lofty hill and vale, and I bowed before his presence.

The boat stopped at Newburgh, and we crossed the ferry to Fishkill Landing. Was I indeed a *stranger?* I felt it not in the pressure of hospitable hands, nor in the dower given by all gracious nature to this magic spot in mountain and valley, river and sky.

A wedding was on foot the next evening, and we went to it. On entering the carriage, we found that our Irish coachman had entered into the spirit of the occasion, and decorated the horses' heads and the windows of the carriage with white and red roses. But there was nothing rural in our wedding; city luxuries were seen on every side, brilliant pyramids, iced fruits, and spiced cakes; no rustic fiddler sat in the pride of ignorance, but a full band from New-York, with a harp accompaniment, set the slippered foot in motion in the airy waltz.

*   *   *   *   *   *   *   *

My window is over a bank which commands the Hudson, and I am drinking in, with unsated gaze, the varied attractions of the landscape. Newburgh, a pretty village on the opposite shore, slopes down on a gentle declivity to the river; cultivated hills are spread out beside it like a map; and the spires of the churches look through the light locust tree on the bank below me. White sails are flitting by on the calm stream, or the lordly steam-

boat, panting and puffing, moves by with its
worldly freight.   At every other point of view
are mountains.   The sun is struggling through
clouds, breaking the mist which has gathered on
their sides, whose gray folds roll up in grotesque
figures, with the wooded green beneath, and the blue
sky above in glorious contrast.   It is beautiful ; but
even while I gaze, some scene on our Southern rivers
rises to my view, with majestic forests clad in their
mingled green and gray, the mocking-bird's song,
the fragrant flower.

THE FAIRY ISLE AND THE LADY ARCHERS.

All is not sublime here ; soft, rural attractions are
scattered in quiet nooks that need only to be sought.
The Matteawan Creek, running in from the river,
goes bounding over rocks, and forms a series of fresh
and sparkling waterfalls ; a little rivulet parts from
it, and circling a grassy spot, meets the creek again,
and leaves in the centre, between waterfalls and rivulets, an emerald bank.   *The Fairy Isle!* Step
with me over this plank.   The rush of the mimic
torrents is heard on one side, the gurgling stream
on the other ; a rustic bridge peeps through the foliage, tall trees are over us, the soft grass below, and
laughing girls, fresh and free, and springing as butterflies, with natural flowers in their hair, are leading the way.   Now view the Fairy Isle in another
aspect ; it is the practising ground of the Ladies'
Archery Club ; but you may not stand here ; climb,
if you can, one of these tall trees, for none but the

favored few can tread this enchanted ground.   They
come in uniform, their snowy dresses girdled with
green sashes, and their white gypsey bonnets tied
with nature's appropriate color ; their white quivers
too are slung with green ; a shield is on the left
wrist, and a three-fingered glove on the right hand ;
their bows, unwieldy to the unpractised arm, are
gracefully poised as they move along.   Exercise
colors their cheeks and lights up their eyes ; they
are nature's children ; they were brought up on her
bosom ; their steps are elastic ; the colder form and
motion of society are gone, the grace and softness
remain.

The following lines, just shown me by a friend,
will aid much in illustrating this enchanting scene :

THE FAERIES' SONG,

Respectfully inscribed to the Archery Club.

Haste! come haste to the Faery Isle,
  Deep in the Highland shades,
Where, Matteawan's clear waters smile
  Around its verdant glades.
Where, silvery-like, the gleaming spray
  Kisses the deep green shores,
There sings its sad and lingering lay,
  And onward, dashing pours.

Haste! come haste to the Faery Isle,
  The wild-vines clamber high
Over the tall old trees that pile
  Their foliage to the sky ;

And soft and sweet the asphodel
Comes breathing in the gale,
Like balmy odors famed to dwell
In Cashmere's fragrant vale.

Haste, come haste to the Faery Isle,
The golden sun sinks low,
And cool and deep the shadows, while
We draw the springing bow!
Then woe to him whose eyes shall see
Us poise our swift-winged dart,
For, quick as lightning's flash, shall flee
That missile to his heart.

The only two Archery Clubs existing this side of the Atlantic, are the United Bowmen of Philadelphia, and the Ladies' Club, called the Mohicans, (the old Indian name of the place,) at Fishkill. The last has been in operation a year. It would be well for our Southern ladies to get up a branch. The greatest difficulty is in procuring suitable bows. The best maker of this article is said to be an Englishman at Philadelphia, where the whole apparatus can be procured. The open lawns on our Southern plantations would be delightful archery fields. If such exercises were more common, they would call a brighter glow into the cheeks of our fair maidens.

THE DOMESTIC SQUIRREL.

A friend here has narrated to me a singular circumstance for naturalists. She perceived from day to day, as her drawing-room was opened, nut-shells, and other little matters, scattered about the room. The apartment was not in use, but after airing it a little while, the door was locked daily. A month passed away, and one day a member of the family saw in the same room a flying squirrel, which was caught, but permitted to go away again. Nothing more was thought about it until, on opening a drawer in the same room some time after, a nest was found with young squirrels. They were of course great pets, but seemed to be cared for by some unseen agent. At length, when the family went one morning to carry their food, they were gone. Their abandoned nest was made of shreds from the hearthrug, paper from a pamphlet in the room, leaves and matter from the forest. It was thought that the visitations of the squirrel were down the chimney, and that she had removed her offspring through the same avenue. On the following season, when the transaction was quite forgotten, the drawer being again opened, the old squirrel sprang out again. Alas! a huge black cat, a family pet too, saw the movement, leaped forward, and the pretty little visitor was decapitated.

I have not seen the moon, which has been obscured through its present stage since its young crescent rose over Gowhannus Bay at Long Island, until last evening. It came over the mountains with an exaggerated glory and size, treading their heights as if they were made for her queenly steps. In vain were gathered shadows, and dark recesses arrayed against her ; her full and glittering splendor fell like a flood upon them, and mountain and valley, river and village, were kindled into a mimic day. A sudden determination was made for a boating party ; shawls were wrapt about us, and we hastened to a private landing. It is not worth while to tell of shoes fastened in the mud, nor of romantic girls sliding against their will down the slippery banks, nor of the fears and tremors in leaping from a ledge of rock to the boat. We were at last seated, the sound of the oars being broken only by laughter or the soft-voiced daughter of song. But I, the only one upon whom the hand of time had been laid, felt the *seriousness* of the scene, and though I would not for worlds have checked the innocent mirth around me, I could not, without tearful eyes, gaze on the sacred loveliness of that hour. I looked to the great and beautiful orb above me for companionship, and my thoughts wandered afar.

DENNING'S POINT, FISHKILL.

Probably one of the most exquisite combinations of natural beauty is here, and it is heightened by the hand of taste. Gardens in luxurious bloom—choice hot-house plants—a lawn of velvet softness on one side the river, on the other, mountains so near as to look down upon the very roses of the garden—and then, the elegant arrangement within—books, music, and the mind's lighter recreations.

Can I leave all this, and give one word to the Matteawan Cotton Factory, that restless, jarring world, where man " the clothes screen," is in his element?

Every thing is neat in the building, and the vil-

lage looks cheerful. At the wedding, which I attended, the Factory children and men crowded to the door,
where they had a glimpse of the fine people within.
I went to look at them ; there was a perfect sea of
faces, though the rain was pouring. How much did
they enjoy our ice-creams ?

WEST-POINT.

Had not my admiration been so long strained
by sights of beauty, I should have more words for
this enrapturing scene. I have drawn my writing-
table to the middle window at the back of the hotel,
the point of view that so many artists have attempted (but oh, how feebly) with their best powers. The
sun has just rolled behind the mountains, and as I
glance from my paper, every moment reveals new
shades and colours in the sky and river.

There was on board the boat as we came here this
morning, a blind German harper, and a young girl
who sings. They are supported by transient listen-
ers, and have an air of decency, as if they gained
at least enough for externals in this precarious way.
As no one seemed disposed to ask them to sing, I
slipped my *douceur* into the girl's hand. She understood it, and they began such sweet melody, that I felt
half ashamed that such a trifle should be repaid by so
much happiness as they gave me. Only think of
the luxury of gliding on the Hudson to the sound of
the harp ! I, who love to give up to fancies when
they will come, thought the hills moved more quickly
to the Orpheus notes. It was better to look at them,

by the way, than at the blind man's face; his gri-
maces were horrible.

We reached West-Point about two o'clock, and
mounted the steep and romantic ascent to the hotel.
Art has had but little to do here; the eye is at once arrested by nature, and as there is nothing in bad taste,
the simplicity in what man has done is attractive.
The piazzas are commodious, the garden pretty, the
walks neat, and the visitor at West-Point asks for
nothing more. But the fare at the hotel is not so
simple a thing : art there is busy enough, and the
sentimentalist is not called, as at some of the Springs,
to live on the elements of water and air. The attendance is excellent, and so far as the wants of the
lower animal are affected, people are made good-
natured, and proceed in good spirits to the enjoyments of the higher nature. After tasting many, to
us, nameless dishes, we sallied forth to Kosciusko's
Garden. The word *garden* seems to be a misnomer,
except the beetling cliff and rugged mountain be a
warrior's garden. It it a spot of wild and romantic
interest, and thrills the heart in itself and in its associations. The monument is chaste, and is dignified with the name of the hero alone.

The cadets are in camp, which gives life and reality to the parade ground. We were invited to repose in a tent, and examined its furniture and arrangements. Like other picturesque objects, it looks
best at a distance; the effect of the whole encamp-
ment, however, is delightful. It occupies a large

space visible from the hotel. I did not expect to see ladies invited to go so freely among the tents.

The evening parade is animating, and the music so inexpressibly fine, one would be willing to be led by it to " victory or death ;" now soft and clear as the note of a bird, then swelling out in perfect gushes of harmony—all is in good keeping ; the wide carpet of grass mellowed by the setting sun, the pure white of the tents in contrast—the erect forms of the cadets moving in measured time—the encircling mountains rising like a heaven-formed battery, and the evening gun, with echo upon echo pouring forth the mimic volley, till it dies away, and the military band bursts out richly on the closing peal !

Darkness came, but, led by the novelty of the scene, we again sought the parade ground ; and here was a change. The restraints of the day were over, and the scene became animated by festivity. Three times a week the band perform, but this was not one of the evenings, and as a substitute, the cadets got up their own music themselves. I think it consisted of a violin, tambourine, and drum. I do not know how much they will feel flattered when I say I fancied myself at home among our negro fiddlers ; at any rate there was music enough to put them in motion. Presently were seen several of them running with short pieces of lighted candles, which they stuck in the grass in a row. One can imagine the effect of this at night. The ladies' benches were placed on one side of the lights for them, as spectators, while the young men danced on the other. I confess I per-

7

fectly sympathized with Black Hawk, who gave one of his satisfied grunts at this scene when he was here. The most perfect propriety was mingled with their hilarity. Yet the waltzing of these upright figures together was odd enough. The contrast between the free, graceful, and ludicrous motions of the dancers, with their stiff, measured, statue-like air on review, was laughable; but the tatoo was beat at the early hour of nine; ladies and cadets retired, and now all is as still as death on that late busy spot. The moon has risen on her gorgeous path among the mountains, and the sentinels only mark her lonely beauty; for no voice is allowed here after this hour.

The sumptuous breakfast over, we were escorted to the parade ground to see the guard relieved, and again that most thrilling music bewitched us with its melody.

One of the cadets pointed out to me the spot where, on a Sabbath morning, an eagle had hovered awhile and then soared away. The circumstance awoke within me the following associations:

THE WEST-POINT EAGLE.

'Tis Sabbath morning; o'er the tented field,
Wild mountain, rock, and grove, the silence broods
Which nature loves. On the far-spreading green,
The tread of martial feet is hushed, or light;
A serious grace chastens the soldier's eye.
The clustered tents stand in still sunshine, white
To the lone hill-top gazer, as the flocks
That wait the shepherd's call. The Hudson sleeps;
The sloop's trim sail flaps on her breezeless way,

And gentle ripples swell and die unheard.
In rugged quietness old Putnam's wall
Ascends; the Crow's Nest pillows the high clouds.
Ranges of nearer hills heave up to heaven
More fixed and clear, while to their wooded sides
Green shrubs reposing cling.   A glittering light
Crowns Kosciusko's column, like his fame.
And listen, on the rocks below soft fall
Still waters, like the ceaseless beat the heart
Gives to its country's champions.
                              But behold,
From yonder height an eagle presses on !
Hither he bends, with pinions spread, and cuts
The azure sky ; and now above the plain
He wheels, and now the rushing of his wing
Is heard careering o er the silent tents.
Like a keen sentinel his quick eye darts
A glance around, then with majestic sweep
He cleaves the air, and o'er the mountain's crest
Fades his dark form.
                         Why com'st thou, noble bird ?
To note if all is well with those who hail
Thee as their emblem ?
                         Loyal youths ? behold !
Look ye to this ; slight not the sacred sign ;
But when the eagle of your country comes,
 Flapping his bold wing on your listening ear,
Still may he find you thus, as on this morn ;
A sabbath calmness resting on your souls,
And strength, unboasting, in each God-nerved arm.

The next thing was to visit Fort Putnam.   Our
Southern party looked up with a kind of alarm at its
distant walls, but after all only rested twice on the
way.   It is a noble, exquisite scene ; but I could not
sympathize with Fanny Kemble's tears on the same

spot ; to me there was rather a soothing association in those far-spread hills, like a modulated harmony. I forget the particulars of her description, but I think it was there she wept simply at nature ; but who shall compare their feelings a moment with her rapid and ever-varying impulses ? One might as well assimilate the smoke of a hamlet with the changing vapors on these glorious mountains. We returned to the hotel, where some sweet private music soothed our fatigue.

Among other things, the courteous and graceful manners of the cadets should not be forgotten. In almost all other large associations of young men, this charm is lost, but the discipline of West Point recognizes the gentleman in the soldier.

I found some of the novices, *plebs* they are called, home-sick, and weary with their discipline. I saw several poor fellows under arrest, some of them for offences of ignorance only. Of course this is all right. But what a change to a young Southerner, for instance, who has been on horseback, the freest position in the world, scouring the wide fields from boyhood, to this limited scene and strict discipline ! Not a word above a whisper spoken after nine o'clock, nor a step taken beyond a certain point without a written permission, and the soft bed exchanged for boards. If this is right, ought not our domestic discipline to conform to it ? Is not the change too abrupt ? To think how old the world is, and yet we cannot say to any given form of early education, this is right—this will best fit us for life and for eternity !

FISHKILL.—EVENING.

The Albany, in which we returned, is the most beautiful boat I have seen. In place of the pannels between the windows in the dining cabin are pictures—striking and interesting views of natural scenery and groups. I could not examine them, for the warning bell for Newburgh soon sounded; we landed, and the noble boat, crowded with passengers, passed on. To-morrow we are to ascend the mountain called the North Beacon, which has a carriage-road to within half a mile of its summit. Fort Putnam is but a baby to this giant.

TROY.

Our excursion to the mountains at Fishkill was defeated by the morning mists, but we were recompensed by a gorgeous storm, the first I had seen in the highlands. I watched it as it came on. New-burgh lay in sight, with its white houses and spires glittering like a gem set in the green hills. The gust moved with the tread of a giant; step by step it trod over the mountains, village, and river, conquering and to conquer, until a long dark range was formed in the heavens of black cloud against a sky of blue; it stood before us awhile in mighty stillness, then came a rush of wind, the rain fell, and the green leaves flew like autumn foliage.

The rain, I confess, was not the sheeted mass of a Carolina shower; for a true specimen of an outpouring of the elements, give me a Southern thunder gust. Simms has described one well in the Partisan. Other

7*

rain in comparison, (as I heard a Western Senator
say of a New-England stream in contrast to the Mississippi, with the fingers of his left hand bent up, and
the palm hollowed as if it might hold it,) is "a cup
full." "Sir, the gentleman's river is but a tea-cup
full!"

The patriotism of gunpowder was astir at twelve
o'clock on the 4th, and sleep was driven from the
usually quiet pillows at Fishkill. Our ladies could
only testify their national ardor by wreathing an additional flower in their hair through the day, and the
gentlemen by a little extra idleness; but at night not
all New-York, with its crowd and gardens, presented a more animated spectacle than we with our six
rockets and countless bundles of crackers. Here
were the unstudied, unchecked shouts and laughter
of woodland excitement; the shriek of the young
girl, as the report was roguishly sounded in her ear
—the playful retort—the first attempt to conquer
fear—the sudden relinquishment at the whizz of the
cracker—the rush as our few treasured rockets shot
up triumphantly—merry hearts gathering around the
fruit repast, and light feet treading the sudden dance.
Desecrated day! would that it could close on all as
innocently!

We left beautiful Fishkill on the 5th, in the
steam-boat Albany, for Troy. A passenger, who
proved a friend, favoured me with the first volume
of Dewey's Journal, "The Old World and the New,"
and the day flew by swiftly, in alternately dwelling
on its pages and the scenery before me. I recog-

nized in the work the same ardent love and hope
for the human race which characterize his sermon
on the Moral Influence of Cities, which I was fortunate enough to hear delivered in New-York.
Though gratified by the sketches in the first volume,
I felt the deficiency to which the most delicate and
conscientious travellers are obnoxious. The more
refined the individual, the less will he unveil that
delicious gossip which reveals public and private
character ; he is obliged to generalize, and thus is
lost the colouring which makes the letters of the
heart so interesting. Mr. Dewey has deliberately
avoided the temptation, and the chief attraction of
his book, now that every one knows Europe like
Broadway, is in his own philosophical views. I
was called from his important discussion on the
state of religion in this country, to look at the town
of Hudson. I have not seen, on the whole, a more
beautifully situated spot. It commands the Catskill mountains, and the river in front ; a graceful
wooded hill on one side, and a promenade of great
local beauty on the other. The only interest I had
in the place was the recollection of the journal called the Rural Repository, a successful periodical,
which has often met my eye, neat in its appearance
and judicious in its selections. Soon after passing
Hudson we met a gaily decorated steamer, a relic
of the fourth, with streamers flying and music playing ; they gave us a salute on one side, while a
troop of boys swimming popped their heads out of
the water, and hurraed on the other.

We arrived at the Troy House, wearied enough, at the close of this burning day. Our supper was in an immense hall, just vacated by the military,

> " Where *Trojans*, Dardans, and auxiliar bands
> Still take refreshment as the hour demands."

We were not in the best humour for the fumes that assailed us, after being spoiled, as we had been, by private hospitality ever since our departure from home. Oh, the crowded loneliness of those forties, " feeding like one," at the immense tables !

I retired to a close and unhome-like bed-room, and wrote the

SONG OF THE WANDERER.

There are sweet plants springing around my house,
    But *I* cannot cull their flowers!
There are green walks asking the feet to roam,
    Where the sun has kissed off the showers!

The wild birds are singing familiar lays,
    But *I* cannot hear their trilling;
The water-fall still on the river plays,
    But it wakes not my bosom's thrilling.

The moonlight sleeps upon rocking leaves,
    But I cannot watch their motion !
The night air freshly the light cloud weaves,
    But I am far over the ocean !

Sunny smiles rest on the lips of friends,
    But I am not there to greet them;
And many a hand in welcome extends,
    But my hand is not there to meet them !

Yet in Him who rules over that fairy home,
  My lone heart is still confiding,
Since wherever on earth my footsteps roam,
  I feel the Eternal presiding.

But I was not long left to make home-sick rhymes. Open-eyed and ready-handed hospitality awaited us there, as elsewhere, ready to strew our path with flowers, and among the first pleasures was a visit to the Cohoes Falls. The romantic interest of the access is somewhat diminished by the utilitarians who have gathered about it; but when standing in front of the cataract, nothing is visible but the wildness of nature, harmonizing well with its ceaseless voice and ceaseless flow; and, though not absolutely a spectacle of grandeur, yet the thought of Deity, which a waterfall almost necessarily awakens in a reflecting mind, comes over one in solemn reverie.

I have never seen canal navigation before, and here the very majesty of canal-ism dwells, wielding his lazy sceptre over the Erie and Champlain channels. There is a remarkable variety of objects along this little region. The cars whirl by on the Troy and Ballston rail-road, mocking the slow canal boats, that peep up from the banks like tortoises; while small boats—for no craft of importance can navigate here—glide over the diminished Hudson, seen among the emerald islands that diversify its tranquil stream.

Nothing could exceed the beauty of our drive from the Falls. A sudden shower had dressed nature in a fresher robe of green and diamonds; a sunset rainbow formed a glorious arch over the villages of Lansingburgh and Waterford, relieved by the sweep of hills beyond ; while the sun gave a yellow tinge to the fields, sparkled on the river, and even lit up the canal with its parting glory.

I visited with great pleasure the Troy Female Seminary, and was indebted to Mrs. Willard's politeness for an opportunity of seeing all the young ladies assembled, amounting to upwards of two hundred, in one apartment, which only occurs once a week for the purpose of reading the compositions. Mrs. Willard's plan to improve the style and judgment of her pupils is, that they should read a selection from some approved author alternately with the original pieces. I was more gratified by this exhibition than I should have been with one of mere memory. Where I find a school of animated, understanding *readers*, I should be willing to trust the intellect of a child. The young ladies here, in emphasis and deliberation, gave a valuable testimony to the judgment of their superintendent. The general air of the scholars was graceful ; and the teachers, whom I saw more familiarly, possessed that refinement of manner so important in feminine culture. The harp, piano, and vocal performances, were in good taste.

According to my usual plan of following up the associations of a place, I looked into Mrs. Willard's journal in Europe. Her design in travelling, was to inspect, as far as possible, European systems of education, and the proceeds of her book were given to the object of female instruction among the Greeks ; two things so highly creditable, as to need no commentary beyond the mention of the facts. The zeal and cheerfulness of this lady make her a beautiful model, as a teacher of youth, an office too often degraded by its being thought mere labor. It grieves me to see people embark in this great object like convicts, when the free spirit of hope and love ought to guide them.

I was happy to observe ladies over twenty years of age being educated for teachers. I have sometimes thought no one should be authorized to instruct, who could not produce a certificate from some authorized body on the Prussian system. Error is deplorably perpetuated in this country by the ignorance of teachers.

We shall have no thoroughly instructed women while schools are so fluctuating ; the progress of a girl's education in most of our cities, is like the frog's in the well. We should have national establishments. How is the system of the Troy Female Seminary to be perpetuated when the intelligent head that now presides there is withdrawn ? What security is there for its perpetuity ?

We rode to Albany over the macadamised road, which is said to be the best in the country, and is delightfully free from the Washington annoyance of dust. This city, in its exterior, which was all we saw, is a heterogeneous mixture of elegance and awkwardness ; the old Dutch slanting roofs mingle oddly enough with the tinned domes and towers of

more modern structure. We tried in vain, in a diligent drive through the streets, to find a music store,
though doubtless they are there.

SARATOGA.

We left Troy at 10 o'clock in the commodious
cars for this place. What a contrast are these airy
and convenient conveyances to the Camden and
Amboy rail-road cars ! The rush of porters on our
arrival, exceeded any thing I have met with elsewhere ; the shouts were perfectly bewildering, as
they recommended the different hotels to which they
were attached. The U. S. hotel, in which we are
located, is at present the most crowded, and perhaps
fashionable ; though I understand some of the others
have better sleeping rooms and better fare. It is in
vain to write here ; there is something in the tone of
things that prevents all fixedness of attention. It
is enough to look at people dressed up for show.—
There is a lovely demi-French family of celebrity,
with five attendants and their foreign friends,—a
Northern Senator, " the observed of all observers,"
about whom the Bostonians cluster ; there is a Carolina party, &c., &c. A foreigner sits in front of
me, who appears to associate with respectable people, wearing a dark check shirt, without a vest, and
whose mustachioes surpass by many degrees the most
extravagant American standard. Near me is an
American lady, with *gold* cable watch-chain and
ear-rings, and *silver* comb and buckle ; but, generally speaking, there is an air of propriety throughout

this large concourse, the manners of the ladies are discreet, their dresses modest, and the men are unassuming.

A paper was circulated yesterday, at dinner, proposing a " hop" in the evening ; signatures appeared to be easily gained, and at eight o'clock our fine hall was lit up brilliantly, and a full band began the preliminary notes. The affair went off languidly, no one group was large enough to form sets, and none amalgamated. The demi-French and foreigners only danced, and they made but one cotillion. It was very warm, to be sure, but that had not prevented the joyous unceremonious couples at Fishkill from " tiring each other down," as gaily as if it had been Christmas eve. Notwithstanding the lively exterior of things at Saratoga, there are more forlorn looking people than I ever met with, if you watch faces ; and there is nothing in the whole compass of yawns like a Saratoga yawn, if you hear one when a gaper is off his guard. The whole man is stretched, inwardly and outwardly. Let no one who values a small mouth risk a gape at the Springs. Still, it is a glorious place, and in fifty years, palaces, and fountains, and gardens will burst forth on its now rude location, and rival in beauty the healing power with which God has blessed it so richly. The site of the Congress springs, naturally beautiful, is beginning now to assume an air of improvement. It is capable of tasteful ornament. A circular pleasure rail-road surrounds a grove on the hill, with a car,

where two persons can sit together, and propel themselves.

We strayed out yesterday to the nearest church.
The Sabbath is very dear to me amid the throng of
strangers, and I would not miss its privileges.   The
church, neat externally, proved to be of the Baptist
denomination, and was attended by the more laborious classes.   A stranger preached with animation
and earnestness ; but as I glanced my eye round, I
found two thirds of the men and several women
asleep ; they were probably rendered drowsy by
their unaccustomed quiet attitude.   Being wide
awake, and most of our party, from principle and
feeling, having the habit of attention at church, the
pastor's attention was attracted to us, and he literally fixed his eyes upon our group until some of us
were embarrassed.   The style of music and the
bass-viol reminded me of my early years, and the
sounding of the key-note awoke a long strain of the
melody of memory.

We left the drawing-room of the hotel as crowded
after dinner as if there were no bell summoning us
to the house of prayer, and went to the Presbyterian
church.   A South Carolinian preached on the admirable theme, a well-balanced Christian character.
In the course of his discourse, he said there was no
such thing as a particular Church of Christ on
earth.   The Church of Christ was composed of individuals of every denomination, who obeyed his
precepts.   Neither of the gentlemen alluded to the
character of the place.   They had probably good

reasons to decline appropriating the healing power
of the Springs to the illustration of religious truth.

We visited, this evening, Saratoga Lake. It is
a placid spot, about five miles from the Springs.
A boat lies temptingly ready for ladies of the lake
and their Douglasses. Our party entered one,
and rowed across to a floating fishing-house, where,
unexpectedly to ourselves, we became engaged,
and successfully, as a "piscatorial party." The
first fish one of us caught was of that species which
Cuvier has named after Dr. Holbrook of our city.
I forget what the name is. What can be said in a
journal when one's carriages roll along over good
roads, when boats are safe, and waters clear, and
skies blue, and fish willing to come to the hook, and
company good-humoured? Absolutely nothing.
One can only fold arms quietly, be grateful, and
fall asleep, or make verses like these :

SARATOGA LAKE.

O'er Saratoga's bright lake we row,
Bathed in the light of the sunset glow;
We dip our oars in the placid wave,
Our hands in the rippling current lave.

There's scarce a cloud in the summer blue
Save one lit up with a rosy hue,
Like the smile that flits o'er a tranquil face
Lending its softness a richer grace.

The shore is near with its girdle green ;
The dim-eyed mountains look far between ;

The twittering bird is heard on the bough,
And the shining fish are chased by our prow.

Light jests fall sportive from hearts at ease,
As buds that burst in the spring's warm breeze,
And our laugh o'er the silent water swells,
Like fountain music in echoing dells.

No traitor-tears for the absent rise,
Though deep in our hearts their image lies,
But a light from the thought of their love upsprings,
Like that which is ushered by angel wings.

Oh! Saratoga's fair lake, adieu,
With thy placid waves and thy sky of blue!
Soft thoughts arise with thy evening ray,
They are thoughts of our home—away! away!

UTICA. (N. Y.)

We left the Springs, saddened by the thoughts of parting with companions who had lent a charm to our visit there. I closed my eyes in the car for a while, and the images of the past week flitted by. There was the graceful foreign party, who had excited passing wonder; their fair girls and boys floating in the waltz, or the elder members attracting admiration by Italian or French music, and their very motions watched as they promenaded the spacious piazza; there were various other groups; but amid many pictures, the Senator from —— was the leading object, moving among the motley crowd among them, but not (apparently) of them. A lady remarked to me, that when she looked on his forehead, it reminded her of Niagara; and there

is really the difference between his head and those
of common men, that exists between the giant of
the waters and minor cascades. This individual
is remarkable for looking neither to the right
nor left; a slight acquaintance must meet him right
ahead to stand a chance of recognition; and not
lay it to the account of pride, because, when perceived, he will receive a gentle and courteous address. This habit, however, contrasted the individual singularly with others at the Springs, whose
heads appeared to turn on pivots in their zeal to recognize and be recognized.

Our car illustrated the American *cacöethes* for
travelling. There was a lady accompanying two lads,
her sons, in their vacation, and a young man from
a straw-bonnet establishment in the Eastern States,
and our own party, all rushing to the Falls as a
matter of *taste !*

We saw nothing of Schenectady, passing directly
into a canal-boat, which, being a novelty, we wished
to test. Upwards of forty persons were crowded
into this small space, there being no restriction as in
stages. Why not? Why should these boats be
crowded indiscriminately? Fortunately for us the
company were respectable. Groups were soon formed, and various occupations commenced. A very
young lady near me produced a perfectly new blank
book, a travelling inkstand, the brass of which was
beautifully bright, and a nice steel pen. Her first
inquiry of her father was, at what hour they started
from home, and the precise moment when they enter-

ed the boat. A disagreement of some minutes in their calculations, put her to a dead stand, and she sat biting the handle of her pen. As I glanced at her, from time to time, for the next two hours, she was hammering away at her brain. At length I detected sundry discolorations on her pure manuscript, to the amount of half a page.

It was impossible to go in the sun on deck, and the air was suffocating below. I was giving myself up patiently to suffering with the traveller's lonely feeling, which is sometimes so strong, if bodily exercise is suspended, when a gentleman in one of the parties commenced reading *The Deformed* in *The Old Men's Tales*, aloud. I soon became interested in the story, which was new to me ; beguiled by the charm of the narrative and his spirited manner, I listened until tears were making their way to my eyes ; *one must not weep before strangers,* so I withdrew to a little distance, where I could see the group without hearing the voice of the reader. The ladies struggled bravely with the pathos of the story, much more so than I could have done : but I saw their eye-lids partially close, their mouths work with a slight muscular contraction, and their fingers busy with a glove or handkerchief. I heard the attempted jest to deprecate the charge of tears, and the scene was fairly winding up, when we were summoned to dine.

Every thing connected with this mode of conveyance had been disagreeable, but the long day at last rolled by, and we went on deck to see the setting sun. When it is possible to be on deck, canal

navigation is pleasant enough. I do not at all object to the bobbing one's head down at the bridges—
it is somewhat exciting, and I dare say gave the
young steel-pen journalist an idea. When we are
all prostrated, I always peep about to see how comi-
cally every body looks, and get up convulsed with
laughter. The constant passing and overtaking
other boats is agreeable; the scenery is sometimes
beautiful, as on this evening, between Schenectady
and Utica; passing the locks, too, has its attraction
from the bustle, and the thought of man's power over
the elements; but I felt deep loneliness and dejection
on this route. My heart was saddened with a stranger's sadness; the sunset on the mountains seemed
dim, and colored not up my fancy as it was wont,
like the twilight clouds. I felt as if even health
could not compensate for the severing of domestic
ties, and longed to press the young forms to my
heart that had lain there from infancy. The sun
sank behind the hills—a gloom, corresponding to my
feelings, spread over creation, the fire-flies came out
like thoughtless companions, as if they could cheer
the darkness with their flitting ray, and a few stars
took their station between the clouds. At this period a song was heard from the centre of the deck
—two exquisite female voices, accompanied by one
of manly richness. The air was plaintive, and the
notes scientifically modulated. I was refreshed and
soothed, and gave this tribute to the scene:

MUSIC ON THE CANAL.

I was weary with the day-light,
　I was weary with the shade,
And my heart became still sadder,
　As the stars their light betrayed;
I sickened at the ripple,
　As the lazy boat went on,
And felt as though a friend was lost
　When the twilight ray was gone.

The meadows in a fire-fly glow,
　Looked gay to happy eyes;
To me they beamed but mournfully,
　My heart was cold with sighs.
They seemed, indeed, like summer friends;—
　Alas, no warmth had they !
I turned in sorrow from their glare,
　Impatiently away.

And tear drops gathered in my eyes,
　And rolled upon my cheek,
And when the voice of mirth was heard,
　I had no heart to speak.
I longed to press my children
　To my sad and homesick breast,
And feel the constant hand of love
　Caressing and carest.

And slowly went my languid pulse
　As the slow canal boat goes ;
And I felt the pain of weariness,
　And sighed for home's repose ;
And laughter seemed a mockery,
　And joy a fleeting breath,
And life a dark volcanic crust
　That crumbles over death.

But a strain of sweetest melody
 Arose upon my ear,
The blessed sound of woman's voice,
 That Angels love to hear!
And manly tones of tenderness
 Were mingled with the song,
A father's with his daughter's notes,—
 The gentle with the strong.

And my thoughts began to soften,
 Like snows when waters fall,
And open, as the frost-closed buds
 When spring's young breezes call;
While to my faint and weary soul
 A better hope was given,
And all once more was bright with faith,
 'Twixt heart, and earth, and heaven.

We sat on deck until ten o'clock, and then what a change to our cabin, three tiers deep, with berths each side! But the difficulty of moving an elbow was mitigated by the perfect good humor of the company—complaint was a mere outbreak of witty remonstrance. The same good-natured feeling governed us as I had perceived in a man who was alighting from a crowded coach in the morning, when he said: "We are so mixed up, I can't pick myself out." Are the scenes I have witnessed really among the same population which English travellers have described? Am I dreaming, when I find only courtesy among the cultivated and quietness among other classes? I confess, however, to the tobacco-horrors on board the North River steam-boats. Why cannot this be remedied as well as smoking, by cards?

Let the warning label appear in boats, hotels, &c.
—*No spitting allowed here.* This would open many
an unconscious eye, or shut many an unconscious
mouth ; for I believe the *spitters* are as unconscious
in their offences as Carlyle's virtuous people are in
their goodness.

We arrived at Utica in time to take a coach for
the day to Trenton Falls. The drive of two hours
and a half was rough, and there is only one very
picturesque view on the way. It is an eminence
from which Utica appears to very great advantage,
as it lies peacefully on the Mohawk ; the bustle of
the canals, and rail-roads, and turnpikes, which are
rendering it so important an inland city, unheard.

I had seen pictures of Trenton Falls. Pictures ?
Mockeries ! The very best of them no more tell
their character, than a drop of water describes an
ocean. Here is not one fall alone, but a succession,
that takes the eye with delicious surprise. Just as
the heart has ceased to beat with the grandeur of
one view, a few steps show another, almost more
beautiful. It seemed to me that nature had prepared a great dioramic display for man. I fancied
that unseen spirits occupied those cliffs, towering
above, as spectators of the gorgeous scene ; and there
is one spot where the prince of the falls must revel.
Those who have visited the place, will remember how
they looked up with awe to that rocky, overhanging
throne. And do they remember a seat jutting out between two cascades, and will they not believe with
me, that some beautiful form sits there, invisible, twin-

ing her hair, which falls in the surf, with her own arbor vitæ leaves, and gracing her fair cold brow with crystals from her own rocks, while she glances upward to the monarch on the cliff, who now hurls down the severed mass, or bathes in the misty showers that rise from its palace of waters?

The sympathy to which I have long been accustomed in joy and sorrow, was not near me at Trenton Falls, and I was comparatively lonely ; for youth seldom fully sympathises with the deeper feelings of maturer years ; perhaps this added to a wild delight, entirely new to me. As my companions advanced, I was left once or twice alone. I cried out to the rocks and waters with a fierce pleasure. One might cry forever there unheard, and one might fall, as did the betrothed girl a few years since, with her lover at her side, in the whirling abyss, and be seen no more, except by a floating garment, shivering and struggling in the whirlpool. We passed this spot safely ; yet one always shudders there, and a deeper horror looks down from the cliff, and upward from the stream :

TRENTON FALLS, NEW-YORK.

My God,
I thank thee for this wondrous birth of joy,
Unfelt and unimagined till this hour !

Was't not enough that thou didst tinge the rose
With delicate glow, —throw silvery whiteness o'er
The lily's cup,—touch the bright sea-shell, like
A spirit's blush, and weave a whisper through
Its spiral folds, like murmuring love-notes, soft—

Arch the rich rainbow into mingled hues,
More beautiful by contrast with heaven's blue,
O'er western skies throw tints of gracious light,
Smooth down the river with a mirror's truth,
And wrap around the fresh and teeming earth
Its lovely drapery of chastened green ?
Was't not enough for me, that from my youth
Mine eyes have bathed in beauty, banquetted
On lovely sights, and listened to sweet sounds ?

    Grateful was I for this; but now I feel
The beauty of the awful and sublime.
My soul leaps upward to these towering cliffs.
And onward with the stream !

                 Father ! and God !
Enlarge my spirit for this mighty gift !
When I consorted with the buds and flowers,
Heard the full choir of woodland melody,
Gazed up in reverie on placid skies,
Or wandered by the pure, meandering stream,
Or prayed beneath the bright-eyed lights of heaven,
Looking serene from out their azure home,
Or blest the moonlight, as it burst in joy,
Like youthful thoughts, enkindling hill and dale
I felt as if a mother's gentle voice,
Called on her child to acts of grateful love.
But now that I have communed with the *vast*—
Seen the veil rent from Nature's stormy shrine,
Heard her wild lessons of magnificence
In cataract voices, 'mid the echoing rocks,
I feel a *louder* call upon my soul—
A trumpet-sound ;—and as a soldier girds
Himself for war, so will I gird my thoughts
For conquest o'er the world !

The memory of Trenton Falls was still vivid, when
I learned that Colonel Thorne's little daughter had

perished there immediately after my return from it. I had but recently seen this lovely child at the Springs, in all the graceful gaiety of youth. Oh, how well could I fancy the horror of her closing hour from my own impressions of the scene ; the shrieks waking the echoes from that group, bound by ties of love and kindred ; the whirlpool before them,—slippery rocks beneath,—and cliffs piled on cliffs above! I could see that wailing procession return, lingering, yet despairing, for *one was not.*

THOUGHTS ON ZERLINA THORNE,

Drowned at Trenton Falls.

And art thou gone, fair, graceful child !
I dreamed not, mid this cataract wild
    Thy form would lie,
When, like a bright and budding flower,
I met thee in a summer bower,
    Life in thine eye!

I saw thee in the airy dance,
With floating step, with kindling glance,
    With happy brow ;
A brother's arm around thee clung,
A parent's smile upon thee hung,
    Where art thou now ?

Oh ! cold and dark must be thy grave
Love-nurtur'd one !—the dashing wave
    Rocks thy death-sleep,
And o'er thy glazed and unclosed eye,
The high-heav'd cliffs, all frowningly,
    Their vigils keep !

But why repine, though summer dews,
And flowers of soft and blended hues
    Deck not thy sod ?

Thy spirit from the wave upsprings,
Scatters the white foam from its wings,
  And flies to God!

AUBURN.

The great west begins to unfold itself in strong
characters at this point of our journey. The flourishing town of Syracuse is one evidence. Let no
one smile at the classic names in New-York. Not
a hundred years will pass before a greater than
Rome will be in this vast region. Considering its
Atlantic and internal commercial advantages, its
canals, its rail-roads, its vast lakes and water-falls,
its agricultural power, &c., it seems to me that this
State combines more power and beauty than any
other.

We are usually waited on at the smaller establishments by young white women, who are modest and
amiable in their deportment. Maps are to be found
in the poorest houses. I always stop when the
horses are watering, and reconnoitre. One sees more
Buonapartes than Washingtons as ornaments to
the walls.

The stage between Utica and Auburn was fatiguing, but it was beguiled by social dispositions
and intelligent minds, opening to the influence of a
cool, unclouded day. One stranger, without any display, unfolded the treasures of an ardent and cultivated mind; he recited to us, occasionally, selections
from standard authors, whose works fill our minds
with the best recollections, as well as more modern

effusions ; and, what was a singular coincidence for me, a Southerner, he repeated a part of an address of the present editor of the Mercury to his classmates.

We found at the Auburn Hotel a pleasant addition to our coach party.   Chance has thrown me somewhat intimately in the way of three of the most eminent physicians of the city of New-York.   They differ entirely, though they have lived under the same influences, travelled in Europe, and would be likely to have the same associations.   They have all contributed, more or less, to the cause of science and literature, and are probably as interesting specimens of their class as can be found.

We snatched an hour to visit the Auburn prison. I could not look at the manufactures, curious and beautiful as they were ; my whole attention was rivetted by the convicts.   I did not see a *small head* there.   There was something sublime to me in the unseen chain which kept in order seven hundred thieves and murderers.   The difference of the Penitentiary of Philadelphia and this prison may be illustrated by their mode of eating.   I have described the custom at the former institution before.   At Auburn, there is an immense hall, with tables, on which are a wooden plate, knife, fork, spoon, and two cups for each individual.   They are marched in, in silence, attended by their keepers, (one, I think, but I am not certain, to twenty.)   The superintendent knocks on the table, and a blessing is pronounced ;—he knocks again, and they commence eating ; again, and they cease, and are returned in silence to their work.

CANANDAIGUA.

This is a truly beautiful city, and, like the other Western towns, is laid out with wide streets. The taste in building, in this quarter of the country, excels that of the Atlantic cities and villages. The hotel, in which I now write, is situated on an open elevation. It is the Sabbath day, and it has been passed by me in grateful repose. We went out this morning to seek a church. The occupants of one looked too finely dressed for us way-soiled travellers, so we entered another, where the open pews are attractive to a stranger. I was disappointed at seeing (to me) the greatest charms of a Methodist Meeting lost, by the forms being merged in the common mode of worship. There was but one Methodist bonnet in the building, the gay world's-ribbon decorated every other; there was nothing of the usual prostration in prayer, there was a feeble and cold *choir*, instead of the noble shout of praise that usually goes up with the united voices of the congregation. The preacher read one of St. Paul's most difficult pieces of reasoning, which he accompanied by a more obscure commentary, instead of those simpler appeals to truth and duty which the common people love.

A young woman in the pew before me was the most inveterate starer I have ever seen, and in that respect entirely unlike the rest of the congregation. She had a strongly marked English air. It was not a furtive glance, directed occasionally, but a close reading. As this became exceedingly annoying, I practised a *ruse*, which I hope was pardonable, by arranging my pocket-handkerchief on the seat so that she might see the name. I knew it was in too small characters for her to decypher, but I was in hopes she would try. She did, and puzzled over it for the remainder of the service.

BUFFALO.

We rose before dawn at Canandaigua, and were kept waiting an hour by the non-arrival of the stage. How little is there on such occasions to realize the descriptions of poesy! Sleepy attendants, damp entries, listless and yawning travellers chewing biscuits or tobacco, dews, not upon flowers but upon trunks ; but the stageman's whip is heard, the horn is sounded, the almost endless luggage is adjusted, we are seated in the carriage, the face of nature changes, out bursts the glorious sun, lighting up the hills, we look into each other faces, and find there the pleasanter glow of social warmth ; but this exaltation soon subsides ; the " hope deferred " of a cup of coffee " makes the heart sick ;" ennui succeeds ; some sleep, some muse on home comforts, some speculate on the nodding heads around. An old gentleman and a young girl, father and daughter, I suppose, were separated on the front seat by a young man, a stranger; it was a warm morning, and the old gentleman soon fell off in the lands of dreams. The young girl's large eyes began to languish ; her head

9*

drooped ; at a jolt of the coach she became suddenly
erect, and looked wild ; again her countenance settled,
the glow of sleep mantled on her pretty cheeks, her
eye-lashes lay darkly on them; again her head waved,
now this side, now that, and at length she sank in
utter unconsciousness, on the shoulder of the youth.
He tried to edge off, but the weight fell heavier and
heavier ; he blushed up to the eyes, and seemed to
feel any thing rather than,

" Oh lovely burden, why not thus forever ?"

He raised his hand once to remove her head, but
it lay solid as Georgia gold ; his distress became
comic to observers, which made the matter worse.
Once she had nearly slipped off, but with natural
instinct she deposited herself more commodiously
and securely. The youth looked as if he would
rather have borne the logs of Prospero than this
fair charge. At length the stage horn was
sounded, the innocent awoke so suddenly that she
was ignorant of the involuntary aid she had received from her neighbor, and understood not our
restrained mirth at his embarrassment.

I ought not to omit to mention the beautiful lakes
which have thrown such a charm over our journey.
Skaneateles, Owasco, Cayuga, Seneca, Canandaigua, &c., showing their placid surfaces, and throwing a soft repose over the traveller's weariness.
Gardens are often formed down to the water's side,
as at Geneva, where vegetation is in rich luxuri-
ance. The wheat fields, and other grain, are turn-

ing golden for the harvest, and the canal peeps up, here and there, like a familiar friend all along the way.

At Rochester we gave a short look at the Genessee Falls. It is a spot of magnificent natural beauty, but man is doing all he can to mar it. The place where Sam Patch finished his wild career was pointed out to us. The most beautiful rainbow I have seen is here. I feel complacency in gazing on these softeners of waterfalls; they speak a language amid the rush and tumult, like that conveyed by the bow in the heavens after a storm.

By diverging northward to Rochester, we were enabled to take the Ridge Road, where, though the scenery is tame, the travelling is good. There is a theory, that Lake Ontario must once have reached this boundary. It made us feel far from home, to think of our vicinity to these great waters. We were glad to repose at the village of Gaines that night, and reached Lockport at noon the next day. I should suppose this place to be situated something like Edinburgh; it has its upper and lower town, and the natural wildness that I have heard attributed to that great city. A resident of the South has been principally instrumental in the prosperity of this wonderful spot. Here the great Erie Canal has defied nature, and used it like a toy; lock rises upon lock, and miles are cut in the solid stone. We passed on for a few hours, and the waters of the Niagara river, or rather strait, came in sight; then the blue waves of Lake Erie were visible in the distance, the mighty beginning of the mightiest cataract of the world.

The enterprize exhibited at Buffalo almost makes one catch his breath, particularly when thinking what the name denotes, and what it was thirty years since, and comparing it with what it is now. I had thought the other western towns great, but at Buffalo I almost rubbed my eyes to see if all was real. You pass through streets of commanding width, lined with noble buildings ; you enter stores as fashionable and extensive as Stewart's in Broadway, and more elegant ; you find omnibuses and four flying about, with horses larger and handsomer than any at the east. Every body is in earnest, yet every body looks good-humoured. There is piquancy and originality about every thing. When we approached the wharf, the porters began their usual cry of, "Any luggage for the U. S. Hotel ?—for the Eagle ?—for the Mansion House ?" A man stood with his back against a post, with a grave look, and when the porters pleaded for the U. S. Hotel, he cried, " Yes, go there, you will have your pockets picked, and take a fresh start !" " For the Eagle ?" " Yes, go to the Eagle, you will be starved in a land of plenty." " The Mansion House ?" " Yes, go there, excellent feed on bread and water ; I reckon you'll see day-light through their beef steaks !" And these jokes were followed by shouts of laughter, while the perplexed travellers scarcely knew which way to turn. Another set of porters were announcing the hour for the coaches and steam-boats to start. An oracle among them cried,

" The *Circus* starts this evening, at half past seven ;
you'd best go in her, she's got the best *horses !*"

We left Buffalo in the morning, having been
amused by the bustle at the Eagle.   I wanted my bed
made at nine o'clock, to retire, and rang the bell.
Up flew an Irish waiter—" Directly, madam, directly !"   I waited a quarter of an hour, and rang again ;
in rushed a German girl, and we could not say a
word to each other.   I pointed to the bed, she disap-
peared.   I waited a quarter of an hour more, and rang
again ; and another Irish woman appeared, with a
pitcher of boiling water, which she affirmed I had ordered.   I protested against taking it.   " Oh, dear,"
said she, " it isn't it, *thin,* and where is she to find
her ?" and scampered away.

On the whole, we have been well served on our
journey, and so far from bribing waiters, they have
been devoted to us *every where.*   Houses are usually
well furnished, and almost every hotel has its piano
forte as a necessary luxury.   While we were at the
wharf, a negro fellow came down to sell one of their
noble looking horses, which he rode with a halter.
I was inexpressibly amused by his comic recommen-
dations.   He seemed to have entered into the Buffalo
spirit of enterprize.

Lake Erie is quite rough just before the waters of
the Niagara rise ; but the river was speedily gained.
We had been advised by the majority to see the
British side of the Falls first, and therefore entered
Chippewa Creek, and were under the government
of her Britannic Majesty.

A passenger asked me if I was going to visit the Falls. I answered, yes. " Well," said he, " you'll find it a pretty piece of scenery, I reckon."

NIAGARA FALLS, (UPPER CANADA.)

When entering the steamer Victoria at Buffalo, I was startled by the question, " Are you going to Great Britain ?" It was the first time I had realized that I was about to be under a different government, and I felt a mighty working of that organ which makes captious travellers. We soon left the blue waters on Lake Erie, and entered on the Niagara river. Grand Island is twelve miles long, and is interesting from the fact of its having been selected as the spot where Major Noah, of New-York, projected the city of Ararat, as a rallying-point for the Jews. That plan failed, and it is now owned by a company of Bostonians for saw mills, &c., and is likely to be an extensive and lucrative concern. A village is already rising there, with its church and school.

I observed a man smoking and spitting on the *quarter-deck* of the steam-boat, and as I had not seen such a spectacle throughout my whole journey from the South, I asked who he was, and was told that he was an Englishman, the agent for the British Hotel. I was lost in astonishment, having taken all my views of such matters from Hall, Trollope, & Co. Of course I entered on my notes, in conspicuous characters, that Englishmen smoke and spit, (a favorite word with English journalists.) As we en-

tered Chippewa Creek, the first object that met my
eyes was an English lady, knee deep in the water,
her sleeves rolled up above her elbows, scrubbing a
naked boy. My surprise was indescribable, and I
entered on my notes (I never kept notes but for
this occasion) the singular manner in which English
women perform their ablutions in open creeks. As
we passed through the village, I observed on one
sign " *Storcage*," on another, " *Travillers*." Is it
possible, thought I, that these are countrymen of
Johnson, and Sheridan? I immediately entered on
my tablets, according to the sweeping custom of foreign journalists, that the Canadian shop-keepers
are ignorant of the most simple forms of orthography.
Dinner was ready on our arrival, and, as the keeper
of the Pavilion had boasted that there was nothing
to eat or to see on the American side, I expected a
great entertainment; more particularly did I feel that
I was in a nation renowned for civilization and silver forks. What was my renewed astonishment
at finding at my plate a dirty steel fork ! I was almost induced to take out my tablets on the spot, and
insert, that in the large hotels in British America
silver forks are not used, and direct teachers to draw
the shade, meaning uncivilized, over that part of the
world on school maps. I afterwards discovered that
about a third of the plates were provided with discolor-
ed washed metal, three-pronged forks ; and I minuted
that at the first British hotel I ever visited, a third of
the visiters can obtain imitation silver forks if they
happen to sit at the right end of the table.

It will be perceived that in detailing these things, I am departing from my usual habit of seeing the good and agreeable wherever it can be found. I have rather done it as a lesson to myself, to show how easy it is to describe isolated things as general ; how easy it is, in travelling, to revel on a few defects, and slight the useful and fair ; but I have not quite wasted my time in the paltry cavilling. My room overlooks the Falls ; I have listened to their roar, I have sprung often to the windows to see the white foam glitter, and rise and die away upwards, like thoughts that blend with heaven, and I have felt a spell on my soul as if Deity stood visibly there.

At the first approach to the Falls, from the smooth river to the Rapids I experienced a sensation of oppression, followed by trembling and fears ; my first full view was at Table Rock, in sunshine. For a few moments I longed for the sombre cliffs of Trenton to relieve the dazzling whiteness of the foam ; but as I gazed, my thoughts became dream-like ; the far distant and dim future, blended together ; I felt an indistinct and troubled joy, like the bright chaos beneath me.

I found that tea was ordered at seven, a summer evening seven, when Nature has holiday, and the gorgeous sun, in his robes of glory, is shedding his parting honors on mist and waterfall. I told mine host that I had travelled thousands of miles to see this spectacle, and he politely promised me mine by candle-light. After a long, long view at Table

Rock, where the waters of lakes and rivers are seen, concentrated, rushing over, and thundering down the chasm, we descended the staircase, and looked upward. In these two views, from above and below, one has an idea of the power of the cataract. While we were there, several persons passed us in India rubber suits to go behind the sheet of water. The dress is green and picturesque, and my imagination was excited as I saw their receding figures, perceived them rebuffed by the roar and the spray, then gain courage, and disappear. It seemed to me like a burial, a flood-death, and a deep solemnity absorbed me. They soon re-appeared; and, wrought up to the highest enthusiasm, I ventured to ask the first individual, with a voice and feeling as if he were an arch-angel from the heavenly veil, what were his sensations.

" Whart, marm?" said he, with his teeth chattering, and spitting out the remains of the water from his mouth.

"I inquired," I answered, a little dashed, " how you felt behind the Fall?"

" It's plaguy cold, I reckon," said he; " but I warn't goin to stick on so fur, without seeing the whole on't."

This interview seemed to cure me of a slight desire I had felt for this undertaking. I observed by the books, that many English travellers performed this exploit—Miss Martineau among the rest. I have heard several persons say that the shock is excessive, and that there is no beauty to repay one for it. We

10

ascended the steps, and turned over the miserable
scrawls which deface the books, where strangers record their names.   They are evidently written by
vain, or idle, or uneducated youths, and are no test
of the mind of our country ; for scarcely a commanding name is found among the writers.   It is a little
remarkable that there were upwards of a hundred
persons at the hotel, and I could not learn that there
was a literary or professional man among them.
This fact shows a love of the beautiful among the
whole mass that must cause some scribbling to be
forgiven.

Two of us only remained at Table Rock at twilight.   There was a fearful beauty in the growing
darkness and loneliness of the scene.   I lay down
on the rock, with my head over the vast abyss.   It
was an hour of deep and mighty feelings—none but
moral struggles can rival them in my soul.   It is
now midnight ; the roar of the waters agitates me.
I have just raised the window, and the white foam
looks like a troubled spirit in the darkness.   I cannot sooth down my heart—it is kindled by deep
workings of the Invisible.

CATARACT HOUSE—*American side.*

My dreams are very wild here.   I am not calm.
A great voice seems calling on me, which I am too
feeble to answer.

I left the Falls, for a few hours, with regret, as a
matter of duty, to visit Brock's Monument.   I never
care to see these tall, ungainly contrivances of brick

and mortar and stone capacity, unless the associations are strongly marked ; and one does not like to
hear the keeper boast of nine hundred American
prisoners being taken. The prospect is commanding, but I love infinitely more a closer and more de-
fined view of nature. The English houses on the
way are neat, and somewhat tasteful. More pains
are taken by the inhabitants than by persons in a
corresponding class on the other side of the river,
to hide the unseemly, and cultivate the agreeable.
At Bridgewater, or Lundy's Lane, we stopped to
see the battle ground of July 25th, 1814. Marks
of balls are still visible on the houses and trees. If
men must fight, there can be no fitter place than in
the neighborhood of Niagara. Strength to do and
dare may well be caught from this spectacle. I
think I could pull a woman's cap to tatters, who
should offend me there.

The Museum, on the British side, is arranged with
peculiar taste and ingenuity. The cases are suffi-
cently capacious to hold large but graceful branches
of trees, which are covered with green and gray moss.
The birds, their nests or their young, are placed on
them in natural positions, and the effect is singularly
living.

The walk from the Pavilion to the Ferry, after
one has seen all the minor spectacles, is a grand conclusion to the visit on the Canada side ; and the
passage across gives a few moments to one's existence, never to be forgotten. It was a wild, cloudy
day, and the scene seemed closely bounded. It is

impossible, in the necessary direction given to the boat to stem the current, not to believe, as it leaps over the rapids, that it is hurrying to the foot of the Falls. The rushing of the cataract, and its roar, which has seemed to me increasing rather than diminishing ever since I came, are brought fearfully near. I closed my eyes an instant, as we approached the Fall, but one cannot afford to lose such moments. I opened them, and gazed, and that view is impressed on my memory forever. We turned the seemingly dangerous point. I felt like a triumphant rider on a battle-field, and as our boat sprang forward, and I looked upward to the mass of waters, they seemed like giant witnesses.

And now I am in the United States again. It is in vain for me to attempt to describe the beauty and glory of this spectacle. I can only tell its effect on me individually. We paused at the foot of the staircase, near the descent of the lesser Fall. My agitation rather increases than diminishes in contemplating them. I have felt, ever since I came, as if the Great Architect were near. I care for nothing but this work of his hand. Human beings, whom I so love and prize, move by me like visions.

We are at the Cataract House, and as agreeably accommodated as persons can be who see the beautiful and sublime giving place to the useful and the low. This site is ruined. It is the prayer of all persons of taste that Goat or Iris Island may be preserved from this desecration. If any building is erected, it should have a classical exterior, with no more clearing than necessity demands, and be devoted to visiters, giving them a short and romantic walk to these glorious exhibitions. I was glad to escape from the sound of the hammer and mill. We registered our names at Bath Island, and paid our little fee. The rapids at the bridge are indescribably beautiful, and have shed over me, I think, as great an amount of delight as any other view. I never pass them without lingering with a protracted gaze, and feeling the growth of thought at every survey; then succeeds the secluded forest isle, in its perfect natural beauty, affording the eye time to repose, before it is again called to bow before the majesty of the Cataract. If there was nothing to be seen on the island but the view at Lunar Bridge, it would repay nature's pilgrim, who comes to worship here. Standing near the current of the lesser Fall, a rainbow appears at either side,—distinct arches of light, reposing on the mist like crowns of glory. We descended the Biddle staircase, and passed some hours on the rocks at the foot of the Great Fall. Here its height and power are fully appreciated. The sun burst forth in radiance, and the sheeted foam glittered like frosted showers in his rays. How hard it is to leave that spot—one lingers, and lingers as over a new-found joy!

Having re-ascended the steps, we rested at the top of the hill, on the grass, gathering green moss, and preparing for a visit to the tower. Shakspeare's injunction,

" Run, run, Orlando, carve on *every* tree,
The chaste, the fair, the inexpressive she !"

has been obeyed to the letter on Iris Island, though
the inexpressive *hes* rather predominate. As I was
resting on the grass, I saw a fat, hard-faced man,
carving his name, and lo! L. P. stood forth on the
unconscious bark, and he became, to his own thought,
immortal !

The tower is boldly placed over the rushing flood,
and is forty-five feet high ; the access is by a bridge,
which projects ten feet beyond the Falls. This view
is the crown and glory of the whole. I felt the moral influence of the scene acting on my spiritual nature, and while lingering at the summit alone, offered a simple and humble prayer. Descending the
Tower, I crossed to the extreme end of Terrapin
Bridge ; there, lying down with my head over the
Fall, I ceased to pray or even to think. I gave myself up to the overpowering greatness of the scene,
and my soul was still.

My mind has been calmed by rambling through
the romantic forest walks of the island, where beautiful, but not overwhelming, views of the rapids and
falls break through the clustering trees. Yielding
myself up to the sensation of a new youth, I lost, for
a while, the excitement of more thrilling scenery,
and passed several hours in that delicious stroll, while
the calm clear sky looked through the branches, and
the shade of the woods softened the summer sun,
soothing the over-taxed senses. Long—forever,

may this gem of nature, Iris Island, remain in its wild
beauty.

This evening we walked, by moonlight, round the
island, and just as I began to be weary with the
length of the way, a young married couple, who had
come to pay true homage to nature, by consecrating
their new happiness at this shrine, commenced singing. Their voices mingling with, and softening the
roar of the Fall, floated richly on the air, and were
in sympathy with the soft light of the moon as the
green leaves trembled in its rays. My weariness
was beguiled, my steps became measured to their
songs, and thoughts of the absent came like brooding doves, and nestled on my heart.

My last look at the great Falls was at the lunar
bow, at the extremity of Terrapin Bridge. If I was
affected at the Gennessee Falls, with the thought of
the tender associations which spring up at seeing
this mighty element softened by its peaceful arch,
how much did the spiritual beauty of this moonlight
creation touch me in a scene of such surpassing power! The lunar bow lies in its shaded white on the
mist, like a thing of the imagination, lending grace
and softness to its majesty. When I had beheld this
spot in sunshine, I was overpowered; now a deep
tide of reflection solemnized and absorbed me. One
feels thoroughly *alone*, while overhanging that thundering mass of waters, with the silent moon treading her tranquil way. I thought of *soul*, and this
mighty Fall seemed as a drop compared to the cataract of mind, which has been rushing from the bosom

of the Eternal, from age to age, through every channel of human nature, now covered with mists, now
glittering in sunshine, now softened by moonlight,
now leaping in darkness and uncertainty, and I trust
in God, destined to flow in many a happy river
around his throne.

KINGSTON, *Lake Ontario, Steamer*
Great Britain.

I have been seriously disappointed in this route.
Instead of keeping along the coast, and having the
friendly eyes of green trees looking on us, we have
been out of sight of land, pitching and rolling as if
we were traversing the Atlantic ; this evil arises
from the necessity of crossing over repeatedly from
the American to the British side, and back again, at
the different towns.   From Lewiston, we swept over
to Toronto, the capital of Upper Canada ; and after
stopping awhile at Coborg, swept off again across this
inland ocean to Oswego ; then crossed again to Lexington, all of which makes a pretty *lengthy* sea
voyage, a thing to protest against when one is travelling purely for pleasure.   In this dearth of out of
door attractions, obliged to lie down from sickness,
I gave myself up to the interests of the cabin, where
a variety of passengers, French, English, and American, amusingly maintained their peculiar characteristics.   Among the group was a beautiful lady from
the West Indies, attended by a little mulatto girl,
with her head wrapped in a picturesque looking tur-
ban, having all the spoilt prettinesses of manner

which is so often seen in Southern colored pets. She had under her charge a squirrel, which was kept prisoner by a gold chain, two yards long. The boat being crowded, we were spread at night three deep over the cabin floor; our countless heads, apparently bodyless, looking like the cherubs in the pictures of the old masters. Just as we were composed (after the combined noises of some young ladies in a frolic, and a West India negro nurse, who, with a curious compound of French and African dialect, was asserting her right to one of the best beds, the Irish stewardess's exercise of lungs, after all, giving out first,) one of the recumbent party screamed out that the squirrel was loose, and had run over her. The poor little animal went whisking his tail over several other faces, upon which mingled cries of alarm, mixed with shouts of laughter, succeeded, and it was a late hour when we slept.

How unnatural has been our Sabbath, with the complaining English, the laughing French, and the half and half Americans! How different from the quiet of our blessed home, where the only task of the soul is to tread onward its heavenly way.

On leaving Kingston, we passed the Barracks, a fine range of stone buildings, and Navy Point, where are two ships of war on the stocks, and soon the thousand isles began to stud the St. Lawrence, like emerald gems, and as we glided around and among them, the imagination could scarcely help recalling in their deep solitude those forms with which classic taste once peopled the woods and waves.

TO THE ST. LAWRENCE.

River of thousand isles! in graceful glee
Has nature thrown around her gems of green,
Where summer skies look downward joyfully,
And sheltering trees erect their wavy skreen,
And waters flow, laving each emerald shrine,
While nature dwells, lone, silent and divine!

Bird calls to bird from out these islets fair,
Unheard man's death-gun, and unfelt his snare,
And flowers spring up, nor fear a cultured doom,
Bright families of beauty and perfume.
Farewell! a first, last gaze I take—a parting spell,
Thou'rt woven round my heart—and now farewell.

We arrived at Prescot in the after-part of the day, and went immediately on board of the Dolphin, which was to proceed in the night. Some of our party visited Ogdensburgh, an American village opposite, a flourishing place, with about a thousand inhabitants, near which is an extensive lead mine, of the purest ore, which promises prodigious wealth. We assembled on deck by a full moon, and sang near

" St. Ann's our parting hymn."

It was pure romance to sit by that " trembling moon," perhaps on the very spot where Moore conceived the Canadian boat song, and hear the beautiful melody swell forth on the silent air; and there were voices and spirits there that would have gladdened the heart of its musical author. It was not on the " Saint of the Green Isle" that I called in that calm and lovely scene, but a thought of the thousand joys

and blessings scattered in my way, touched my heart
with gratitude to a higher power, in that evening
song.

Full of the romantic associations of the evening,
we determined to see the sun rise on the St. Lawrence. The theory of the morning sun on the water
is beautiful, but the reality of wet decks, the chill of
the early air, the drowsy looks of the work people,
who do *not* rise for the picturesque, and the cravings
for a cup of coffee, which follows the inhalation of a
sharp morning breeze, are prodigious drawbacks;
nevertheless, the lines of light breaking through the
clouds, and coloring up the placid river, touched
me with their beauty, and my heart sang its morning hymn of thanksgiving and trust.

MONTREAL.

Glad were we to take the stage, on the fine Canadian roads, though the appearance of poverty at
Long Sault, the first settlement we passed, was painful. Hut upon hut arose almost more squalid than the
last; while the half-clothed children, and one entirely naked, in the bleak morning air, excited sympathy.
They were evidently the habitations of emigrants.
A little farther on, was a canal, where the men were
employed. At the distance of twelve miles from this
settlement, we again took the steam-boat to Coteau
de Lac; after this, stage and steam-boat, alternately, through the Cascades and La Chine, to Montreal.
We stopped a few moments at the Indian settlement
of St. Regis. As soon as he saw our approach, an

Indian boy threw off his blanket, leaped into the
river, and swam by the side of the boat an incredi-
bly long time. Another lad leaned on an oar in a
canoe, with that earnest, *unsmiling* look, which we
remarked in the boys who ran after the stage in our
route to the Falls. Before entering Montreal, we
were saluted in the twilight by shouts, and one or
two balls of dirt were thrown into the stage.

On entering Montreal, the narrow streets and
gloomy looking dwellings were unfavorably contrasted with the recollection of our more airy cities in
the States. We visited the Cathedral, attracted by
its imposing exterior. It is an immense building,
sufficiently capacious to hold ten thousand persons.
The interior produces disappointment, there being
not only imitation marble pillars, but bad imitations.
The painted glass windows behind the altar, representing the twelve Apostles, were new to me, and I
liked the effect ; but the pictures are really not worth
describing. We were interested in visiting the Sa-
cristy, and looking at the priests' garments. The
vestments of the bishops were gorgeous beyond description, wreaths of flowers of every hue being
delicately wrought in gold and silver, with the sym-
bolical Lamb in the centre, of most exquisite workmanship.

After a drive through the principal streets looking
in at one or two wards of the General Hospital,
where every thing wore an air of comfort, passing the
Hotel Dieu, the Seminary, and Nelson's Monument,
we went quite round the mountain, from which the

city takes its name. Though a rural and agreeable drive, the only point particularly worthy of admiration is that which embraces a fine view of Montreal, the Faubourg St. Antoine, where the bishop resides, with the wide-extended country around. On our return we visited the convents of the Gray and Black Nuns. Whatever may be the speculative views of visitors to these institutions, their hearts must be softened as they see the pure and graceful nuns gliding about, administering, with the quietness of daily duty, medicine and food to the most, apparently, disgusting sufferers, objects from whom the world's children would shrink in dismay.

QUEBEC.

After some repose we obtained admission to the Museum of Montreal, belonging to a society of gentlemen. This is a small but promising collection. As far as I could understand by inquiry, it is the *only* literary or scientific association in Quebec or Montreal. After a day passed agreeably in these various objects, we embarked in the evening in the Canada for Quebec. The passage of the St. Lawrence is really delightful; the dwelling-houses, and uncultivated grounds along the shore being so frequent as to make it appear almost like an unbroken street; the churches, which are numerous, giving an additional charm to the varied and attractive scenery. Soon after leaving Lake Rouge, the towers and citadel of Quebec opened to view, situated on a rock 345 feet in height, called Cape Diamond, from

11

the quality of the crystals found with the granite
beneath its surface.   The view of the city is
unique.   I know of nothing like it.   Point Levi appears on the right, a rocky precipice, covered with
white dwellings, and commanding the citadel of
Quebec from the opposite shore.   Passing Wolf's
Cave, Wolf and Montcalm's Monument, the Parliament House, and Martello Towers, consisting of
four circular forts, forty feet in height, situated on
the Plains of Abraham, half a mile in advance of the
wall of fortifications, we landed at the wharf, and ascended the precipitous hill; our party distributed in
four *caleches*, which are uncouth looking articles of
the chaise kind.   As we looked back on each other,
in this sudden change of vehicle, we could not keep
our countenances until we were sobered by the martial air of the Highland centinels in full costume,
who were stationed on the way.   Then we began to
feel that we were in a fortified city.   We were fortunate enough to obtain lodgings and front rooms
at the excellent hotel opposite the parade ground.

As the Canadian dinner hour is 5 o'clock, and
we were anxious to see the Falls of Montmorenci,
we immediately took carriages to visit them.   Passing out of town, through the suburbs, every window
was full of heads.   As there was nothing either *outré*
or *distingué* in our air, we set it down to the habits of
the people.   On entering the French village of Beau-
port, which appears to be simply one long street, the
dogs issued from every yard, barking and snapping;
as we passed on, the tumult increased, and as there

was certainly nothing peculiar in our air in common coaches, we concluded this to be the habit of the dogs. How civilized beings can see strangers assaulted thus, is inconceivable to me.

The Falls of Montmorenci inspire none of the solemn and mysterious awe of Trenton or Niagara. The stream descends in silvery threads, over a perpendicular precipice two hundred and forty feet in height, and in connection with the surrounding scenery, the tree-crowned summits and overhanging precipices, is extremely picturesque and beautiful. Having viewed them from the window of the mill, the brow of the hill, and the bed of the river, and gazed with a lingering look of delight at the distant prospect, we returned in season to escape a heavy shower, which seemed almost kindly to delay, to gratify our love of nature.

This morning we visited the Catholic Church, a spacious stone building, the interior of which is decorated with better paintings than those at the great Montreal Cathedral. Near this is the Chapel of the Seminary, where the paintings seemed in still better taste. On returning to our lodgings, we were delighted with seeing the regiment of Highlanders, with their bagpipes in full play, pass our door. It was worth going to Quebec to have one's old associations and imaginings thus realized. We remained an hour at the Esplanade, seeing the change of guard, which it was particularly interesting to me to compare with West Point, and listening to the music, while an obliging and intelligent gentleman of Quebec obtained tickets of admission for us to the citadel.

This stupendous fortress includes the whole space on the highest part of the Cape, and is intended to accommodate the garrison as a residence, and to contain all military stores. The armory is beautifully arranged, and is said to be a perfect miniature representation of the Tower at London. One file of muskets is kept for presents to friendly Indians. After mounting the wall, and viewing the prospect from the highest point on the Cape, we proceeded to the flag-staff and telegraph stand, and looked through the telescope, by which the signals are adjusted; from thence we went to the inclined plane, which is five hundred feet long, extending from the wharf to the summit of the Cape, where the perpendicular elevation is three hundred and forty-five feet above the stream. This plane is used by government to convey stores, and other articles of great weight, for the use and erection of the fortress. On one occasion, a heavy load of stone was raised, when the chain broke, and it was precipitated with such force as to be carried over two boats without striking either. Near the lower end of the rail-way is the spot where General Montgomery was shot in attempting to ascend the bank when proceeding to the assault of Quebec.

The fortress is still unfinished, although immense sums of money have been expended upon it by government, and though it is, undoubtedly, the Canadian strong-hold. The quarters of the soldiers are comfortable, and family groups, about sitting down to dinner, added cheerfulness to the scene.

Having the happiness of joining a delightful party from Charlestown, (Mass.) we sent our cards and letters to the two Ursulines, who had taken refuge in Quebec, but had little hope of being admitted into the Nunnery, as we learned from all quarters that none but the dignitaries of the kingdom were allowed to go over the institution on account of the interruption it occasioned to the instruction, and of the disagreeable intrusion of mere curiosity. The least we expected was a conversation with the two sisters in the parlor. What was our pleasure and surprise to find ourselves welcomed with the cordiality of dear friends. When I hesitated to proceed with some strangers, who had joined us, the *religieuse* exclaimed,

" You are welcome! you are welcome! The names of ******** and ** will ever be a passport to this community."

Tender was the gratitude and warm were the blessings that greeted those names. Preceded by a sister with an hour glass, who accompanied us afterwards, we were conducted to the reception room, where the Superior received us, and introduced us to the other members of the community, with the exception of those whom we saw in their respective rooms afterwards, attending to their pupils. After a few moments' conversation, we were attended by the Superior and several nuns, through the various apartments; the simplicity and cheerfulness of our fair conduct-

11*

ors, and the neatness and good taste of the establishment, charming us at every step.   In the room devoted to drawing and painting, were some really
beautiful specimens of the work of the pupils.   In
the sitting room of the community is a painting of
Christ, which evinces the genius of an artist, by a
novice.   There are several interesting paintings in
this room, among them the portraits of the foundress
of the Convent, and of the *religieuse* who came with
her to Canada in 1639.

After visiting the school-room, where about fifty
blooming girls received us standing, we passed to the
music room, which contained a harp, pianos, and
guitars ; from thence to the various apartments devoted to different branches of instruction, where we
found the teachers, all with the same happy countenances and pure attire, attending to their pupils.
We then were led into the refectory and the kitchen,
and were more and more delighted with the neatness
and order which pervaded every part.

We were introduced into the chapel of the Convent, unaccompanied by the Nuns.   I did not ask
why ; but I presume, from their serious attitude, as we
entered without them, that they thought it improper to
go in but for religious purposes.   The altar is a highly ornamented piece of gilding, executed by the Nuns.
The paintings appeared to me superior to those in
the cathedrals.   There is a simple monument and inscription to Montcalm ; and an old Nun is now living, who witnessed his interment, to whom we should
have been introduced but for her extreme age and

infirmities. The following is the inscription referred to :

> Honneur a Montcalm !
> La destin en lui dérobant la victoire
> La recompensé par une mort glorieuse !

On quiting the Chapel, we passed the hall where
the charity scholars were assembled in great numbers,
and both teachers and pupils looked happy. If any
of our party entered with prejudices, they must have
been dissolved by the touching interest of the scene,
from the moment of our reception, to the warm and
affectionate farewell.

TO THE URSULINES.

Oh pure and gentle ones, within your ark
    Securely rest!
Blue be the sky above—your quiet bark—
    By soft winds blest!

Still toil in duty and commune with heaven,
    World-weaned and free ;
God to his humblest creatures room has given,
    And space to be.

Space for the eagle in the vaulted sky
    To plume his wing—
Space for the ring-dove by her young to lie,
    And softly sing.

Space for the sun-flower, bright with yellow glow
    To court the sky—
Space for the violet, where the wild woods grow,
    To live and die.

Space for the ocean, in its giant might,
    To swell and rave—
Space for the river, tinged with rosy light,
    Where green banks wave.

Space for the sun, to tread his path in might,
    And golden pride—
Space for the glow-worm, calling by her light,
    Love to her side.

Then pure and gentle ones, within *your* ark
    Securely rest !
Blue be the skies above, and your still bark
    By kind winds blest.

On our return from the Nunnery, we were introduced to Mrs. Montgomery, mother of the late Superior of Mt. Benedict, Charlestown, who is about to follow her daughter to New-Orleans. We could not quit Quebec without visiting the Plains of Abraham, to which we were politely accompanied by two Montreal gentlemen. We passed the spot where was formerly to be seen the rock against which Wolfe leaned when he died, and which, to his shame be it recorded, an American caused to be blown up and buried, on account of the injury caused to his grounds by visiters. A small monument has been erected by the Governor of Canada, who purchased the land ; and now pilgrims can come without fear of intrusion, and breathe and pray on the sacred spot.

Spenser Wood, a seat owned by an English gentleman, was shown to us as a specimen of English taste. It is beautiful spot, but by no means excels the country residences of Massachusetts or the cultivated plantations of the South.

MONTREAL.

The rain, which seemed to have held back until we had gratified our curiosity in the interesting city of Quebec, poured down in torrents as we left it, but in the comfortable quarters of the steamer Canada, which lay at the wharf to start at early dawn, we enjoyed a happy repose. Being obliged to tow two vessels, crowded with emigrants, our progress was slow ; the emigrants were animated by music, and the gay strains of the violin swept occasionally on the breeze to us, and when we stopped at *Trois Rivières*, I saw a father and his two young sons playing together. We went ashore, visited the Ursuline Convent, to convey a message from a Quebec Nun. The Sister only appeared behind the grate, with her veil covering all but a round and benevolent looking chin ; but her voice was sweet, and her air graceful. It was Saturday, and about nine o'clock in the morning ; but as it is a charm in Catholic churches that they are always open, we entered one on the way. It seemed to me, though small, the most beautiful that I had seen. We walked lightly, that we might not disturb the two or three worshippers, who had gathered for quiet devotion.

It was the last day of the Races at Trois Rivières, and as these races unite the jockeys of Montreal, Quebec, and the surrounding country, we received considerable additions to our company in the boat,

beside the winning mare, *Brunette*, whose name was
changed to *The King's Own*, from her having gained the purse, the first which William had appropriated to this object at this place. I heard something about her being akin to some Southern racer,
which I have forgotten. Among the gentlemen,
were nearly all the officers of the 32d regiment, from
Montreal, and a distinguished Irish lawyer. The
commander of the regiment, Capt. Smith, is one of
the most elegant men I have ever seen. He is brother
to the celebrated Miss Penelope Smith, who recently married the Prince of Capua. Having a very
elegant piano in the ladies' cabin, belonging to one
of the gentlemen, we became united through this delightful medium, and had the singular good fortune,
passing travellers as we were, of agreeable intercourse with some of the intelligent and interesting
society in Montreal. Oh, how often has music, in
this long journey, been a bond of sympathy!

We arrived at Montreal on Sabbath morning, and
proceeded directly to the Catholic church; and
when there, in that vast and silent assembly, though
not sympathizing either in principle or habit with
the forms, yet I gave myself up willingly to the influences of the scene; nor can I conceive that any
mind of reflection or sensibility should regard them
with coldness or ridicule. Perhaps if I saw the eyes
of the congregation fixed on the flower-robed priests
or tinselled altars, I might feel lightly; but no, among
those thousands every eye and knee were bent in
prayer or meditation, and the decorations passed for
what they are, mere symbols.

I thought within myself, God makes not only the snow-drop in its pale beauty, and the ring-dove in her modest plumage, but he paints the gorgeous robe of the tulip, and sends the oriole glancing like a ray of light through the forest ; and though I will worship in the spiritual and simple form of my fathers, I will not pluck one ornament from your gayer shrine.

In the afternoon, one of our polite fellow-travellers accompanied us to the English Church, where every body agreed that we ought to go, " because the regiment and the band would be there." I could not but smile at the stress laid upon these things in a place of religious worship. How sincerely we responded to the petitions for King William and the royal family, I am not bound to tell ; but my own heart went up in thankfulness for God's goodness, and in that dwelling I erected a passing altar to the Lord.

BURLINGTON, VT.

We left Montreal in the steamer Princess Victoria for La Prairie, where we took the cars for St. John's, and from thence the fine steam-boat Franklin for Lake Champlain. I have seen nothing, either in boats or hotels, to compare with the elegance and neatness of this boat. Among other matters of taste are excellent waiters ; handsome youths, in uniform, with stylish caps, from which a silk tassel depends, and in the purest white aprons and jackets.

This is altogether a most exquisite sail. Plattsburgh, on the west side of the lake, is a handsome village ; and one looks with interest on McDonough's farm, consisting of one hundred acres, which was granted him by the Legislature of Vermont. Near this location is the island where prisoners were confined during the war. The most glorious sunset I have ever seen, colored up the lake, the hills, and valleys, on this lovely evening ; and as we passed the spot where the dead lay, foe with foe, who had struggled here, I fancied a cloud gathering there, separated itself from the bright and beautiful rays around ; but one learns to sympathize with valor, and as I gazed, light came upon the cloud and tinged its edges, and it grew brighter and brighter until it faded away to a heavenly blue.

THOUGHTS

On passing Plattsburgh on Lake Champlain.

Hush, this is sacred ground,
　　Sacred the wave ;
Here were true warriors bound,
　　Here is their grave !
Blue mountains dimly smile
　　Over each little isle,
Passing clouds pause awhile
　　Over the brave.

Foeman sleeps near the foe,
　　Silent and cold !
Passions all hushed below,—
　　Tales that are told !—
Flowers the green-sod have crowned,
Summer birds softly sound,
Murmur the waves around,
　　Peace to the bold !

Bellows' Falls, Vermont.

We arrived at Burlington too late to enjoy the extensive view afforded by its elevated site, and left it with the dawn just opening on the handsome square in which our hotel was situated; but the rising sun shone on Lake Champlain for many a mile, contrasting its tranquil beauty with the mountains towering on every side, while Otter Creek River peeped into many a valley. Mountains! mountains! mountains! For two days I have been realizing a wish of my life, to be shut out from all things but lofty summits and the sky. Our stage companions on this route were incommunicative. I was glad to enjoy this tranquil breathing-place, and during the long days I cherished the associations of the scene in silence. The memory of the Green Mountains will follow me to my dear but level home, and their verdant tops will be a resting-place for thoughts which cannot pass away.

The rapidity with which we travelled prevented me from seeing the Green Mountain Boys; but one little trait of New England character occurred which amused me. As we stopped at Leicester, a tall and strong featured old man, in a blue farmer's frock, with a somewhat gouty walk, was on the tavern piazza.

" How d'ye do, Major?" said one of the passengers.

" Just steppin', thank ye, Captain," was the answer. " Pleasant weather !"

"Too pleasant for some folks," said the passenger—"We eat more than our peck of dust."

"Folks are always worryin' about something," answered the Major. "*It's my candid opinion* that mankind is just about the hardest to please of *any of God's creation.*"

There is but little remaining of natural beauty at Bellows' Falls. The dashing waters have gone to aid a slow canal; mills are working over the rocks, and a bridge hides the most beautiful portion of the cascade.

WATERTOWN, Mass.

We passed through a corner of New Hampshire, and the two meals we ate at Walpole and Fitzwilliam were the richest on one whole route. "Honor to whom honor is due."

As several ladies, from preference or necessity, had taken seats on the top of the stage, in our New England journey, I was disposed to try it from Keene to Fitzwilliam, before breakfast.—The scenery was picturesque, the mountains gradually softening down to hills; a little nameless stream, a tributary to the Connecticut, leaping among stones or gliding along over the sands, accompanied us all the way; the morning was bright, nature all fresh from a shower, and with six horses before, the driver snapping his long whip beneath, and the landscape stretched around, I felt the same excitement as if riding on horseback, while the great circle of hills, and woods, and meadows, glowing in the morning light, were all my own.

As we passed through a small village, the driver stopped to take in a woman and her son.   She came running to the house door, wringing out the water from a pair of pantaloons.

"Oh lud! Oh lud!" cried she, "what *shall* I do? I ha'nt but jest done sudsing Nat's pantaloons! What will he do to go to meeting with?"

Nat stood by in silence, twirling his hat, evidently not with his best pantaloons foremost.   There was a pause.

"Suppose we let her hang her pantaloons out of the coach window," said a young man, who seemed to like the fun.   It was put to vote among the passengers, and carried by acclamation.   The good woman ran to the rinsing tub, and wrung them out as quick as thought, a pretty girl from within the house brought her bonnet and bundle, she scrambled into the stage, hung out the pantaloons, and the unconscious legs kicked off, in freedom, at every jolt, in a more unconstrained manner than those which were cramped up in the vehicle.

An evident change is perceptible soon after entering Massachusetts; the mountain grandeur disappears, except where Wachusett, or some lesser eminence, lifts its rounded height, and a garden cultivation is over the whole country.

At ——, I found myself in the stage with eight of women-kind, the gentlemen being obliged to take the seats outside.   Silence prevailed for a little while, when a middle aged lady, with a buff-colored, glazed gingham frock, said to her neighbour—

" If it won't inconvenience you, I should be glad to *set* by the window a spell, as I feel a little qualm-ish."

The removal was effected, and there was a pause.

First Passenger. It's dreadful to be *sea-sick* ridin'.

" Dreadful !" said two or three.

Second Passenger. My sister Sally is the worst off of any body I ever see ridin'. She was two days travlin' in the Jarseys, lookin' as white as a sheet, and when her head warnt out o' winder, she was obleeged to lay flat on her back in the folks laps, in a kinder faint.

First, third, and fourth Passengers. Mercy ! Dreadful ! Did you ever ?

Fifth Passenger. *I* always feel fainty, like, ridin.'

Second Passenger. It makes *me* kinder squeam-ish, but I aint nothing so bad as sister Sally.

First Passenger. I've seen folks turn as white as a rag just ridin' a mile. Deacon Jones always dooz. Do you feel any better, marm ? (to the sick lady.)

Glazed Gingham. I dont expect to feel no better tell I feel worse.

Fifth Passenger. It always makes me keep spittin' and spittin' to ride. I'm obleeged to set by a win-der, constant.

Glazed Gingham, (faintly.) I woul'nt grumble an atom, if it warnt nothing but spittin' with me.

Ninth Lady. Is there any cure for this kind of sickness?

Eighth Lady. A draught of hot spear mint—and a handful put on the chest, gives some relief.

First Lady. I've hearn tell suckin' a lemon was good. Have you fur to go, marm?

Glazed Gingham. I calculate to git as fur as Borston.

First Lady. Do you calculate to be poorly all day?

Glazed Gingham could not answer, but her mouth, drawn down at the corners, looked unutterable things, and she leaned her head out of the window.

After this the party were silent, some in sleep, some in reverie; and as the stage rolled along, scenery, familiar to my youth, began to appear, touching thrillingly on the thousand chords of memory, and my thoughts framed themselves to words like these:

RETURN TO MASSACHUSETTS.

The martin's nest! the martin's nest!
  I see it swinging high,
Just as it stood in distant years,
  Above my gazing eye;
But many a bird has plumed its wing,
  And lightly flown away,
Or drooped its little head in death,
  Since that—my youthful day!

The woodland stream! the woodland stream!
  It gaily flows along,
As once it did when by its side
  I sang my merry song.

12*

But many a wave has roll'd afar,
  Beneath the summer cloud,
Since by its bank I idly poured
  My childish song aloud.

The sweet-brier Rose! the sweet-brier Rose
  Still spreads its fragrant arms,
Where graciously to passing eyes
  It gave its simple charms;
But many a perfumed breeze has past,
  And many a blossom fair,
Since with a careless heart I twined
  Its green wreaths in my hair.

The Barberry bush! the Barberry bush
  Its yellow blossoms hung
As erst, where by the grassy lane
  Along I lightly sprang;
But many a flower has come and gone,
  And scarlet berry shone,
Since I, a school-girl in its path,
  In rustic dance have flown.

My sisters dear! my sisters dear!
  And ye still live and dwell
Among the scenes where early life
  Once threw its gentle spell:
And, God be thanked! though some *young* joys
  Have flown from your soft nest,
The wanderer finds a welcome still,
  And in your arms is prest.

CAMBRIDGE.

The annual commencement at Harvard College
collects one of those great intellectual assemblages
that brighten the eye and thrill the heart of an am-

bitious speaker. The orators, on this occasion, were grave and respectable, and realized the description given in Winthrop's Journal of the first *nine* students who graduated in 1642. "They were young men of good hope, and performed their acts so as to give good proof of their proficiency in the tongues and arts."

It is seventeen years since I attended this celebration; my thoughts chiefly rested on the audience, and were drawn away from the speakers by the throng of memories that clustered so richly over the scene. There were many changes. The old Puritan meeting-house was gone, and had given place to one of elegant and classical structure. How the mind struggles between a love of the beautiful and a love of the familiar—a desire for improvement and regret at change ! It seemed to me that I would have relinquished the advantages of the present building, if a magic stroke could have restored the old edifice, with its coarse architecture, its rattling windows, its little balustrades at the top of the pews, by the twirling of which I had beguiled many a long sermon in my girlish days, and I would even have sacrificed the full-toned organ for the bass-viol, with its preliminary twang. As the bonnetted ladies entered and thronged the galleries, I thought of the waving veils and flower-wreathed curls, which once made the seats look like a garden with white banners. I went back to the time when, on the night previous to Commencement, the then scanty wardrobes of the Cambridge girls were ransacked for their little finery to grace the day. That gallery presented then a beautiful sight, and they who saw it, felt that night was not wanting to bid the eye sparkle and the cheek bloom ; that beauty was even lovelier when the rich sun-light developed its intellectual grace, as flowers are charming by the evening glare, but fruit glows more richly in the day.

The first object I missed, though well replaced by the present graceful and dignified incumbent of his office, was President Kirkland, of whom it has lately been beautifully said, that " his face is a benediction." My eyes wandered over the stage where bright locks had become grey, and the silvery hair more thin. Some had departed, all were changed ; buds of promise had bloomed, blossoms had given fruit, some had laid their young heads in the grave, and some stood ripely ready for the harvest in a good old age. There mingled those good, wise men ; yet I thought what waves of trouble had flowed over each and all ; how passion had swept across their souls ! I heard a voice rising from that tranquil body, telling the common lot of man. They have had days of strife and nights of bitterness ; they have wrestled with the world, with themselves, with God ; seeming friendship has mocked, ambition has lured them on its bitter pleasures, eating the heart it fed ; death has crushed their hopes, and life has been a toil, sanctified only by the promise of a home, where man shall lay down these cares, where the skies shall not darken, nor the leaf drop in autumn winds, nor the flower perish ; but all that is beautiful and good,

and, God be thanked, there is still beauty and goodness on the earth, shall look up and smile, and breathe
heaven's atmosphere of love.

After musing awhile on these things, until the
voices of the speakers sounded, dream-like, amid the
deeper voices of the past, my attention was rivetted
by one conspicuous individual.   I had seen that subdued glance years ago, at his first college exhibition ;
it was the same—the same slow raising of the clear
blue eye, the same deferential bow at honors confer-
red.   The cheek of the man was pale ; on the boy's
was a crimson spot, where genius seemed feeding ;
time had laid his hand on the head of the man, the
boy's fair hair was glossy and full ; the limbs of the
man, though not large, were firm, the boy was slender, so slender that it was feared mind would master
him, and that he would be one of those plants that
die early.   Why God so often takes the prematurc-
ly ripe, we know not ; but we know that the respon-
sibilities of such moral agents as he permits to remain, are fearfully great.   The eye of heaven must
look searchingly down on the individuals it has gift-
ed so unsparingly.

At the Commencement of 1811 he again appeared, still a boy, bearing off the honors of a man.
There was another lapse of time, and he stood before the Phi Beta Kappa Society as a poet ; and
the lips of the fair opened in praise, and friends gathered and fluttered like butterflies around the opened flower, and old men shook their heads in pleasant
surprise, or gazed upon his modest brow, and bade

him God speed. A few years passed, and he stood
to be ordained in the holy character of a Gospel
minister. I shall never forget that day. As his fathers in the ministry laid their hands on his head,
he looked too slight for so tremendous a charge ; but
when, at the close of the service, he pronounced a
blessing on the audience, there was a tremulous depth
in his voice which spoke of ardent communings with
duty.

Another period elapsed, and he visited Europe, to
glean from its fields pleasure and improvement. In
the Chapel of Harvard College, on his return, I heard
his first discourse. It was a brilliant summary of
interesting things. Since then he has walked the
halls of statesmen ; his various orations have risen
like a line of beautiful hills on the literary horizon,
and he has been crowned with civil honors.

But are the performances of the day really closed ?
Have fathers strained their eyes and ears in half
terrified joy, and mothers shrank into themselves,
and sisters blushed, and smiled, and wept, as the
young orators trod the stage ? Have the diplomas, which seem like the rolls of fate, been given,
freeing them from collegiate duties, and launching
them off to untried scenes ? Has the benediction
been pronounced by the sweet and tremulous voice
of the patriarch of the scene, and the brazen tongues
of the band sent out their thrilling harmony, while I
have been lifting the curtain of the past ?

The pleasure of Commencement day is greatly
heightened by the attractive levee at the President's.

It would be ungrateful to allow this opportunity to pass without a tribute to the dignified courtesy, the graceful hospitality, of the lovely family who contribute so fully to the happiness of their guests. None are overlooked or forgotten, where the charm of good-nature is added to the refinement of polished manners. There stood on the centre table a grape vine in a jar, bearing rich and beautiful fruit. The outside of the vase was ornamented by flowers confined with a string passed round several times, so that the vessel itself looked like a beautiful flower. This tasteful gift was from the garden of Mr. Cushing, of Watertown, whose costly and cultivated grounds, which I have had the pleasure of visiting, attract the notice and admiration of strangers. One of the curiosities is a China wall, the tiles of which were brought from Canton at immense expense. The hot-house presents the most rare East India plants. Many of the attendants are Chinese, and dress, in part, in costume of their country. The grapery is extensive, and as the clusters hung invitingly before me, in the temperated apartments, while a raw east wind was scattering the leaves out of doors, I could not but think how our sunny South repays, with one half the expense and labor, the efforts of the careful planter, and yet how few specimens are to be found of fruit culture. But we must be patient; the "Southern Agriculturalist" regularly issues its voice of instruction and experiment, and private enterprise is awaking with public improvements. After all, the question may be asked, why not let all who can spend their means in travelling, do so ; and instead of wearing out money and health in our warm summers, visit gardens like Mr. Cushing's. There they will not be called to mourn over a rare fruit or flower frost-nipped or broken ; the laborer works for their eye unpaid ; they may tread on the gravelled paths or marble walks, and inhale the odour of rare exotics, and for the time being, throw up their hats and shout hurra, this is mine ! As I saw the China wall, and the East India plants, and the huge broad Chinese hats of the servants, I thought it might be a pretty whim in the rich people of this country to copy the style and costume of Europe in their country seats. Let one man have an Italian villa, and all its accompaniments ; another, a Russian retreat ; let a third select some romantic site for a Swiss cottage ; another might fancy a Dutch flower garden. When we shall dart across the Atlantic in our steam-boats in ten days, these imitations will doubtless increase among the wealthy, and it is probable the taste of the laboring classes, too, will be more English. The little vegetable garden will be ornamented with flowers, the trelliced window show forth its honeysuckle or clematis, instead of here and there a straggling bean, which is all that greets us now ; and the merry bird sings out its notes from sheltering trees, surrounding cottages that now stand uncovered in the summer sun. But then, alas, new modes of evil, new motives to sin, will come along with these improvements ; are we prepared,

as a nation, to avail ourselves of one without yielding to the other?

PHI BETA KAPPA CELEBRATION.

There can scarcely be a more imposing audience
than that which assembles on this occasion. Fashion and intellect bow together at this shrine. I was
glad of an opportunity to see and hear President ——,
having read his printed discourses with profound respect for their elevated character. His appearance
is grave and dignified, his action graceful, and his
voice deep-toned; but no man should apologize for
a performance which is accepted a year in advance.
Then it seemed to me that it was not the place for
an essay on faith. I am exceedingly sensitive about
running any risk of the abuse of sacred things, and,
as a matter of taste, should like to avoid the introduction of sacred topics, treated metaphysically,
where the mind of an audience would be likely to
receive them coldly or lightly. Not that a religious
tone should be avoided; for there may, and should
be, in every performance, those appeals to our higher
nature, which, mingling in with less elevated themes,
sanctify and ennoble them.

Never were two beings in stronger contrast, in
every point of view, than the orator and poet. The
first, a massy Gothic edifice; the latter, a Corinthian temple. There was something almost sublime,
however, in the expansion of the poet's slight figure,
and the rolling of his large eyes, while he heaved up
pearls and *sea-weed* from the little ocean of his mind.

13

His performance, which lasted an hour and a half, was entirely committed to memory.

CAMBRIDGE, Sept. 8. }
morning.

This memorable day is ushered in by clouds, but I cannot bring myself to believe that they will not disperse.   Every thing should be bright on this great anniversary, the two hundredth year since the foundation of Harvard College.   The beautiful repose which characterizes Cambridge still rests over the verdant common and the tasteful buildings scattered around it, though thousands of individuals are gradually collecting to join the great Jubilee.   The noble elm of Washington, the tree beneath which his tent was pitched in the revolutionary war, is waving quietly in the breeze not far from my window, the only object in the whole circle of my view, which saw the infant day of Harvard; the colleges stand in the early light, silent testimonials of the wisdom which planned, and the energy which has sustained them ; nothing breaks the stillness of the morning but the light or loitering step of the passing students.

The great subject of excitement for the last week has been, whether ladies should be permitted to hear the addresses within the tent.   There was a strong and powerful party in favor of the measure among the Committee of Arrangements ;—it was contended that the daughters, and wives, and mothers of the sons of Harvard, had an interest in common with the Alumni ; that it was a scene for the affections, which the jar of politics and the grossness of forensic debate could not reach, and that it would be an appropriate opportunity to indulge them in witnessing a style of public eloquence to which their peculiar habits render them necessarily strangers. So strong was the desire to effect this object among the gentlemen, that it was given up only at the last moment, from the apprehension of too limited a space for the numbers that would probably have pressed in.   The only substitute therefore for the ladies was to visit the tent, yesterday, after its completion, and call upon their imaginations to locate Webster, and Everett, and Legaré, and the other Mercuries of our country, in their respective seats.

The site for the tent is well chosen on a green enclosure, forming a natural amphitheatre.   The covering of the Pavilion is supported in the centre by a pillar between fifty and sixty feet in height, gradually descending in a slope in the Pagoda style, until it meets eight pillars supporting a frame work from which the canvass reaches to the ground, where it is fastened as a protection from air and observation. The pillars are covered with white cloth from the base upward, and garlanded with flowers and evergreens, while festoons hang gracefully from different quarters of the arch.   The seats for the President of the day and the invited guests are placed on a platform in the lowest part of the amphitheatre, while semicircular ranges of tables for the alumni, in classes, occupy the whole rising ground, and are so arranged that every individual will face the President of the day.

On this array we, poor ladies, looked like Eve when driven from Paradise, and half turned Wolstonecraftians on the spot as we fancied the intellectual treat which we could not share.

Next to a view of Niagara has this day thrilled my soul. The sun *did* break out in beauty and gladness over this noble scene like a sent blessing. Tears of emotion have been in the dim eyes of age, trickled down the cheek of manhood, and glistened on the face of youth, and every woman who witnessed that mighty wave of the intellectual ocean of our country, felt proud of her connexion with Harvard.

By nine o'clock there was a crowd of ladies at the church door, waiting for its opening. The key was turned within, and in we rushed. I should have been badly seated, after all, had not one of the seats reserved for the President's family in the gallery been kindly offered me. From that point of view I saw every thing to the greatest advantage, and watched with eagerness the procession which entered in the following order :

Students of the University.

Band of Music.

Chief Marshal and Aids.

Committee of Arrangements.

President Quincy and Chaplain of the day.

The Corporation of the University.

Ex-President Kirkland, and President Humphrey of Amherst College.

His Excellency the Governor and Suite.
The Vice-Presidents of the Day.
Senators and Representatives in Congress.
Judges of the United States and State Courts,
and Attorney General.
Benefactors of the University, distinguished Stran-
gers, and other Guests specially invited.
The Overseers of the University.
Professors, Tutors, and Officers of the University.
Gentlemen who have received honorary degrees, and
who do not come under any regular
Class of Graduates.
Graduates of the University in the order of their
Classes, from the oldest class present, to 1836.
Students of the Divinity School, Law School, and
Medical School, who are not included
above.

There were no ladies on the lower floor, but countless beaming eyes from the galleries testified their interest in the human mass that was collecting below,
filling every point of the building, wave upon wave.
The Rev. Dr. Ripley of Concord, ninety years of
age, commenced the services by prayer.   There was
none of the listlessness perceptible that usually pervades a promiscuous audience, in this often desecrated
service.   "The age that was past" seemed speaking to one and all from his time-worn form with ora-
cular energy.   Then the following Ode, by the Rev.
S. Gilman, was performed by a select choir :

Fair Harvard! thy sons to thy Jubilee throng,
  And with blessings surrender thee o'er,
By these festival-rites, from the Age that is past,
  To the Age that is waiting before.
O Relic and Type of our ancestor's worth,
  That hast long kept their memory warm!
First flower of their wilderness!   Star of their night,
  Calm rising through change and through storm!

To thy bowers we were led in the bloom of our youth,
  From the home of our free-roving years,
When our fathers had warn'd, and our mothers had pray'd,
  And our sisters had blest, through their tears,
Thou then wert our Parent,—the nurse of our souls,—
  We were moulded to manhood by thee,
Till freighted with treasure thoughts, frendships and hopes,
  Thou didst launch us on Destiny's sea.

When, as pilgrims, we come to revisit thy halls,
  To what kindlings the season gives birth!
Thy shades are more soothing, thy sunlight more dear,
  Than descend on less privileged earth:
For the Good and the Great, in their beautiful prime,
  Through thy precincts have musingly trod,
As they girded their spirits, or deepened the streams
  That make glad the fair City of God.

Farewell! be thy destinies onward and bright!
  To thy children the lesson still give,
With freedom to think, and with patience to bear,
  And for Right ever bravely to live.
Let not moss-covered Error moor *thee* at its side,
  As the world on Truth's current glides by ;
Be the herald of light, and the bearer of Love,
  Till the stock of the Puritans die.

There was a felt stillness as the sentiment and mu-

sic sank in every heart, and at the close each man
folded his printed copy carefully like a thing to be
cherished and carried to his home.

President Quincy's discourse was an interesting
revelation of the early history of the College. As
I walked to the Church in the morning, I saw the
name of *Dunster* with others enwreathed over the
College gates, with a dim feeling of ignorance of his
character; after the address, on my return, I looked
at it again with changed impressions. I had become
acquainted with the first President of Harvard. His
hopes, his struggles and trials had been revealed to
me by the orator, and I cast my eyes with tenfold
interest on the grave yard where his remains had
so long since mingled with the dust. There was a
happy mixture of graceful good humor mingled with
the more serious matter of Mr. Quincy's essay, and
a general smile lit up the countenances of the audience to whom bequests of thousands of dollars were
familiar, to hear him read records of donations to
the College of an iron spoon and pewter cup, or similar articles.

Dr. Homer of Newton, an octogenarian of the class
of 1777, made the concluding prayer. The services
were then closed by a doxology in which every individual appeared to join. The voices, perfect in
harmony, came on the ear like a tuned tempest, in
their solemn fulness and power.

Most of the ladies rushed from the house to see
the procession move to the Pavilion; a few, perhaps
half a dozen, were detained accidentally in the gal-

lery, and the formation of the procession in the Church, which they witnessed, constituted one of the most interesting and affecting scenes of the celebration. The marshal of the day called " the class of 1759." There was no response,—the only survivor, a gentleman from Maine, being incapacitated from attendance. Successive classes were summoned ; there was a hush over that immense concourse that would have made a foot-fall seem loud. At length " the class of 1774" was called ; a feeble old man stepped forth, and passed along the aisle *alone*. A reaction was experienced, and a burst of animated cheers followed his tottering footsteps. It was a grand moment. I know nothing finer in the poetry of life.

But as life is full of variety, so after awhile there was a little touch of the ludicrous. The printed order made it requisite for the marshal to call on " *Distinguished Strangers*" to join the procession. At this there was a great deal of half blushing and fidgetting as Northern gentlemen bowed and signed to Southern gentlemen, and middle State gentlemen were bowed to and bowed in their turn. They might perhaps have been bowing to this day, had not the foremost been gracefully hustled off the stage, and the remainder followed naturally as they stood. It was a glorious procession when they were all formed, and brought the pulse of the spectator higher than military or civic grandeur could do. Thirteen hundred persons passed before the eye, who had all drank from the same intellectual fountain. It was a serious procession, for this would never meet again, I scarcely saw a smile.

There were several private circles which were entertained by the hospitality of the Cambridge ladies at dinner ; and many from them, to beguile the time before the President's levee, walked to the Pavilion. As we endeavored to press within I could compare ourselves to nothing but chickens trying at every crevice to get at their dam,—now the faint echo of a song would reach us,—now the tones but not the words of a familiar voice,—now huzzaing and clapping of hands, and then that silence prevailed, which showed absorbed attention to some low tones of eloquence which we could only fancy.

But the time approached for the interdict of separation to be taken off, and we retired to dress for the President's levee. At twilight the first lights appeared, and by eight o'clock the illumination of the Colleges, the Law School, the Church and other buildings in the vicinity began to attract the throng. Invited guests passed and repassed from the President's fashionably filled rooms to the College grounds, as suited their inclination. There was no restraint, and one could scarcely say which was more attractive, the music, the refreshments, and elegance of the saloon, or the brilliant lights abroad, shining on groups of happy, yet quiet throngs of all conditions and ages. One of the most beautiful combinations at an illumination is the effect produced by the light on trees. There is a kind of unearthly beauty, a mystery in the waving of their green boughs, that attracts me more than the glow of the lights; and the elms in the College yard seemed from their elasticity to partake unusually of this wave and hue, which are so exquisite.

It is now near midnight,—all is still; the artificial blaze is extinguished, man has exhausted his brief brilliancy, and closes his eyes in rest, but there, above and around me shine the stars unfading and untiring; the northern lights shoot up their meteor rays in silvery glory, as they did when creation was young; the little fire-fly prunes its light wing, and flits as freshly as the day's butterfly; the breeze too is untired, as when it first fanned the wings of the seraphim in Paradise, and passes by my window busy with its own appointed task.

Oh sleeping man, how thou dost struggle for thy little brief authority over nature and time, and how helpless art thou! Yet what if thy "brief candle" be quite extinguished here, not only by sleep but death, it shall be lit again from new urns of living light where no feeble mottoes and inscription shine in momentary mockery, but where, kindling in gem-like hues, illuminating myriads and worlds, shall blaze forth on the eternal arch in " buildings not made with hands," *Immortality.*

But my far-wandering thoughts are recalled by the rustling of the wide-spread arms of Washington's Elm, whose green leaves wave as lightly as when its buds were formed *before we were a nation;* and my busy musings ask for measured words.

WASHINGTON'S ELM AT CAMBRIDGE.

Much hast thou seen, brave tree,
  Since thy young holiday of early leaf,
When thy slight branches struggled to be free,
  And thy pale root was brief!

More than the common share
  Has fallen to thy wondrous lot, I guess,
Great antiquarian of an age most rare,
  Of trial, hope, success!

Take me among thy boughs,
  Good tree; I to thy vast experience soar!
More than book knowledge can thy whisperings rouse,
  A sterner, richer lore!

I hear an answering tone
  In the long waving of thine aged limbs,
And the wind's low and softly uttered moan,
  Like spirits' midnight hymns.

Did not the Indian's dart,
  When roving wild, make thy young trunk its aim?
And some brown girl, beneath thy branches, start
  The fire-fly meteor flame?

Dost thou remember, tree,
  Harvard's *first* sons?   Came they beneath thy boughs
With study pale—or wandering carelessly,
  Dream of fair maiden's vows?

And does not every leaf
  Stir with the strong remembrances of *one*,
The immortal—the unconquerable chief—
  Thine own—thy Washington?

To think that he did lay
  His weary limbs beneath thy very shade,—
That here he mused, and planned, and thought by day,—
  That here he nightly prayed !

To think that here his soul
  Writhed in some stirring of war's agony—
Or with a strong, prophetic, deep control
  Looked through to victory !

Yes ! 'tis a hallowed spot !
  Here for my country a new pulse beats high,
And woman's feeble nature all forgot,
  Here too even I could die.

Without possessing the romantic characteristics
of many of the neighboring towns, Cambridge has a
peculiar charm from the associations connected with
it ; it may be that beside its literary interest and be-
witching hospitalities, my heart wakes up at the
sight of the school-house where I conned my lessons,
the dwelling around whose humble porch I twined
the honey-suckle, and the walks where I strolled
with my schoolmates. I remember one of those
schoolmates ; she was called early to her rest, but
a brighter mind never shone in heaven's spiritual
constellations, than that which dwelt in the slight
figure of Mary Ann B.   Some who read these pages
may yet remember her,—her laugh " that rang from
the soul ;" her wit, that sparkled like stars in the
shade of common minds ; her strong good sense,
that triumphed over her tendency to satire ; her varied powers, that made

"the long summer's day
Seem too, too much in haste."

Mary Ann was the life of the masquerades at Cambridge. It may surprise many, but it is a fact, that masquerades in college, exclusively confined to the students however, were permitted as an annual amusement so late as 1809. The maskers felt themselves authorized to enter any house, under any disguise they chose, throughout one appointed evening. There might be seen the Cambridge girls, usually so retired, dressed with more than usual care in the slight ornaments of their unpretending wardrobes, while unannounced soldiers entered and knelt at their feet; fortune-tellers gazed on the lines of their extended hands; Indian chiefs brandished their hatchets in their quiet parlors; pretended Frenchmen, with snuff and broken phrases, raised easy laughter; lumbering Falstaffs, who had despoiled their beds of pillows, came glorious with clumsiness instead of wit; while here and there a youth betrayed himself by an amphibious bow, in attempting a courtsey as a fair maiden.

There was another occasion where Mary Ann· B. was the soul of our girlish joy, in May day excursions to Sweet Auburn. Shutting up our books on the first propitious day, we sallied to that delicious retreat, and gazed on the page of nature. Doubtless our hearts grew on those lovely jubilees, and the young eye that seemed listless in its carelessness, was drinking in thought like the breath of heaven. Hap-

py period! when the heart, in its soarings, perceives
that the Deity has commenced his first felt spiritual
creations on the soul, and in gentle visitings stamps
there pure thoughts and holy affections! I can remember nothing more delicious than this young
spirit of piety, this offering up of the unstained
thought to its Maker in his solitudes! Let those
who live in cities carry their children, sometimes,
to a retreat of idleness; let them pause in the hurry
of the locomotive sweep of modern education, and
teach them by hill-side and rivulet. I can hear
now, though the din of life has long been sounding
in my ear, the murmur of the beech trees as I sat
a child at Sweet Auburn on Moss Hill. Who can
recall these emotions without thinking of eternity?

But what a change is here! The city does indeed
throng to the spot so sacred to my early associations, leaving the dusty world behind. Daily, hour-
ly, a line of carriages stands at its lofty gate, and
countless guests pause at the solemn inscription—
  "*The dust shall return to the earth as it was, and
the spirit shall return to God who gave it,*"—
and then enter to meditate among the unrivalled
varieties of Mount Auburn, or to recall the following graceful and descriptive language of Judge
Story at its consecration:

  "A rural Cemetery seems to combine in itself all
the advantages which can be proposed to gratify human feelings, or tranquillize human fears; to secure
the best religious influences, and to cherish all those

associations which cast a cheerful light over the darkness of the grave.

"And what spot can be more appropriate than this, for such a purpose? Nature seems to point it out with significant energy, as the favorite retirement for the dead. There are around us all the varied features of her beauty and grandeur; the forest-crowned height; the abrupt acclivity; the sheltered valley; the deep glen; the grassy glade; and the silent grove. Here are the lofty oak, the beech that 'wreathes its old fantastic roots so high,' the rustling pine, and the drooping willow; the tree, that sheds its pale leaves with every autumn, a fit emblem of our transitory gloom; and the evergreen, with its perennial shoots, instructing us that 'the wintry blast of death kills not the buds of virtue.' Here is the thick shrubbery to protect and conceal the new-made grave; and there is the wild-flower creeping along the narrow path, and planting its seeds in the upturned earth. All around us there breathes a solemn calm, as if we were in the bosom of the wilderness, broken only by the breeze as it murmurs through the tops of the forest, or by the notes of the warbler pouring forth his matin·or his evening song.

"Ascend but a few steps, and what a change of scenery to surprise and delight us. We seem, as it were in an instant, to pass from the confines of death to the bright and balmy regions of life. Below us flows the winding Charles with its rippling current, like the stream of time hastening to the ocean of eternity. In the distance, the city—at once the object of our admiration and our love—rears its proud eminences, its glittering spires, its lofty towers, its graceful mansions, its curling smoke, its crowded haunts of business and pleasure, which speak to the eye, and yet leave a noiseless loneliness on the ear. Again we turn, and the walls of our venerable University rise before us, with many a recollection of happy days passed there in the interchange of study and friendship, and many a grateful thought of the affluence of its learning, which has adorned and nourished the literature of our country.   Again we turn, and the cultivated farm, the neat cottage, the village church, the sparkling lake, the rich valley, and the distant hills, are before us through opening vistas ; and we breathe amidst the fresh and varied labors of man.

"There is, therefore, within our reach, every variety of natural and artificial scenery which is fitted to awaken emotions of the highest and most affecting character.   We stand, as it were, upon the borders of two worlds ; and as the mood of our minds may be, we may gather lessons of profound wisdom by contrasting the one with the other, or indulge in the dreams of hope and ambition, or solace our hearts by melancholy meditations.

" Who is there, that in the contemplation of such a scene, is not ready to exclaim with the enthusiasm of the poet,

' ' Mine be the breezy hill, that skirts the down,
  Where a green, grassy turf is all I crave,
With here and there a violet bestrown,
  Fast by a brook, or fountain's murmuring wave,
  And many an evening sun shine sweetly on my grave!' "

* * * * *

" The voice of consolation will spring up in the midst of the silence of these regions of death. The mourner will revisit these shades with a secret, though melancholy pleasure. The hand of friendship will delight to cherish the flowers and the shrubs that fringe the lowly grave, or the sculptured monument. The earliest beams of the morning will play upon these summits with a refreshing cheerfulness; and the lingering tints of evening hover on them with a tranquillizing glow. Spring will invite thither the footsteps of the young by its opening foliage; and autumn detain the contemplative by its latest bloom. The votary of learning and science will here learn to elevate his genius by the holiest studies. The devout will here offer up the silent tribute of pity, or the prayer of gratitude. The rivalries of the world will here drop from the heart; the spirit of forgiveness will gather new impulses; the selfishness of avarice will be checked; the restlessness of ambition will be rebuked; vanity will let fall its plumes; and pride, as its sees ' what shadows we are, and what shadows we pursue,' will acknowledge the value of virtue as far, immeasurably far, beyond that of fame.

"But that which will be ever present, pervading

14*

these shades like the noon-day sun, and shedding cheerfulness around, is the consciousness, the irrepressible consciousness, amidst all these lessons of human mortality, of the higher truth, that we are beings, not of time but of eternity ; ' that this corruptible must put on incorruption, and this mortal must put on immortality.' That this is but the threshold and starting point of an existence, compared with whose duration the ocean is but as a drop, nay the whole creation an evanescent quantity."

There is something very touching in the predominance of white flowers around the graves. They speak, amid the darker foliage of the grove, a language like hope in our shaded world. No one should visit Mount Auburn without a tribute of respect to Hannah Adams, its first occupant. I saw her often, in my early life, and as I stood by her grave, recalled her modest worth, her strong integrity, her Christian hope. Probably her humble taste would have chosen some violet-covered bank for her last resting place, rather than the monumental shrine that admiring friends have awarded her. She humbled herself, and is exalted. I remember a little trait of modesty which in any one else would have seemed affectation. About the time of her writing the History of the Jews, she was praising the poetical attempts of a very young girl, who, feeling the compliment deeply, said, " Oh, Miss Adams, to think that you, who write on such profound subjects, should like my rhymes !" " My dear," answered she, earnestly, with her rapid and somewhat lisping tone, " my writings have nothing original ; they are *mere compilations !*"—yet this woman's works were then in the libraries of the learned.

The site chosen by Fanny Kemble for the interment of a relative, is beneath cedar trees, and is surrounded by sweet-brier ; but the sweet-brier cannot thrive without the sun, and looks withered and seared.

Spurzheim's tomb is attractive in its simplicity ; he followed soon the tender appeal of the orator at the Consecration—" Here let the teacher of the philosophy of nature come !"

Yet to me no spot is more beautiful than that which covers the gathered forms, beloved by the orator himself. His affecting call has been often sadly answered in his own experience, for " youth and beauty, blighted by premature decay, have dropped like tender blossoms into the virgin earth," and the hand of affection has " cherished the shrubs and flowers that fringe their graves."

Yet probably few persons, of contemplative minds, now visit this sacred spot, without feeling that there is too much *life*, too much of the world collected there. Idle questions of childhood, flippant jests of the gay who have none to mourn for, criticisms over the model of monuments where affection longs to come and lie down and weep alone, press on the ear with painful dissonance to the still harmonies of nature. I joined in the cry, *It is great ! It is beautiful !* But when it was *Sweet* Auburn, and I strayed there in my lonely childhood, I heard lessons in the springing and falling leaves, in the undisturbed chants of birds, in the rushing of winds, as eloquent as those which cluster over the monuments on the spot that classical hands and affectionate hearts, combining with its surpassing natural beauties, are tending to make another wonder of the world.

The incongruous combinations at Mount Auburn are illustrated by a group whom one of our friends saw greatly puzzled over the word *fecit*. "Who is that Fecit family?" said one; "there seem to be a great many on 'em!" By the way, it is curious to observe how long this Latin word has adhered to grave stones; probably, as some punster cunningly said, because it is a *dead* language!

SWEET AUBURN.

NOW MOUNT AUBURN CEMETERY.

Sweet Auburn! when a gay and happy child,
Playing with nature like a favorite toy,
I loved thy haunts,--thy bowers so altered now!
Nine summers only on my eyes had smiled,
When to thy wilds, all unaccompanied,
Frequent I strayed, slighting more cultured paths,
Where glowed, mid wary steps, the weeded flowers.
I sought thy mossy banks—raised a green throne,
And wielding there the willow's flexile twig,
Sang idle songs, such as ring wildly forth
In carol light or sad from untried hearts.
To Woody Dell I strayed; not then the voice
Which since, in manly eloquence, has woke
Its echoes, met my ear, but the gay birds

Sent up clear notes of joy from bough to bough,
Unconscious, that those notes in after years
Would change to funeral hymns.

    I climbed thy Hill,
Whose noble height look'd down o'er art and nature.
The city's spires stood out, bathed in the glow
Of distant sun-light, while the gentle Charles
Lay like a nursing child outstretched in joy,
Soft murmuring, beneath the waving boughs.

  Then with a light but not unthinking mind,
A glancing eye, and busy foot descending
The wooded Hill, I sought the Giant's Grave,
On whose extended mound the wild flowers rose.
The soft anemone stood peeping there,
To woodland gaze the gentle snow-drop's peer,
And violets that owe their witching charm
To kindred with an azure eye,--and heaven.

  And can it be the hand, the same small hand,
That with its soft and twining fingers loved
To cull the flowers on Auburn's leafy slopes,
That presses oft in serious thought my brow
Beneath the star-beam of a Southern sky ?

  Thou, too, how changed, sweet Auburn! then of life,
Now of the grave thou tell'st—thy bloom is mourning!
And with the wild bird's song the sob of woe
Mingles most sad.————————

    I ask no monument,
Or lettered urn, within thy classic shades.
Be thou to me as in my childish days
Clustered all o'er with bright imaginings.
Though solemn words have sanctified thy Dell,
Linking its grassy clods with thoughts of heaven,
Though with fastidious taste affection's hand
Has piled the costly marble on thy hills,
And carved it in thy vales : though the great dead,
Great in the intellect that cannot die,
Have made their bed with thee, to me thou art

Sweet Auburn, and I love thee as the nest
From whence I joyed to plume my youthful wings
And soar to man's high nature from the child's.
    I ask no monument within thy shades.
The rustling branches of our Southern groves
Shall sooth my sleep of death, kindly as minds
That circle through thy famed and cultur'd bow'rs;
The Southern flower spring up as soft and pure
As thine; bright Southern birds a requiem pour
As rich and mournful as thy plumed quire ;
And Southern hearts, God knows how fervently,
Breathe prayers and blessings on my humbler grave.

WATERTOWN, Mass.

The general traveller hurries though the main street of this village without comment, though its historical interest and local beauty might call on him to pause if he reflected on one, or but glanced at the other. I, on the contrary, linger along its river-banks, where the Charles rolls on in placid bright-ness, or ascend its rounded hill, where the woods cluster like a loving family, looking calmly down on the residences that are scattered below, or visit its neighboring country seats, where taste and wealth have made Edens of beauty. The general traveller has no associations like mine. It was not here that he sojourned, when leaving school he began to feel the pressure of duty and responsibility mingling in with the elastic spirit of hope and enjoyment; he tuned not his guitar on the slope of that *hill*, nor saw the sunset beam up in his evening rambles; he has not trod Sabbath after Sabbath through wintry snows and summer heats to yonder old Meeting

House, offering up the heart's prayer in its young developements.   To be sure, as the Sartor Resartus saith, in the days of which I speak, "those same Church clothes had gone sorrowfully out at elbows, nay, far worse, many of them had become mere hollow shapes or masks under which no living figure or spirit any longer dwelt;" the subduing hand of disease was on the Pastor; we were at the mercy of a bass-viol and clarionet that "ganged their ain gates," the chief merit of the performers being physical power, aided, as the Village Choir describes, by their stripping off their coats, and beating time in their shirt sleeves.   There was no stove to comfort the chilled devotee in winter, nor trees to shade him in summer.

Yet the congregation kept together.   The strong love of some tie between man and his Maker often surmounts and conquers the most adverse circumstances, and while externally all seemed nipped and chilled in this garden of the Lord, "religion was weaving for herself new vestures wherewith to re-appear and bless," and behold, she has re-appeared and blessed!   A new and beautiful temple has arisen, crowded with attentive worshippers.   A choir more full and harmonious than can often be met in country towns, utters hymns of praise beneath its dome.   An organ rises in noble symmetry, and peals its triumphant notes as if glad to be an instrument of God's glory; and his oracles are unfolded by one of the brightest minds he has created.

I have attended the dedication of this very chaste

edifice. There is something exceedingly affecting
in leaving the church of one's familiar worship.
The old building stands with a solitary and almost
human look of appeal to those who cast it off to
lonely decay. The grave-yard, too, what a language it speaks ! No ground can seem so consecrated as that where our first tears have fallen ; and all
the monuments of Mount Auburn, rising in the vicinity, are not so touching to me as the now deserted
tomb of two bright boys, whom I saw laid in this
grave-yard by hearts breaking with the tumult of
their *first* woes. Can it be more than twenty years
since those children were covered like shut-up
blossoms beneath that sod ? Sometimes in looking
over my relics of the past I see a soft light curl.
I took it from the brow of the elder as he lay beautiful in death ; his perfect features still and fair as
chiselled marble. I had watched his slow decay ; I
saw the dimpled hand grow thin, the blue eye become
dim, and the smile that once lit his face beam slow
and sickly. His little arm could no longer clasp
my neck ; he lay passive in my arms, and so he died.
What a struggle has he escaped ! How often might
that severed curl have lain upon a throbbing temple ;
how often been pressed by a hand, whose pulses
beat to sorrow and despair !

These thoughts came upon me in the solemnities
of the dedication of the new temple, yet I soon began to sympathize with those who felt a happy pride
in their religious ark ; who had wafted it along by
noble efforts and had come up to give their vows

and take shelter for their souls ; nor can I deny myself the pleasure of recalling some of the high and beautiful thoughts with which their pastor, the Rev. Convers Francis, led their devotions.

"It is a poor philosophy and a narrow religion," said he, "which does not recognise God as all in all. Every moment of our lives, we breathe, stand, or move in the temple of the Most High; for the whole universe is that temple. Wherever we go, the testimony to his power, the impress of his hand, are there. Ask of the bright worlds around us, as they roll in the everlasting harmony of their circles; and they shall tell you of Him, whose power launched them on their courses. Ask of the mountains, that lift their heads among and above the clouds; and the bleak summit of one shall seem to call aloud to the snow-clad top of another, in proclaiming their testimony to the Agency which has laid their deep foundations. Ask of ocean's waters; and the roar of their boundless waves shall chant from shore to shore a hymn of ascription to that Being, who hath said, ' Hitherto shall ye come and no further.' Ask of the rivers; and, as they roll onward to the sea, do they not bear along their ceaseless tribute to the ever-working Energy, which struck open their fountains and poured them down through the valleys? Ask of every region of the earth, from the burning equator to the icy pole, from the rock-bound coast to the plain covered with its luxuriant vegetation; and will you not find on them all the record of the Creator's presence? Ask of the countless

15

tribes of plants and animals; and shall they **not**
testify to the action of the great Source of Life?
Yes, from every portion, from every department of
nature, comes the same voice; everywhere we **hear**
thy name, O God; everywhere we see thy **love.**
Creation, in all its length and breadth, in all its depth
and height, is the manifestation of thy Spirit, and
without thee the world were dark and dead. The universe is to us as the burning bush which the Hebrew
leader saw; God is ever present in it, for it **burns**
with His glory, and the ground on which we **stand**
is always holy.

"How then can we speak of that Presence as peculiarly in the sanctuary, which is abroad through
all space and time?

*   *   *   *   *

"Yet it is interesting to contemplate the progress
of Christianity in respect to the external accommodations enjoyed by its disciples.   We look back on the
little and friendless band of the Saviour's followers,
just after they had returned from the memorable
scene, at which their Master bade them farewell, **to**
go to his Father and their Father, to his God and
their God.   They turned away, as we may suppose,
with heavy hearts, and when they reached Jerusalem, assembled in 'an upper room,' where they continued 'with one accord in prayer and supplication.'   What holy and touching associations does
imagination attach to that room, where were gathered the small company of God's messengers, from
whom the word of life was to go forth subduing and

blessing the world! Time rolled on, and that little band grew into a large body of believers, holding 'the unity of the spirit in the bond of peace,' and carrying with them the power that was to effect the greatest moral revolution in the annals of the world. During this time, they had stated places of meeting, though not such as were then denominated temples. As their numbers increased, and as they found periods of peace and favor from the civil power, they built their churches. These were multiplied rapidly, insomuch that when the edict of Diocletian went forth for the destruction of such edifices, there were more than forty of these *basilicæ* in the city of Rome alone. Christianity passed through its seasons of sunshine and of storm, ever growing, ever reaching forth to wider conquest, till a Christain emperor was seated on the throne, and the banner of the cross became the banner of empire. Then architecture, in its most costly and magnificent forms, was summoned into the service of the religion of Jesus; and, when Constantine had finished a church at Jerusalem, the bishops were gathered from the various parts of Christendom, to perform with due magnificence the solemn rites of dedication. From that time the spread of the religion was accompanied by the multiplication of edifices adorned with solemn beauty, and consecrated to the services by which the soul, in visible forms, manifests its relation to the Infinite One and to spiritual being.

"And now, instead of that one 'upper room,' where the little company of heart-stricken disciples

met, surrounded by a hostile world, we look abroad
on those parts of the earth which are most distinguished by all the refinements of life, and in which
the great intellectual power of mankind resides, and
see them abounding in the splendid memorials of
Christian worship, which echo to the prayers and
praises of countless multitudes keeping the holy day
of the Gospel. The traveller lingers with reverent
delight among the venerable temples and time-hal-
lowed cathedrals of the old world; and our own
fair land, a new. and glorious conquest for the Gospel, is covered with churches, whose towers and
spires glitter in her crowded cities, or point peacefully to heaven on the hills and along the valleys of
her beautiful villages."

I congratulated an old inhabitant, after the services, on the finished beauty of the building, the
crimson hangings, the noble organ, and the various
accompaniments of convenience and taste, and we
were naturally led to the discussion whether religious
services were more faithfully attended now, than when
long walks and thin walls tested the sincerity of the
worshipper. She lamented that with all the luxurious
aids of modern times, an indifference was manifested
now-adays towards attendance at church, that would
have made our stricter forefathers groan in spirit.
Her grandmother had told her, that no distance or
inclemency of weather had prevented her from going
to *meeting* when a girl; that mothers took their in-
fants when but four weeks old, and wrapping them
in their arms, travelled through snow and sunshine

to the ordinances of religion. There were seats provided in the broad aisle for those who had babies, and they generally brought apparatus for feeding them. My informant was obliged to confess, however, one accident that occurred in this church nursery, which more fastidious modern taste has avoided. A dog prowling about the porringers of pap and fennel-seed in the broad aisle, came to a pitcher of milk, and thrust his head in. As if to punish this sacrilegious theft his head stuck there, and unable to relieve himself he ran from pew to pew with the pitcher attached to him, drawing away the attention of the congregation from the 7thly and 8thly, with which they ought to have been edified.

WORCESTER, Mass.

The cars left South Boston, a part of the great metropolis destined to hold an important weight in this region, between three and four P. M., for this exquisite town. It was a brilliant summer's afternoon; the beauty of the scenery would have been almost charm enough to one who loves to watch the varying lights and shades in the bird-like flight of a rail-road, but I was blessed beyond the joy of external nature in the presence of friends whom absence had not chilled, and whose tenderness threw a mellow freshness on the heart, like the sun's rays that began to slant in yellow glory around us. Journeying in Massachusetts is a good deal like reading Thomson's poetry. As cultivated fields, and gentle slopes, and miniature streams, and mimic lakes flit

15*

by, a gentle and dreamy repose steals over the mind, opposed, and perhaps not unpleasantly, to the sterner beauties of more Northern scenery. Two hours' excursion, I think, brought us to Worcester, and it has seemed to me, in my short and happy visit of twenty-four hours here, that I am in a garden. I have been in no place where the cultivation of externals appeared so much the fashion. It is a real gift to the stranger to decorate one's windows and porches with flowers, and let him peep into open fences where nature and art are busy, instead of shutting up their products within massy walls.

A stranger, of course, is carried to the rooms of the Antiquarian Society, and there, as he turns to the books, and likenesses, and relics, he feels that even an American begins to have a peg on which to hang national reminiscences. The two first bibles published in America were issued at Worcester in 1791. As I was turning over the file of an old colony newspaper, I was struck with an advertisement, the force of which can only be felt by one who has travelled through our country, and seen the time-pieces that decorate the most common establishments. It was to this effect : " A clock-maker from London may be expected to travel in July next, through Philadelphia, New-York and Boston, for the purpose of repairing old clocks !"

The Hospital for the Insane exhibits one of the most beautiful of all charities in the greatest possible perfection. It seems to me that no one, with the proper control of his reasoning powers, can see our asylums in this country without deciding that they should be his refuge if destined to the calamity of insanity. We found most of the patients employed and cheerful. We were introduced by the attending physician, to whose politeness we were much indebted, to several interesting individuals. After a very courteous reception from one, who was told that we came from South Carolina, he said, abruptly, " Have you felt any of my earthquakes there lately ?"

On one of the party replying in the negative, he frowned, and said,—

" I knew it. I have an enemy. Ice—ice—Why, I ordered one of my best earthquakes for your part of the country ! It was to have ripped up the earth, and sent the Mississippi rushing into the Gulf of Mexico. Look here," he continued, pointing to a slight crack in the plastering, his arm stretched out with an air of importance, " that is one of my earthquakes. What do you think of that ?"

Passing by a variety of characters, we came to an apartment on the women's gallery, where sat a very neatly dressed female. She welcomed us with peculiar grace, requested us to be seated, and one of our party said, " I am glad to see you so happy."

" Happy !" exclaimed she, " Oh am I not happy ? Providence has been too kind to me. I am loaded with blessings ; my heart," (and she pressed it fervently) " is overwhelmed with mercies. I have every thing that I want, and oh, much more than I deserve ! Yes, one thing I *do* want, ladies," (in

a low tone) " *the tear of gratitude* ; it will not flow, I
am surrounded with blessings, yet my eyes are dry.
Oh, ladies, for *the tear of gratitude !*" We left her
with her hand on her heart, and her bright glaring
eyes upraised to heaven.

I think it was at the Hospital in New-York, I was
congratulating one of the insane who had been conversing with me very rationally, upon her comfortable quarters, when she turned to me abruptly with a
knowing wink, and whispered close to my ear,—

" Suppose you come and try how comfortable it
is !"

CAMBRIDGE.

I left beautiful Worcester with regret, for beside
its imposing location and tasteful residences, and
admirable institutions, there were minds near which
I should have joyfully lingered. I had my usual
good fortune in delicious weather. Again the rail-
cars darted on, and again the setting sun shone gladly over glowing nature, and I reached Boston after
this formerly long journey as quickly as a fairy on a
moonbeam, and prepared for an evening party.
Why can I say so little about parties, even in Boston ? There was the brilliantly illuminated room
that cast no shadow, the soft and courteous salute, distinguished strangers, stately ladies, graceful girls,
ornaments lavished by taste and wealth, fruits rich and
tempting ; all that the eye seeks when it asks for fashion and splendor ; nothing that the heart wants
when it yearns for answering sympathy ; nothing that
the mind cherishes when it seeks intellectual food.

Parties are levellers of intellect; even wit, that light ball, gets lost in a crowd, however high the skilful hand may toss it; and as for wisdom, she, poor thing, hides behind the fold of some damask curtain and moralizes in silence.

There is, however, in Cambridge, a very pleasant association of ladies and gentlemen, called the Book Club, which is an exception to the above charge. It is composed of twenty families, and a meeting of the members takes place the first Thursday evening of each month, at their respective houses, in regular order. A subscription of five dollars per annum is paid by every family, and this amount is laid out in the purchase of recent publications of any value. These books are circulated in regular succession to all the members of the Club. A certain number of days are allowed for the reading of a book; at the expiration of the time it is forwarded to another member, and thus they are kept in circulation through the year. If the book is retained over the time allowed, a fine is laid at five cents per day during the period of detention. This regulation has a tendency to make the members punctual.

At the annual meeting the members have a sale of the books on hand, by an auction among themselves, and the proceeds are appropriated to the purchase of new books for the following year. This association has existed several years, and it has been found to exercise a very happy influence on society. The evening on which they meet, passes in agreeable conversation, and as the refreshments are simple, and give little trouble in the preparation, there is less of formality and ceremony than in most parties. Strangers are invited, and it affords them an opportunity of seeing the refined and literary society of Cambridge. The members are chosen by ballot, and the choice must be unanimous ; by this arrangement great harmony prevails, and it preserves the character of a *select society*. The circumstance that the same books are read and enjoyed by so many, gives an interest to the members, affords topics of conversation of a cheerful nature, and a knowledge of the passing literature of the day at little expense of time or money.

SALEM, Mass.

I must begin with a protest against the joke of *table drawers* in this good city, as I hold it from repeated experience to be a great libel; better dinners or more hospitable hearts are rarely to be found ; but as every one may not understand the allusion, I must mention, that it has been handed down as a kind of traditionary characteristic of the Salem people, that they keep their food in table drawers at meals, that when a knock is heard at the door it may be slipped in, lest they should be expected to ask visiters to partake !

The drive to Salem from Boston is over an excellent road, and occupies but two hours; this however is too slow for modern habits ; nothing but a rail-road will answer in our hurrying era. I confess the turnpike affords but little in its scenery to attract the eye, since long ranges of sterile land are almost all that is visible. Now and then the ocean is in sight, and sometimes a green spot where the eye revels, as much from contrast as for its natural beauties. It is a little singular that I should have heard the same two anecdotes told by the passengers in the stage on this drive, that I did some years ago on the same road.

" Did you ever hear," said one, " of a man who robbed himself near this bridge ?" (the floating bridge.)

" No," was the answer, " that sounds oddly."

" As a traveller was passing this spot," said the first speaker, " he heard groans of distress and cries for assistance. Alighting from his vehicle, he searched the neighboring fence, where he found a man lying prostrate. He had been attacked, he said, by robbers, who had taken from him a large sum of money with which he had been entrusted, bruised and beaten him, threatened his life, thrown him over the fence, and had then run away. The good stranger assisted him to rise, sympathized in his misfortunes, and carried him on his way. Suspicions were afterwards excited, he was arrested, and proved to have robbed himself in order to keep the money !"

" You have hearn the story of the pump, I reckon," said another traveller. Most of us smiled, but one had not, and asked for it.

" Well, one night," said the passenger, " a gentleman was ridin' from Borston, and it might be a little darker than this, just a kind of glimmer you

know, when folks dont see real. This is a plaguy
pokerish road o' nights, and about them times there
was stories of highwaymen about. Well, this gentleman got pretty nigh home, and was despert scar-
ed to see a figur standing right at the road side with
his arms out, tryin to stop him with a pistol cocked ;
so he rammed his hand into his pocket, and took out
his purse, and says he, 'Sir, spare my life and take
my money.' Well, he threw the purse slat upon
the ground, at the robber's feet, and rid on in a jif-
fey.* When he got home he told how he had been
attacked by robbers, and made such a to do that the
folks double locked their doors. The next morning
as another person was ridin' along the turnpike, he
seen a well-filled purse lyin' down under the nose of
a pump by the road side !"

When our laugh had subsided, the driver stopped
a moment, and we heard, not a robber's but a child's
voice asking us to buy pond lilies, and one of the
passengers, a stranger, gallantly purchased all and
presented them to us. These little acts of courtesy
are the poetry of travelling. How many I have met
on my way !

It was late twilight, and I could not see the beautiful flowers, but their odour was enough for me. I
was wafted back to childhood, beside a still pond,
where I saw their white petals and yellow stamens
floating on the waters.

The city authorities which have been organized

* At a quick rate.

only a few months, and have lately finished the pressure of their duties, with a true *esprit du corps*, have
made an excursion together among the islands round
the harbor, with a few gentlemen *strangers*. This
is really an interesting circumstance, and perhaps
it would soften many a heart if men of business
would sometimes steal a day from the city, and look
thus on nature. Some of them went fishing, some
black-berrying, others laid under the shade of trees
in pleasant intercourse until the main party returned with their fishing trophies, and they all partook
of a repast, giving themselves up to the lighthearted-
ness of youth with the additional spicy wit of maturer age.

Salem is justly proud of her Museum, and its peculiar value has arisen from the marine taste of the
people, who have contributed to it for a long series
of years, mostly from the East India voyages. It is
singular that the charge of penuriousness should belong to a town where there has always been a large
complement of seamen, a race of men notorious for
their warm hearts and open hands. This generosi-
ty is very perceptible in the elegant contributions
which have been lavished on this pet of the community. But while the scientific eye ranges with
delight over such vast collections, I feel a weariness
of head and feet in the well-filled galleries. One
bird flying in solitary freedom over the green trees,
one shell tinged with its rich natural painting, one
flower throwing out its perfume, one insect hum-
ming in the sunshine, one painting hanging without

16

competitors, where I can take in the whole expression, one relic of antiquity bringing up the strong
associations of the past, give me more delight than
the most crowded halls.

It may be that the smallness of the number attracted my admiration, but I have rarely seen a collection so brilliant as one of entomology in Salem, disconnected however with the Museum. I think it is
kept by a private association. Were it not for the
savage spears that impaled them, these insects would
have seemed ready to fly.

The scenery around Salem is not picturesque, but
we enjoyed a delightful drive through Lynn to the
mineral spring. Lynn, which is recorded in the
geographies as only remarkable for shoe-making,
has taken great strides in wealth, and also boasts
its literary associations. In the last year no less
than six hundred houses have been erected. An intelligent gentleman informed us of one peculiarity
of this place. The shoe-makers are its aristocracy,
that is, they stand higher than store keepers, &c.
This would furnish a good hint for a political econo-
mist.

The burial ground at Danvers is remarkable as
being the resting place of the heroine of one of our
earliest American novels, Eliza Wharton. Eliza
Wharton was written by Mrs. Foster of Brighton,
Mass. about fifty years since, and relates, under that
name, the history of an unfortunate girl, over whose
melancholy fate many tears have been shed. It is
said that some years after she had died of a broken

heart, a stranger came to Danvers, passed one night in loneliness and lamentation over her grave, and went away without communicating his name. In youth, in my days of romance, (who has not had them?) I once strolled over this burial ground as I passed through the village, and gathered some wild flowers.

The pond by the mineral spring at Lynn is a spot of great loveliness. After wandering along the banks, a portion of our company were induced to step into a small sail boat that lay very temptingly at hand, and with the excitement usually attendant on such enterprises, pushed off. The scene was as bright as a rich setting sun on the clear water and waving trees could make it; but unfortunately the wind changed as we were about to return, and then, instead of holding up our " happy human faces" to take in this rich scene, it was nothing but tack, tack. Our nice bonnets were wedged down to let the boom pass over us, and we gained about a foot only at each movement; and what added to the ridiculous in our situation was, that our friends ashore were envying us, thinking that it was prolonged from choice, and that we were playing with the winds and waters.

Dr. Brazer's church in Salem is one among the most attractive looking buildings I have yet seen. It is constructed of a rich, dark granite, the stones carefully split and cut in blocks of a uniform size, but not hewn or polished. This plan gives to the whole structure a massy effect.

The church, now under the pastoral charge of the Rev. Charles Upham, claims to be the First American Congregational Church. The second Century Lecture was delivered there in 1829. In turning over the pages of this interesting discourse, I was struck with the following exquisite lines of Hugh Peters, one of its ministers in the first century :

HUGH PETERS'S WISH FOR HIS DAUGHTER.

> I wish you neither poverty
>   Nor riches,
> But godliness, so gainful
>   Without content ;
> No painted pomp nor glory that
>   Bewitches ;
> A blameless life is the best
>   Monument ;
> And such a soul that soars a-
>   Bove the skie,
> Well pleased to live, but better
>   Pleased to die,

I cannot resist adding the following synopsis of Hugh Peters's work, written during his confinement in the Tower,—" *A dying father's last Legacy to an only child,*" which is extracted in Mr. Upham's notes :

> Whosoever would live long and
> Blessedly, let him observe these
> Following Rules, by which
> He shall attain to that
> Which he desireth.

Let thy {	Thoughts	Divine, Awful, Godly.
	Talk	Little, Honest, True.
	Words	Profitable, Holy, Charitable.
	Manners	Grave, Courteous, Cheerful.
	Dyet	Temperate, Convenient, Frugal.
	Apparel } be {	Sober, Neat, Comely.
	Will	Constant, Obedient, Ready.
	Sleep	Moderate, Quiet, Seasonable.
	Prayers	Short, Devout, Often, Fervent.
	Recreation	Lawful, Brief, Seldom.
	Memory	Of Death, Punishment, Glory.

Salem has been, and is, as distinguished for her politicians and men of science and professional superiority as any quarter of our country, and female intellect has there expanded in full bloom. In looking back on her literary history, there is a blank on her poetical page. I will not even except the volume of one of her judicial sons, (Salem claims his earlier powers,) since he, as he stands now on his high eminence, grasping the key of legal knowledge, pronounces poetry the sin of his youth. According to my theory, the *perfect*, in whatever it may consist, is poetical, and thus the learned Judge belongs to the Muses in jurisprudence if not in rhyme.

CHARLESTOWN, MASS.

The objects which have made a day and evening

16*

pass off with interest, and left a long train of associations for me connected with this place, are the Dry Dock, the Monument at Bunker's Hill, the Lunatic Hospital, the ruins of Mount Benedict, and an evening party.

The Dry Dock was constructed by Loammi Baldwin, Esq. who resides in this place, and was the architect for the basin at Gosport. I felt anew the admiration which was excited by that great work. By the politness of friends we were carried over the United States' vessels, now repairing; nothing, however, excites me more, than to look up to a vessel on the stocks in a ship-house, and see the huge thing modelled by such a comparatively diminutive object as man ; and yet there is one object greater in mechanical power,—this mass tossing and dashing on the ocean, yet capable of being governed by the touch of a child. Mechanical power gives me a clearer idea of the Creator than moral power ; and the reason probably is, that mechanism, as far as it goes, is perfect, while moral effort is almost always mixed with selfish alloy.

The unfinished Monument is as sublime and interesting an object to me as if it were reared in the hurrying spirit of the age. Why hasten it ? Why not let years roll on, and the men, women, and children of successive periods carry it to its projected height ? Is there any danger that New England will forget this noble task ? There will always be the same interest, the same pride. If the pillar of Absalom was raised stone by stone, by an offended nation, who threw on the pile as they passed, their touching reproof of final ingratitude, cannot a monument be erected through successive years, even if it were stone by stone, for those who have become immortal as true sons to their country? There is nothing alarming or ridiculous to me in the present delay of this noble pile. The citizen of Rome does not value St. Peter's the less for having been a long series of years in building.

The general Lunatic Hospital of Massachusetts, in this place, vies with its sister establishment at Worcester in beauty of location and completeness of arrangement. It has one advantage, however, over any I have seen; an intelligent and graceful lady has devoted herself, personally, to the amelioration of the wants and sufferings of the female inmates. What more delightful thought can Christianity offer, than that these wandering minds, when called to their eternal, spiritual home, shall recognize such a benefactress?

But a more appalling picture than the wreck of mind awaited me at the ruins of Mount Benedict, the former residence of the Ursuline community. Physical infirmity produces sadness, but moral obliquity, horror. I have seen instances where the love of the picturesque has induced persons to erect seeming ruins in our young country, but there is no need of this artificial effort here. These blackened walls tell a story of deep and awful pathos. I walked on the broken terrace, where the sisters and their young pupils used to sit of a summer's afternoon, while the

traveller on the road below paused a moment at the
sight of their graceful forms as their dresses fluttered in the wind ; I passed the wall over which the
frightened creatures leaped at midnight by the light
of their burning home ; and I saw the rifled tomb,
which the mob left empty, as it is now ! On the
few walls that are still standing, one may see mottoes and words indicative of the feelings of the portion of the community who destroyed them. It
will hardly be believed that a couplet like the following is one of the least vulgar and blasphemous
there :

> " The Priests go to hell
> While the Yankees ring the bell."

There are epithets connected with the names of
some of the former inmates, whose grossness is
enough to madden a sensitive mind. I scarcely
know whether to wish the whole ruin levelled and ob-
literated, to avoid the accusation it seems to speak to
the mind of a stranger, or to let it stand as a solemn
warning to the descendants of those Pilgrims who
sought on this very soil—

> " Freedom to worship God."

I should not have enjoyed the brilliant evening
circle, which was assembled in a Charlestown drawing-room, had I not heard, almost every where, a
protest against this outrage. Even amid the glow
of beauty and fashion many voices still deprecated
the mob-spirit which has brought upon this region a

stain that time will hardly wipe away; and among the few with whom it was my happy lot to meet intimately, I know that if generous and devoted friendship could have saved the *community*, they would have been saved.

QUINCY.

I was glad to make a pilgrimage to this shrine, the associations of which are dear, not only to New-England but to all Americans, from its having been the residence of John Adams and Josiah Quincy. It throws a peculiar charm over the spot to find the descendants of these distinguished men still enjoying the elegant retirement of their ancestors, and dispensing their graceful hospitalities. I believe the sturdiest republican cherishes this feeling at heart. A likeness of one of the earliest members of the family of the great patriot and orator Quincy still hangs in the sitting-room, and one can trace his mild and benignant expression through his descendants.

A friend informed me, that when a boy of eleven years of age, he visited John Adams with a gentleman of his acquaintance. Having read and heard discussed the violent politics of the times, and knowing that Adams and Jefferson were on the very opposite sides of the political wheel, he was astonished, as Adams stood on a little knoll beside him, to hear him break out into a beautiful eulogium of his rival. " It taught my youthful mind a lesson," said the narrator, " which I have never forgotten."

Mr. Dowe's Library at Cambridgeport.

The traveller is fortunate who obtains access to this singularly beautiful collection of books and engravings. Gov. Everett, in one of his public addresses, has noticed this library and its owner, who, amid the laborious employment of *leather-dressing*, has been able to collect volumes, the beauty of which honors the white-gloved hand of the most delicate lady, while their rarity is grateful to the inked fingers of the student. Mr. Dowse's rooms have been the admired resort of his friends for many years, and his kindness in permitting them to gratify strangers, is as beautiful a trait of the heart as fine taste is of his mind. His collection is almost exclusively composed of the *belles lettres* department of literature. If you wish to go back to the fount of English poetry, or renew an early love of the British classics, or find the choicest translations of admired works, or taste the later effusions of modern novelists and rhymers, or search the fields of history, biography, or travels, there you may revel to your heart's content; and no musty, worm-eaten old book, or thumbed and dirty recent favorite, will shock you, but you will find rich binding and clear type wooing your eye; and while you visit larger establishments, you will look back on those precious rooms as a literary gem polished to all possible perfection.

BOSTON, Mass.

Every thing material, moral, and religious in this great city is in motion. Houses that many other

places would be proud to possess, or be years in
building, are pulled down, and palaces rise in their
stead in as many months ; theories and speculations,
from which other regions shrink, are here received
and examined, and antiquity guarantees no repect
for creeds. Boston is a rival to Philadelphia in
beauty, but varies as a brunette from a blonde.

At a dinner party yesterday, I heard the subjects
of Swedenborgianism and Animal Magnetism discussed by advocates of the truth of both. There
are many individuals here inclining to a belief of
the latter mystery. He to whom I allude on the
present occasion, had not only witnessed the operation, but was himself a magnetizer. The patient
he described was a middle-aged woman, who had long
been an invalid, and who had given her consent to the
experiment.—The magnetizer followed the custom-
ary mode. He stood or sat immediately in front of
her, looking in her eyes, with the palms of his hands
open towards her, passing them up and down before
her person. I think there was no contact, but the
approach was as near as possible without it. This
is the act which induces the magnetic sleep. The
first day it was several hours before the patient slept ;
the next period was much shorter, and on the day
when this relation was given, the period had not
been more than a quarter of an hour. When in
the magnetic sleep, the subject is conscious only of
the acts and words, and sometimes thoughts, of the
magnetizer. The gentleman stated that a pistol,
fired off directly by the ear of the patient without

any previous knowledge of the intention on her part,
produced no start or change of pulse; while she
answered not only whispered questions of the magnetizer, but questions whispered in the *entry* with
the door *shut.*

This account was given by a grave scientific
man, who had no other interest in the subject than
one of medical inquiry. He affirmed nothing of
his belief, but only stated what he had seen and
done. I have read the statements of the abuse of
this power among the French in the English journals, and my prejudices were all against it; but I
was induced to pause at least, and, if not actually
to believe, to inquire, when a man of thinking mind
and cool temperament gave such a testimony. Entire scepticism is weaker than credulity.

If the truth of this theory should be established,
the great question of its safety and propriety must
be agitated. The most unsafe period will be this of
experiments; once establish its philosophy, and bring
it to bear on medical science, and checks will be instituted to deprive it of evil results. There is no
danger from truth, but from ignorance. Animal
Magnetism has been introduced into Boston by a respectable Frenchman, and every one should be glad
that the physicians of that place are testing it.

The French appear to be carrying into operation
with the physical, somewhat the same course that
the Germans are in the metaphysical world; and
the great experiment of cures without medicine is
now being acted on, upon their system, in the Bos-

ton Hospital. I was assured, by an individual connected with the institution, that the treatment was sa-
tisfactory. The latest medical statistics in France
show the same result, the amount of recoveries without the use of medicine being strikingly larger than
those with.

Farewell, then, to phials and boluses! Methinks
I see the defeated genius of medicine, with his dis-
comforted face drawn down as if by ipecacuanha influences, striding off through clouds of powders, and
dashing castor-oil, that inexpressible abomination,
upon the earth! But then, alas! what, among other
things, will become of the first and last pages of American newspapers, if advertisements and certificates
are exploded, and the mild sway of baths, and gum-
water, and herb teas is to resuscitate the land?

Mr. Alcott's School.

I pass by any description of the Athenæum and
other prominent objects, which have been so often
the theme of notice from others, to those less known,
but not less interesting. Mr. Alcott's school comes
under this class, and whatever may be the practical
effects of his system, I am confident no one can pass
a forenoon in observing his process of mental culture,
without imbibing new thoughts, and respecting the
unbending perseverance with which he adheres to
his principle of self-development in childhood. But
perhaps the only way of throwing any light on his
system here, is to describe its course in the few hours
during which I had the pleasure of witnessing it.

17

Mr. Alcott's room is a commodious one in the Masonic Temple. He sits in an elevated situation, and his scholars are so arranged that he can see them all at a glance. The quarter had but just commenced, and some of his pupils were in the country; many were new scholars, for very few people have patience to follow out his system, and children unfortunately are apt to be withdrawn before it is fairly tried. There were about twenty scholars present, the eldest I should judge not over twelve years of age. The writing books were exhibited, in the early stages of which the children follow their imitative faculties almost without rule; the improvement, however, was very distinctly marked. We were then allowed to examine the journals. Each child keeps one daily, which is left to his own taste in its subject and arrangement. At length Mr. Alcott commenced reading. The subject he selected was allegorical; but he modified, explained, and asked questions and opinions, until it was made plain to the comprehension of his pupils.

When reading something respecting punishment, he asked—

"Do you think people ought to be punished?"

Several hands were held up, to show that answers were ready. Mr. Alcott heard them in turn. Some said, "I do." One said, "I don't," with rather a low voice and roguish look; others said, "When people are naughty, they ought to be punished."

Mr. Alcott then asked, "When you are punished,

are you sorry because it hurts you, or because you have done wrong ?"

One said, " I don't like to be hurt." Another said, " I don't like to have my parents angry with me." Two or three said, " I am sorry that I did wrong."

After this subject was fully discussed, Mr. Alcott introduced that of *justice,* and when many opinions had been given on the abstract question, he said, " If any of you think I have been unjust, you may tell me so."

Several hands were raised, and many voices said, " You did not give us as many minutes at recess yesterday as usual."

Mr. Alcott confessed that he had not, said that he had good reasons for it ; and to show that he wished to make restitution, told all the scholars they might remain out as long as they chose, and go home if they preferred.   In ten minutes they were all back, some in less.   When seated, they commenced analyzing, which is conducted on the plan of parsing, except that it goes into the meaning of words and into abstract principles.

" What is mother ?" he asked, after several other words had been examined.

" A noun," was the answer.

" Is mother a material or spiritual object ?" he asked.

Several hands were held up—some said mother was " spiritual," some " material ;" one said, in a low tone, " both," but Mr. Alcott did not hear him.

" How can mother be spiritual ?" said Mr. Alcott ;
" hands and feet are not spiritual."

" No," said one, " but hands, and feet, and face
are not my mother. Soul is my mother."

" If your mother were dead, should you have a
mother?" said Mr. Alcott to all.   They answered
variously ; but she who said soul was her mother, replied—

" Yes, I should have a mother even if my mother
were dead."

I observed the countenance of one boy greatly
agitated during this conversation ; at length he burst
into tears, and sobbed out, " If my mother were dead,
I should not have a mother."

Mr. Alcott changed the subject, and mentioned to
me afterwards that this boy's parents were distant
from him.

The teacher and the pupils, (he informed me,) have
sometimes been so much interested in following out
a subject in this way, as to spend a whole forenoon
upon one word.   Some portion of every week is passed in conversations on the New Testament, and Mr.
Alcott has compiled them as " evidences of the truth
of Christianity from the testimony of childhood."
There probably has never been a book written
which will convey so curious a mental picture.

I have given this little sketch as well as my memory will allow, for the purpose of attracting some attention to the subject at the South.   Mr. Alcott is
probably the *ultraist* of his class of teachers, yet every
one must confess that there is so much of mere

memory culture in common schools, that the heart, affections, and even understanding, are neglected. Still, though I was witness to the graceful confidence of the pupils, and the untiring patience of the master, I can imagine that from day to day there should be almost as much *parrot-ism* in the answers of children on this system as in any other. The few, as in other schools, will take the lead, and work out bright answers; while the rest will either copy doggedly, or wait for the natural developments of time and observation.

Swedenborgian Chapel.

I was desirous to witness the service of this peculiar people, from many interesting associations. I knew a Swedenborg lady in early life, and her character left the stamp which goodness always will leave on the memory. Her mind was one of great symmetry, though but little power; and it was therefore more remarkable, that amid ridicule, and sometimes harsher language, she collected around her the ponderous tomes of her spiritual master. She attended the Episcopal church with her husband and children, but her heart was in Swedenborg's heaven. I saw her stemming trials with firmness, bearing rebukes with meekness, and holding a conversation above the world; and from that time, such is the power of virtue, I have continued to respect what I could not believe. She has since gone where truth is no longer dimmed by clouds.

The Swedenborg chapel is a neat edifice, respect-

17*

ably filled. The music consists entirely of chaunts of the Psalms; it is very tender and sweet. A quiet, attentive air pervades the assembly, I was desirous of hearing a discourse characteristic of the views of this religious community, and was amply gratified. The preacher selected one of the wildest portions of the prophetic writings of the Old Testament, in which is embodied a description of a battle field after defeat. Nothing could be more *material* than this picture to an unenlightened eye, until he spiritualized it. The Hebrew, I confess, would have been quite as intelligible to me as his paraphrase.

Sacred Music.

I have not been more delighted with any thing on my journey, than in the improvement in psalmody in this region. The influence of the Handel and Hadyn Society has produced a change that I feel most strongly. I have remarked that punctuation is observed in common psalmody, and that it gives great beauty and force to the sentiment.

The want of uniformity in the posture of many of the congregations is displeasing. Were this principle of choice of position carried out, each person would be at liberty to make the sermons and prayers subject to the same irregularity.

Children's Church.

Boston stands pre-eminent in its religious facilities for the poor, and is also distinguished by having a church for children. A great number attended on the Sabbath, and were addressed in language suited to their capacity. The pulpit was decorated with brilliant flowers, and the preacher seemed as if about to expatiate on them, but his discourse was on the death of Jesus. He endeavoured to associate death with every thing tender and pleasing, and to avoid the gloom with which it is usually shrouded. He exhibited some butterflies beautifully pressed, and the chrysalis from whence each sprang ; and at the close of his remarks, recited the following ballad :

MOTHER, WHAT IS DEATH?

" Mother, how still the baby lies,—
    I cannot hear his breath ;
I cannot see his laughing eyes—
    They tell me this is death.

My little work I thought to bring,
    And sat down by his bed,
And pleasantly I tried to sing,—
    They hushed me—he is dead.

They say that he again will rise,
    More beautiful than now,—
That God will bless him in the skies—
    Oh, mother, tell me how !"

" Daughter, do you remember, dear,
    The cold, dark thing you brought,
And layed upon the casement here,—
    A wither'd worm you thought ?

I told you that Almighty power
  Could break that withered shell,
And show you, in a future hour,
  Something would please you well.

Look at the Chrysalis, my love,—
  An empty shell it lies ;—
Now raise your wandering thoughts above
  To where yon insect flies !"

" Oh yes, mamma ! how very gay
  Its wings of starry gold—
And see ! it lightly flies away
  Beyond my gentle hold !

Oh, mother, now I know full well—
  If God that worm can change,
And draw it from this broken cell,
  On golden wings to range ;

How beautiful will brother be,
  When God shall give *him* wings,
Above this dying world to flee,
  And live with heavenly things.

If it were ever justifiable for a thrill of grateful
pride to go through an author's heart, it would be at
the selection of her humble effort at such a moment,
herself unknown.

The children sang together very sweetly, and the
services closed by their repeating the Lord's prayer
after their pastor.

The Bethel Church.

I found myself at the very antipodes of the calm
and spiritual repose of the Swedenborg chapel, as I

followed the crowd to the Bethel Church. It was not without its interest to me that this edifice stands on the spot where I was born.

When I entered the building, Mr. Taylor, the pastor, whose reputation for eloquence is so widely extended, was walking about the pulpit in great anxiety and concern, arising from the fear that the seamen would be crowded from their seats. Leaning over, he stretched out his hand, and called out, with a loud and earnest voice,—

" Don't stir, my brethren! not a seaman must go out."

The occasion was one of peculiar solemnity. A service of communion plate had been presented, and this was the first opportunity for appropriating it. Having heard Methodist preaching frequently at the South in its most fervid tone, I was probably not so much impressed by the sermon as a Bostonian would have been. Mr. Taylor's changes, like those of his denomination generally, were rapid, varying from the boldest rhetorical flights, to the most commonplace expressions. The sermon being over, he descended to the altar, and called two individuals to the rite of baptism. One was a middle-aged seaman, the other a little girl of five years of age, led by her mother. He had not proceeded far, before I saw and felt the power of his natural eloquence; his audience were soon in tears. He grasped the hand of the seaman, and welcomed him as one who, from sailing on stormy seas, had reached a safe harbor. After the usual invocation and form of baptism, he again took his hand, and smiling on him kindly, said, " God's baptism be on thee, my brother ; go in peace." Then turning to the woman, he exclaimed,

" And the widow did not come alone ; no, she did not come alone, she brought her baby with her."

He took the wondering but passive little girl in his arms, and raised her so that we could all see her. After the silence of a moment, he said,

" Look at the sweet lamb ! Her mother has brought her to Christ's fold !"

There was another pause ; he touched her forehead with the baptismal element, pronounced the invocation to the Father, Son, and Holy Spirit, and saying solemnly, " A baptism from heaven be on thee, my pretty dove," kissed her flushed cheek tenderly, and placed her by her mother's side.

The congregation were then invited to kneel at the altar, and partake the communion. The seamen went first, file after file, pressing respectfully on, while their pastor addressed to each words of caution and encouragement.

" Brother, beware, take heed," he said to one whose face bore marks of worldly cheer, " the tempter is ever ready." And to one who looked dejected, he said soothingly, " Come to the Lord, my brother ; the yoke of Jesus is easy, lay your cares on him."

When the seamen communicants had all visited the altar, others followed, and as circle after circle

knelt around, the good man was often obliged to
pause in his addresses. Weeping and agitated, he
walked the chancel, exclaiming, with broken sobs,—

This is the happiest day of my life. Oh my God,
the happiest day that I have seen since I was
born !"

I went with the rest, and there, on the spot where
God gave me being, dedicated him anew my faculties
and hopes, and asked his blessing on the homeward
path upon which I shall enter on the morrow.

Beautiful New England, farewell ! How often, in
my happy sojourn here, has the following description, dear to me from many associations, risen to my
memory :

ODE

*For the Anniversary of the New England Society in
Charleston, S. C.*

BY S. GILMAN.

New England ! receive the heart's tribute that comes
  From thine own pilgrim-sons far away ;
More fondly than ever our hearts turn to thee
  Upon this thine old festival day.
We would rescue, with social observance and song,
  Awhile from oblivion's grave,
The lov'd scenes of our youth, and those blessings recall
  Which our country and forefathers gave.

We have gazed on thy mountains that whiten the sky,
  Or have rov'd on thy tempest-worn shore,
We have breathed thy keen air, or have felt thy bright fires,
  While we listened to legends of yore.

We have gathered thy nuts in the mild Autumn sun,
   And the gay squirrel chas'd through thy woods;
From thy red and gold orchards have plucked the ripe store,
   And have bath'd in thy clear-rolling floods.

When thy snow has descended in soft feather'd showers,
   Or hurtled along in the storm,
We have welcom'd alike with our faces and hearts
   Its beauteous or terrible form.
We have skimm'd o'er thine ice with the fleetness of wind
   We have reared the thick snow-castle's wall,
And have acted our part in the combat that rag'd
   With the hard-press'd and neatly-form'd ball.

We remember the way to those school-houses well,
   That bedeck every mile of thy land;
We have lov'd thy sweet Sabbaths that bade in repose
   The plough in its mid-furrow stand.
We have joined in thy hymns and thy anthems, that
     swell'd
   Through Religion's oft-visited dome,
We have blest thy Thanksgivings, that summon'd from far
   The long-parted family home.

Can distance efface, or can time ever dim
   Remembrances crowding like these,
They have grown with our growth, and have minister'd
     strength
   As the roots send up life to the trees;
Then be honour'd the day when May flowers came,
   And honour'd the change that she bore,
The stern, the religious, the glorious men,
   Whom she set on our rough native shore.

And oh, Carolina! full gladly *thy* name
   In our green wreath to-day we entwine;
If New England awakens the thought of the past,
   Our present and future are thine.

Thy interests, thy rights, we acknowledge our own,
　On thy soil we are destin'd to fall ;
Thy just confidence lend, and accept in return
　Our love, our devotion, our all.—

We have been favored with a rapid and favorable passage from Norfolk ; Charleston light-house bore in sight, and the pure and beautiful thoughts conceived on the same spot by a popular author, came to my memory, aiding and mellowing the happiness of return :

THE LIGHT OF THE SOUL.

Written off Charleston Light at evening.

BY B. B. THATCHER.

Over winds and waves, far out
　From the shadows of the shore,
I see the mariner's beacon
　Its silvery splendor pour.

And sweeter is the sight
　Than all the wealth, untold,
That o'er the Orman grottoes,
　Breaks forth in blazing gold.

Yet, built on earth's low strand,
　That light may only show,
Where the fields of *time* are greenest,
　And its blooms the fairest blow.

O dearer and diviner flame!
　O changeless, changeless *star!*
Thou mind'st me of the one that shone
　O'er the magi's wandering far.

Oh! shine for me, ye starry hopes,—
Immortal hopes in *Him!*
Ye are holier, and ye give more light,
As the mortal grow more dim.

And now the level shores of Carolina appeared, and soon, at a distance, St. Michael's spire, the seamen's beacon, awoke tender thoughts of home. The vast and the lovely in distant scenery was forgotten, and the affections invested the objects of my love with a beauty and proportion that eclipsed fairer scenes. It was under such influences of local affection that I penned these lines to

ST. MICHAEL'S SPIRE.

St. Michael's spire! St. Michael's spire!
How fair thou risest to the sight—
Now, glittering in the noon-sun's fire,
Now softened by the "pale moonlight!"

Dread storms have thunder'd o'er the sea,
And crush'd the low and rent the high;
But there *thou* standest, firm and free,
With thy bright forehead to the sky.

Fierce fires in rolling volumes came,
But gleam'd innocuous on thy tower,
War's cannon roared with breath of flame,
Unscathing thee, career'd its power.

Symmetric spire! Our city's boast,
In scientific grandeur piled!
The guardian beacon of our coast,
The seaman's hope when waves are wild!

Palladium! on thy lonely height
The faithful watchman walks his round,
While rest and safety rule the night,
And stillness, as of holy ground.

All sleep but thee—Thy tuneful bells
    Hymn to the night-wind in its roar,
Or float upon the Atlantic swells,
    That soften summer on our shore.

Soother of sickness! Oft thy chime
    A gentle voice to darkness lends;
And speaks a language deep, sublime,
    When love o'er dying virtue bends.

Thou guid'st the youth to classic hours,
    The labourer, to his task confin'd;
The maid, to joy's resplendent bowers,
    Th' ambitious, to the strife of mind.

Thy Sabbath summons, not in vain,
    Calls the mixed city to their God;
Each gravely seeks his chosen fane,
    And treads the aisle his sires have trod.

And nobly do thy pæans flow,
    When patriots shout the annual strain,
That echoes from far Mexico,
    To where St. Lawrence holds his reign.

Gliding along bold Ashley's stream,
    Or Cooper's, hung with mossy grace,
We turn to gaze upon thy beam,
    And hospitable joys retrace.

And tender are the thoughts that rise,
    When, sea-bound from thy level shore,
The tear of parting dims our eyes
    Till we can view thy point no more.

And when, returning to our land,
    The summer exile nears his home,
How beats his heart, and waves his hand,
    As first he greets thy welcome dome.

St. Michael's spire! I close my lay,
  Touch'd by the moral thou hast given,
Though duties throng my earthly way,
  My look, like thine, shall be to Heaven.

END OF A NORTHERN EXCURSION.

SOUTHERN

LOCAL SKETCHES,

BY

CAROLINE GILMAN.

18*

EXCURSION UP COOPER RIVER.

My rocking chair, thou velvet luxury! I come to thee from the odorous Mocha beverage with the morning paper in my hand. Delicious summary! On these four pages are pleasures that require no preparatory trouble, pains that ask no sympathy. I see nations moving on thy broad leaves, coming and going in silent panorama. Why, here are kings and warriors, poets and statesmen, for my companions; I sail over oceans, I travel continents, I make my bed in the air—the world is mine! And what possessions does thy typed tongue give, possessions fit for the luxurious occupant of a *rocking chair?* I scarcely glance at the word "cheap," but leave to the sitters on wooden seats the balanced advertisement of prices. I leap over "cut-nails and brads," and scorn the "14000 lbs. small hams," for "preserves" from the West Indies, "sparkling champagne and sauterne." "Muscatel raisins" cluster around me, and "figs" drop at my feet. Lace, fine as a Peri's robe, is thrown over my shoulders, my feet rest in satin slippers, pearls are on my neck, the bird of the air is stripped to fan me, the beast of the wilder.

ness to clothe me. " Chickering & Nun's best" are
vibrating on my ear ; gilt mirrors reflect my polished furniture.   I almost feel the softness of " French
handkerchiefs," and the purest blonde lies in folds
over my brow.   How much can a little imagination
make of a newspaper in a rocking chair !   I sometimes fancy what will be the compensation for these
vehicles of thought in a more spiritual state of existence.   There, perhaps, mind will rush to sympa-
thetic mind from unknown distances—doubt, if it
can exist, be answered by whispering spirits almost
in anticipation—and the speculations, which here
are surrounded by the mists of earth, be solved in
words of light and glory, beaming from the fount of
thought.

It is a summer's noon ; the light is shut out, except
where the sweet South steals through that half-open
window.   What a soft drowsiness comes over me,
as with head thrown back on thy protecting form,
my rocking chair, objects mingle before me.   They
fade—the vase of flowers, the books, the ornaments
of my table, the waving curtains, all fade away ; only
one object remains—a picture by Osgood.   Her
blue eye seems closing, her rich lips soften in their
serious smile, her white brow darkens, her fair hand
relaxes from her fairer temples—I see her no more.
Gone, gone to the land of dreams !

Sickness has thrown me into thy kind arms, my
rocking chair.   Tender friends are around me—my
eye rests on proofs of absent kindness.   I know the
hand that sent that beautiful bouquet.   It is the hand

that loves to throw flowers on the path of the weak
or sorrowful, the hand that takes strangers to its bosom, that makes acquaintance feel like friends, and
friends like brethren.   Amid a thousand I would
say *that* hand sent those flowers!   God will bless
that hand! I love to lean my languid head on thy
breast, my rocking chair, and inhale the perfume of
these blossoms, and trace their hues, God's gifts of
tenderness to man.

It is twilight; the cares of the day are over, and
I return to thee, the rest of my sweet home.   Let
me draw thee nearer to the window, where the dying
day can give me its last look.   The gay laughter
of those grouped girls will not disturb the repose of
the hour.   Sport on, young ones! There is time
enough for you to watch the dying day in sadder
times.   A star advances through the growing gloom,
and a voice at my side tells its opening thoughts,
and asks questions of the far-off sky; a young form
rests on my lap, and I feel a hand, affection's own,
tried, faithful hand, pressing mine.

It is night, and

   " Friends drop off as leaves forsake the flower,"

the kind good-night is given, the watchman's voice
announces the hours, an occasional step sounds ring-
ingly on the pavement.   Again I throw myself into
thy arms, my rocking-chair; and thou biddest me
welcome with thy gentle motion.   The memory of
the past day unfolds its wings, and lingers around
me.   Has active goodness been borne on its pinions?

I thank God; and a pure repose rests on my spirit. Are its brooding edges made heavy with sin? I pray and weep, and then God soothes me with an answered prayer; and musings come, and as my head falls on thee, my rocking-chair, soft visions arise, dreams of re-united spirits, and bright hopes that daylight scarcely knows. But I must rouse myself from these musings, and recall the scenes of yesterday.

I am surprised that more persons do not visit Cooper River now that the facilities for going are so great. Until the establishment of a steam-boat, our citizens had no opportunity to see a southern harvest, and it is truly a surprise to witness those immense tracts of land, more extended than the domain of many a feudal baron, arranged with almost military order and neatness; the golden rice waving beneath the glowing sun, the beautiful river asking to its smooth surface the world-worn citizen, the tasteful residences scattered at wide distances along its banks, and more than all, the stillness of nature, so desirable to those whose summer location, like ours, is in the confinement and bustle of a city.

I went as far as Mulberry Castle, which is an old building on a picturesque spot, erected by one of our Governors at an early period of the settlement of this country as a defence against the Indians. I have never been so struck with earthly possessions as with the extent of some of the plantations on the river. As the boat flew on and on, and I still saw them filling the gaze, I could not but mentally exclaim how much human happiness those planters have in their power!

Mulberry Castle is a more substantial looking building than one can often see of modern workmanship, and its interest within is heightened by quite a gallery of old family pictures. As I was examining them, a gentleman said to me, here is one which bears evidence to the brutality of the British soldiery. You observe it is a likeness of an American officer—one of the dastards in the late war thrust his sword through the eye to show his contempt for us.

I am sorry to spoil so good a story, said another; but that feat was performed by a roguish American boy, who climbed up and dug out his ancestor's eye.

It was a bright spectacle to see our town's people recreating on this romantic spot. Here you might view a party with the keen appetite of an irregular meal partaking refreshment under a tree; now a white dress, floating among the trees, told of some romantic rambler, and again the shout of laughter came softened on the ear; then I heard the sound of music, and drawing near, perceived a group singing the following Ode, originally composed as a national song for the anniversary of our Independence.

The history of this Lyric is interesting to our community. It has been engraved on a silver vase, and presented to the author; on one side is

THE ODE.

Hail, our country's natal morn,
Hail, our spreading kindred-born!
Hail, thou banner, not yet torn,
    Waving o'er the free!
While, this day, in festal throng,
Millions swell the patriot song,
Shall not we thy notes prolong,
    Hallow'd Jubilee?

Who would sever Freedom's shrine;
Who would draw th' invidious line;
Though by birth one spot be mine,
    Dear is all the rest:
Dear to me the South's fair land,
Dear the central mountain-band,
Dear New England's rocky strand,
    Dear the prairied West.

By our altars, pure and free,
By our Law's deep-rooted tree,
By the past's dread memory,
    By our Washington;
By our common parent tongue,
By our hopes, bright, buoyant, young,
By the tie of country strong,
    We will still be ONE.

Fathers! have ye bled in vain?
Ages! must ye droop again?
Maker! shall we rashly stain
    Blessings sent by Thee?
No! receive one solemn vow,
While before thy throne we bow,
Ever to maintain, as now,
    Union, Liberty!

On the reverse is the following inscription :

To the Author
of the National Ode written
for the 4th of July,
The Rev. Samuel Gilman,
and as a tribute of affectionate respect
for the Patriot, the Scholar,
and the Poet,
the friends of National Union
have presented
This Vase,
Charleston, S. C.

The Vase was wrought and engraved in Charleston, and is chaste and elegant ; while the Ode, adapted to the tune " *Scots wha hae*," is sung annually at the celebration of the 4th of July.

I was attracted by the crow-minders as we passed the plantations ; they are chosen from the young or infirm, and have a picturesque air in their extended solitude.   They are kept in the fields all day, having no actual labour to perform ; others go away when their tasks are ended.   The crows know their voices, and wheel off at the sound without alighting.

It may excite a smile that I should find poetry in a crow-minder, but I make a faithful record :

THE CROW-MINDER OF THE SOUTH.

Alone, amid the far-spread field he stands,
Heaven's arch above, an amphitheatre
Of woods around. Wide his domain, and fair ;
But no companionship hath he, for he
Must scare the very birds away, whose notes
Are meet for company.

The Mocking bird,
Herald or partner of his walk, must leave
Him here ; nor shall he list again its note,
'Till, warbling near his lowly hut, the bird
Pours forth orchestral tones ambitiously,
At midnight hour, upon his drowsy ear.

The Lizard, creeping on the blighted tree,
The lazy Worm, unearthing its slow length,
The Ant, which builds its sandy monument,
The Butterfly, a passing traveller,
And e'en the Snake, that shines in motlied hues,
Or Frog, retreating from the burning sand,
Or shining Beetle, will he welcome now.

Few are his cares, nor irksome his employ.
Just far enough remov'd to watch his prey,
His bird-trap tempting lies—the Oriole there,
The Goldfinch, Wax-bird, and like forms of grace,
He snares, to gain a trifle for the prize.
The prison of the finny race he weaves ;
Or, on his basket's growing plaits he toils,
Counts o'er his gains, and whistles out his joy.

The forest trees, that stand like centinels,
Send out a murmur pleasant to the ear.
The Turtle Dove, that seems to mourn, but whose
Low tone is whisper'd tenderness, is there.
From thence the venturous Ground-Pigeon comes,
And with a little band of feathered friends
Steals cautious to the rice-fields' tempting range,
When, faithful to his charge, the " minder" shouts,
With arms uprais'd, and frighted they retire.

There the Blue-Jay, the " feather'd harlequin,"
Trims his rich crest and pipes his mimic song :
While, hidden mid damp brakes, the Cuckoo's note
With harsh monotony assails the ear.
There the Woodpecker, busy Epicure,
Bores with his beak the insect's barky home,

Affrights them with his feign'd but startling cry,
Then coolly riots with his darting tongue,
And taps at intervals the hollow tree.

But the field-minder, idly busy, heeds
Nor knows the sounds sweet to the Poet's ear;
Tho', when the Crow's coarse note is nearer heard,
And his dark form wheels o'er the sunny field,
Or varied pilferers, glide with stealthy wing,
In softer guise, to rob the planter's toil,
Then lifts he high again his warning voice,
And waves his tawny arms, and beats the air,
While the foil'd plunderers turn in circling flight,
And seek the forest's screening shades again.

What are his thoughts, that lone one, as the Sun
O'er-tops the pines, and wakes the woods to joy?
What are his thoughts, when thro' the long, long blaze
Of summer's noon, he sits in solitude?
Right glad is he, when the dark laborer comes,
With hoe upon his arm—his task well done,
And gives a passing greeting to the boy.
Full glad to see the mastiff from the chase
Run with his whining welcome; and willingly,
With passing negro, or with truant dog,
Shares the plain food, cook'd near his blighted tree.

Think not the boy is vacant in his mood;
He muses on relationship and friends;
He plans the evening game, the sabbath prayer,
•He learns from nature's volumes lessons true,
Foretells the storm, the harvest too—and things
That 'scape the world's philosophy, he knows.
There, *more* than in the city's jostling throng,
He feels a present Diety. The moon,
Flooding his homeward track with gentle rays,
Looks in his bosom on a sky-bound soul;
And the far stars, those light-houses of heaven,
Tell him of hopes beyond their glittering sheen.

As we returned, a passenger undertook to teach us a German glee. The whole company assembled on deck, and entered into the spirit of the occasion. I must confess there was more laughter than music. Our entertainer was a foreigner ; we Americans, coolly calculating how far we may go without compromising our dignity, may well copy that social impulse which forgets itself in the thought of pleasing others.

We reached town just as an early moon was lighting up St. Michael's spire.

And yet people rush off to the North and West, unconscious of the attractions around us ; but that belongs to human nature. I know those who live within a few days' journey of Niagara, who hurry off to Europe without even hearing the roar of its waters, and will enter with great complacence in their journals accounts of lakes and streams that would seem like a spoonfull compared to our giant torrents.

THE PLANTATION ON ASHLEY RIVER.

A BALLAD.

19*

CHATSWORTH, ASHLEY RIVER.

The following simple but minute picture of Southern country life, written in the quiet of the scene it describes, may not be uninteresting to those who are not familiar with our local circumstances. Probably the whole circle of romance cannot furnish sadder spectacles than those which arise from the unfitness of our low-country residences to the New-England constitution; yet yearly victims are renewed The white men who do survive on our plantations, look cadaverous and unhealthy.

THE PLANTATION ON ASHLEY RIVER.

A BALLAD,—PART FIRST.

Farewell, awhile, the city's hum,
    Where busy footsteps fall,
And welcome to my weary eye
    The Planter's friendly Hall.

Here let me rise at early dawn,
    And list the mock-bird's lay,
As warbling near our lowland home
    He waves the bending spray.

Then tread the shading avenue,
    Beneath the Cedar's gloom,
Or Gum tree with its flicker'd shade,
    Or Chinquapen's perfume.

The Myrtle tree, the Orange wild,
　The Cypress' flexile bough,
The Holly, with its polish'd leaves
　Are all before me now.

There, towering with imperial pride,
　The rich Magnolia stands,
And here in softer loveliness,
　The white bloom'd Bay expands.

The long gray moss hangs gracefully;
　Idly I twine its wreaths,
Or stop to catch the fragrant air,
　The frequent blossom breathes.

Life wakes around—the red bird darts
　Like flame from tree to tree;
The whip-poor-will complains alone,
　The Robin whistles free.

The frighten'd Hare scuds by my path,
　And seeks the thicket nigh;
The Squirrel climbs the Hickory bough,
　And peeps with careful eye.

The Humming-bird with busy wing
　In rainbow beauty moves;
Above the trumpet-blossom floats,
　And sips the tube he loves.

Triumphant to yon wither'd pine,
　The soaring Eagle flies,
There builds her eyrie mid the clouds,
　And man and heaven defies.

The hunter's bugle echoes near,
　And see, his wary train,
With mingled howlings scent the woods,
　Or scour the open plain.

Yon skiff is darting from the cove;
　And list the negro's song,
The theme, his owner and his boat,
　While glide the crew along.

And when the leading voice is lost,
　Receding from the shore,
His brother boatmen swell the strain,
　In chorus with the oar.

There stands the dairy on the stream,
　Within the broad oak's shade,
The white pails glitter in the sun,
　In rustic pomp array'd.

And she stands smiling at the door,
　Who *minds* that *milky way*,
She smoothes her apron as I pass,
　And loves the praise I pay.

Welcome to me her sable hands,
　When, in the noontide heat,
Within the polish'd calibash
　She pours the pearly treat.

The poulterer's feather'd tender charge
　Feed on the grassy plain:
Her Afric brow lights up with smiles,
　Proud of her noisy train.

Nor does the herdsman view his flock
　With unadmiring gaze,
Significant are all their names,
　Won by their varying ways.

Forth from the Negroes' humble huts
　The labourers now have gone;
But some remain, diseas'd and old—
　Do they repine alone?

Ah, no. The nurse, with practis'd skill,
  That sometimes shames the wise,
Prepares the herb of potent power,
  And healing aid applies.

While seated at his hut's low door,
  The convalescent slave
Gazes upon his garden store,
  And sees the young corn wave.

On sunny banks his children play,
  Or wind the fisher's line,
Or, with the dext'rous fancy-braid,
  Their willow baskets twine.

Long ere the sloping sun departs,
  The labourers quit the field,
And, hous'd within their sheltering huts,
  To careless quiet yield.

But see, yon wild and lurid clouds,
  That rush in contact strong,
And hear the thunder, peal on peal,
  Reverberate along.

The cattle stand and mutely gaze,
  The birds instinctive fly,
While forked flashes rend the air,
  And light the troubled sky.

Behold yon sturdy forest pine,
  Whose green top points to heaven.
A flash! its firm, encasing bark,
  By that red shock is riven.

But we, the children of the south,
  Shrink not with trembling fears;
The storm familiar to our youth,
  Will spare our ripen'd years.

We know its fresh, reviving charm,
    And, like the flower and bird,
Our looks and voices, in each pause,
    With grateful joy are stirr'd.

And now the tender rice up-shoots,
    Fresh in its hue of green,
Spreading its emerald carpet far
    Beneath the sunny sheen.

Tho' when the softer ripen'd hue
    Of autumn's changes rise,
The rustling spires instinctive lift
    Their gold seeds to the skies.

There the young cotton plant unfolds
    Its leaves of sickly hue,
But soon advancing to its growth,
    Looks up with beauty too.

And as midsummer suns prevail,
    Upon its blossoms glow
Commingling hues, like sunset rays—
    Then bursts its sheeted snow.

How shall we fly this lovely spot,
    Where rural joys prevail,
The social board, the eager chase,
    Gay dance and merry tale ?

Alas! our youth must leave their sports
    When spring-time ushers May ;
Our maidens quit the planted flower,
    Just blushing into day ;

Or, all beneath yon rural mound,
    Where rest th' ancestral dead,
By mourning friends, with sever'd hearts,
    Unconscious will be led.

Oh, Southern summer, false and fair!
   Why from thy loaded wing,
Blent with rich flowers and fruitage rare,
   The seeds of sorrow fling?

PART SECOND.

THE OVERSEER'S CHILDREN.

Three fleeting years have come and gone
   Since Ann Pomroy I met,
Returning from the district school,
   Ere yet the sun was set.

With her, her brother Francis stray'd,
   And, both in merry tone,
Were saying all the rambling things
   Youth loves when tasks are done.

The mountain tinge was on their cheeks;
   From fair Vermont they came,
For wandering habits led their sire
   A southern home to claim.

Fresh with the airy spring of youth
   They tripp'd the woods along,
Now darting off to cull a flower,
   Now bursting into song.

Oh, Ann Pomroy, thy sparkling eye
   Methinks I often see,
When some young face, in loveliness,
   Beams up in smiles to me.

And when light rounds of boyish mirth
   Laugh out uncheck'd by fear,
It seems to me that Francis' voice
   Is floating on my ear.

I said the hue of health they bore,—
   Her's was the nect'rine fair,
And his the deep pomegranite tinge,
   That boys of beauty wear.

They walk'd at early morn and eve,
   And as I yearly paid
My visit to the Planter's Hall,
   I saw the youth and maid.

At first, by simple accident
   I came upon their walk;
But soon I lov'd to pause, and seek
   The privilege of talk—

Until my steps were daily turn'd,
   But how I scarce can say,
When Ann and Francis came from school,
   To meet them on the way.

They told me of New-England hills,
   Of orchards in the sun,
Of sleigh-rides with the merry bells,
   Of skating's stirring fun;

And sometimes of a grave they spake,
   And then would sadder grow,
In which a gentle mother slept
   Beneath the wintry snow.
*   *   *   *   *

When April's changing face was seen;
   Again from town I flew,
To where the sleep of nature wakes
   To sights and odours new.

All things were fair—the plants of earth
   Look'd upward to the sky,
And the blue heaven o'erarch'd them still
   With clear and glittering eye.
20

I sought the walk I us'd to seek,
    And took the little store
Of toys, that from the city's mart
    For Ann and Frank I bore.

A rustling in the leaves I heard,
    But Francis *only* came,
His eye was dim, his cheek was pale,
    And agues shook his frame.

He saw me—to my open arms
    With sudden gladness sprang;
Then rais'd a thrilling cry of grief,
    With which the forest rang.

Few words he spake, but led me on
    To where a grave-like mound,
With young spring plants and ever-greens,
    In rural taste were crown'd.

And there he stood, while gushing tears
    Like summer rain-drops came,
And heavings, as a troubled sea,
    Went o'er his blighted frame.

I did not ask him *who* was there,
    I felt that Ann was gone,
Around his drooping neck I hung,
    And stood like him forlorn.

"I soon shall die," the mourner said,
    "Here will they make my grave,
And over me the Cedar trees
    And moaning Pines will wave.

None then will come to tend the flowers
    That blossom o'er her bed;
None sing for her the twilight dirge
    When I am with the dead.

I cannot join the school-boy sports
  My head and heart are sad ;
When Ann is in the silent grave,
  Oh, how can I be glad ?

And when I say my studied tasks,
  Or gain the once-loved prize,
I weep, and softly pray to Heaven
  To lay me where she lies."

I kissed his pale and suffering brow,
  By early sorrows riven ;
I talk'd to him of her he lov'd,
  And rais'd his thoughts to Heaven.

And when the call of duty came,
  To take me from his side,
He told me, with a sickly smile,
  " 'Twas best that Ann had died."

*   *   *   *   *

Another annual season roll'd
  Its cares and joys along—
Again I sought the country's charms,
  Deep woods and caroll'd song.

And there I found two silent graves
  Amid the vernal bloom—
I ne'er shall see those forms again,
  'Till Heaven unseals the tomb.

Oh, Southern summer, false and fair,
  Why, on thy loaded wing,
Blent with rich flowers and fruitage rare,
  The seeds of sorrow bring ?

I have raised my chamber window to admit the
odour of morning, and the song of a mocking-bird,
which has been varying its multiplied notes, like the

tints on the early sky. This exquisite songster has enjoyed frequent and various homage, but I have never
met a tribute so beautiful as one from a Charleston
poet.   Except that he is chary of his song, he might
be fancied to be the prototype of our Phœbus of the
forest.   Those who read the following lines will feel
their rich Miltonian flow, and doubt not the *poetry*
of travelling at the South, if it unfolds such scenes
and creates such genius.

A SOUTHERN SCENE.

The scene which most delighted me in youth
Was round me still—A broad and winding lane,
Its natural carpeting, of emerald
'Broidered with flowers of a thousand hues—
The wild rose clustering with the jessamine,
In beautiful confusion, quite shut out
The world and its entanglements—above,
The loveliest of the southern forest, formed
Meet roof for such a temple, from the oak
Rejoicing in its never-fading green,
And huge fantastic limbs—to the slight myrtle
Studded with bright blossoms—here and there
A lofty sycamore would raise its head,
Most fearful of the woodland, last to trust
To the soft wooings of the smiling spring,
And first to cast its foliage to the ground,
Before the breath of winter—but when high
The sun rides in his summer majesty,
Proudly the laggard Sycamore puts on
Its garniture of silvery green, and waves
Its crisp leaves to the zephyrs, with a sound
Like murmurs of far waters—It was summer,
A Carolinian summer,—when the eye
Shrinks dazzled from the blue of the clear Heavens.

Unless, as now, it falls upon the sight,
Flickering the waving verdure—Nor did lack
Sweet music to the magic of the scene.
The little crimson-breasted nonpareil
Was there, its tiny feet scarce bending down
The silken tendril, that he lighted on
To pour his love-notes,—and in russet coat
Most homely, like true genius bursting forth
In spite of adverse fortune, a full choir
Within himself, the merry mock-bird sate
Filling the air with melody—and at times
In the rapt fervour of his sweetest song
His quivering form would spring into the sky
In spiral circles, as if he would catch
New powers from kindred warblers in the clouds.

20*

MARY ANNA GIBBES,

THE HEROINE OF STONO.

ST. PAUL'S PARISH, STONO RIVER.

EVERY year that rolls away will add a new charm to travelling in the United States, for even where the scenery has no attraction, the hand of genius, busy as that of old Mortality, will be clearing up the records of our national story, and bringing to light names hidden by the gathered moss of time. How little did I ever care for this uninteresting stream, until it was associated with the name of Mary Anna Gibbes! Now it is crowded with vivid associations. Our poets and painters have a glorious field before them! Already the graphic touch of Simms has filled our Southern woods and plains with beings, that, like the mythology of the ancients, give a tongue to inanimate nature.

The authentic anecdote connected with this portion of the country which now occupies my thoughts, is recorded by Major Garden. It is poetry itself without the aid of measured words, but I should be glad if I could make our young Carolina heroine known even to one individual. Colonel Fenwick, distinguished in the war of 1812, was the person saved.

MARY ANNA GIBBES;

THE YOUNG HEROINE OF STONO, S. C.

        Stono, on thy still banks
The roar of war is heard; its thunders swell
And shake yon mansion where domestic love
Till now breathed simple kindness to the heart;
Where white-arm'd childhood twined the neck of age,
Where hospitable cares lit up the hearth,
Cheering the lonely traveller on his way.
    A foe inhabits there, and they depart,
The infirm old man, and his fair household too,
Seeking another home.—Home! Who can tell
The touching power of that most sacred word,
Save he who feels and weeps that he has none?
    Among that group of midnight exiles, fled
Young Mary Anna, on whose youthful cheek
But thirteen years had kindled up the rose.
A laughing creature, breathing heart and love,
Yet timid as the fawn in southern wilds.
E'en the night-reptile on the dewy grass
Startled the maiden, and the silent stars,
Looking so still from out their cloudy home,
Troubled her mind. No time was there for gauds
And toilette art, in this quick flight of fear;
Her glossy hair, damp'd by the midnight winds,
Lay on her neck dishevelled; gathered round
Her form in hurried folds clung her few garments;
Now a quick thrilling sob, half grief, half dread,
Came bursting from her heart,—and now her eyes
Glar'd forth, as peal'd the cannon; then beneath
Their drooping lids, sad tears redundant flowed.
    But sudden mid the group a cry arose,
" Fenwick! where is he?" None returned reply,
But a sharp piercing glance went out, around,
Keen as a mother's towards her infant child

When sudden danger lowers, and then a shriek
From one, from all burst forth—"He is not here!"
   Poor boy, he slept, nor crash of hurrying guns,
Nor impious curses, nor the warrior's shout
Awoke his balmy rest!   He dreamt such dreams
As float round childhood's couch, of angel s face
Peering through clouds ;—of sunny rivulets,
Where the fresh streams flow rippling on, to waft
A tiny sail ;—and of his rabbits white,
With eyes of ruby, and his tender fawn's
Long delicate limbs, light tread, and graceful neck.
He slept unconscious.—Who shall wake that sleep
All shrink, for now th' artillery louder roars ;—
The frightened slaves crouch at their master's side,
And he, infirm and feeble, scarce sustains
His sinking weight.

                    There was a pause, a hush
So deep, that one could hear the forest leaves
Flutter and drop before the war-gun's peal.
Then forward stood that girl, young Mary Ann,
The tear dried up upon her cheek, the sob
Crushed down, and in that high and lofty tone
Which sometimes breathes of woman in the child,
She said, " He shall not die "—and turned *alone*.
   Alone ? oh gentle girlhood, not alone
Art thou, if ONE, watching above, will guard
Thee on thy way.

                    Clouds shrouded up the stars ;—
On—on she sped, the gun's broad glare her guide!
The wolf-growl sounded near,—on—onward still;
The forest trees like warning spirits moaned,—
She pressed her hand against her throbbing heart,
But faltered not.   The whizzing shot went by,
Scarce heeded went—Pass'd is a weary mile
With the light step a master-spirit gives
On duty's road, and she has reached her home.
Her home—is this her home at whose fair gate

Stern foes in silence stand to bar her way?
That gate, which from her infant childhood leap'd
On its wide hinges, glad at her return?
Before the sentinels she trembling stood,
And with a voice, whose low and tender tones
Rose like the ring-dove's in midsummer storms,
She said,

    " Please let me pass, and seek a child,
Who, in my father's mansion has been left
Sleeping, unconscious of the danger near."

While thus she spake, a smile incredulous
Stole o'er the face of one,—the other cursed
And barr'd her from the way.

      " Oh, sirs," she cried,
While from her upraised eyes the tears stream'd down,
And her small hands were clasp'd in agony,
" Drive me not hence, I pray.   Until to-night
I dared not stray beyond my nurse's side
In the dim twilight; yet I now have come
Alone, unguarded, this far dreary mile,
By darkness unappalled;—a simple worm
Would often fright my heart, and bid it beat;
But now I've heard the wild wolf's angry howl
With soul undaunted—till to-night I've shrunk
From men;—and soldiers! scarcely dared I look
Upon their glittering arms;—but here I come
And sue to *you*, men, warriors;—drive me not
Away.   He whom I seek is yet a child,
A prattling boy; and must he, must he die?
Oh, if you love *your* children, let me pass.—
You will not?   Then my strength and hope are gone,
And I shall perish ere I reach my friends."

And then she press'd her brow, as if those hands,
So soft and small, could still it throbbing pulse.
The sentinels looked calmly on, like men
Whose blades had toyed with sorrow, and made sport
Of woe.   One step the maiden backward took,

Lingering in thought, then hope, like a soft flush
Of struggling twilight, kindled in her eyes.
She knelt before them, and re-urged her plea.
  " Perchance you have a sister, sir, or you,
A poor young thing like me ; if she were here,
Kneeling like me before *my* countrymen,
They would not spurn her thus."
                        " Go, girl,—pass on "—
The softened voice of one replied, nor was
She checked, nor waited she to hear repulse,
But darted through the avenue, attained
The hall, and springing up the well-known stairs
With such a flight as the young eagle takes
To gain its nest, she reached the quiet couch,
Where, in bright dreams, th' unconscious sleeper lay.
Slight covering o'er the rescued boy she threw,
And caught him in her arms.   He knew that cheek,
Kiss'd it half-waking, then around her neck
His hands entwined, and dropp'd to sleep again.
  She bore him onward, dreading now for him
The shot that whizz'd along, and tore the earth
In fragments by her side.   She reached the guards,
Who silent op'd the gate,—then hurried on,
But as she pass'd them, from her heart burst forth—
" God bless you, gentlemen !" then urged her way ;
Those arms, whose heaviest load and task had been
To poise her doll, and wield her childhood's toys,
Bearing the boy along the dangerous road.
Voices at length she hears—her friends are near,
They meet, and yielding up her precious charge,
She sinks upon her father's breast, in doubt
'Twixt smiles and tears.

21

FORT MOULTRIE,

OR

SULLIVAN'S ISLAND.

SULLIVAN'S ISLAND.

THIS is a wild and uncultivated spot, desirable only for its patriotic associations, and the sea-breeze that brings health in its current. For about two months in midsummer the public boarding-house is thronged ; now, at the close of August, I am quite alone.

The steam-boat has its afternoon crowds, but they only ramble on the beach, and return to the city. The aspect of the individuals hurrying thither for health or pleasure, and the historical recollections of the scene, have induced me to beguile my loneliness by embodying my thoughts in lines adapted to the tune of *The Emerald Isle.*

HURRAH FOR SULLIVAN'S ISLE !

Our Fair Steamer cuts swiftly the wave,
    And her smoke tells our track on the sky,
As we steer where the noble and brave
    Once assembled to conquer and die !
And still hallow'd to us is the spot,
    Where Liberty first gave her smile,
Nor be the Palmetto Fort ever forgot
    As we gather to Sullivan's Isle.
        Then Hurrah for our Sullivan's Isle !
        Hurrah for our Sullivan's Isle !
    Nor be the Palmetto Fort ever forgot,
        As we gather to Sullivan's Isle !

21*

Oh, Fair Steamer, be true on our seas,
 For the gentle and lovely are here,
The wan infant revives at the breeze,
 And the young mother wipes off her tear.
When thou bearest the aged and young,
 To where health brings its ravishing smile,
Let not the Palmetto Fort e'er be unsung,
 As we gather to Sullivan's Isle!
  Then Hurrah for our Sullivan's Isle!
  Hurrah for our Sullivan's Isle!
  Let not the Palmetto Fort e'er be unsung,
  As we gather to Sullivan's Isle.

 * * * * * *

There are two churches on the island, connected with the Presbyterian and Episcopal persuasions. I was one of *twelve* worshippers at the latter this morning. There is something deeply impressive in the low murmurs of the summer ocean mingling in with man's tones of penitence and thanksgiving, while the waves, the winds, the flowers, the birds speak their language of natural joy.

THOUGHTS AT GRACE CHURCH,
SULLIVAN'S ISLAND.

Praise is around.
The bounding waves swell on,
 Giving their rushing voices to their God,
And ere, commingling with the deep, they've gone,
 Throw incense-foam abroad,
  With solemn sound.

Praise on the winds!
Borne on their countless tongues,
 They tell the story of creative power,

While the wild music of their sacred songs,
    In many a shrub and flower
        A listener finds.

        Praise from the flower!
Tho' few and scatter'd here,
    Yet even *here*, among these sands they bloom;
Like pious thoughts, when hearts are bleak and drear,
    To heaven they give their color and perfume,
        Their innocent dower.

        Praise from the bird!
The garden songster wakes
    His long, rich notes of Sabbath minstrelsy—
His stealthy step the white crane lightly takes,
    And the wild curlew floats on quietly,
        With wing scarce stirr'd.

        Praise from my soul!
By holy prayer upborne,
    Come hither, *Faith*, that seeks the Deity,
And *Penitence*, of earthly trappings shorn,
    And her best partner, gentle *Charity*,
        Me still control.

        My prayer is this:
Though toss'd on time's dark sea,
    That I may reach at length that blessed shore,
Where waveless, passionless, yet free,
    The tumult of the world all o'er,
        We rest in bliss.
*   *   *   *   *   *

Though there is something stimulating to the frame
and exciting to the spirits in an ocean day-scene,
the heart is subdued by the wave-dash that returns
again and again in darkness; there is a supernatural

brightness in the stars, gemming their far and wide
canopy; and the waters, tinged by moon-beams, seem
like deathly upturned faces.   It is late.   I am lonely, and as I gaze on Charleston, where all I love repose, I feel an awe and tremor as if its distant spires
could tell me secrets of its few wild wakeful, or thousand unconscious dreaming ones.

> She sleeps, my own fair city, and the moon
> Looks down with guardian eyes, as clear and still
> As a fond mother's o'er her infant child—
> As still—as wakeful.   How profound her sleep!
>   The Light-house fire burns on, emblem of Him
> Who rests not 'mid the slumbering, but on high
> Holds his bright torch o'er yet uncounted worlds.
> Peace is around in nature—peace and joy!
> Scarcely a cloud is seen save one, which like
> A veil o'er beauty, lends a softer ray
> To heaven's bright eyes, that look out through the stars,
> While the west wind, in gentle breezes, sweeps
> The gentle wave.
>
>   How *distant*, yet how *near*,
> Seems the great city—near, for I have heard
> The sounding bell when the tenth hour was toll'd;—
> Near, for I see the fading lights retire,
> As one by one men seek oblivious rest.
> The old man goes to sleep through dreamless hours,
> Unless perchance a thought of youth steals in
> And opens the far past;—and childhood sleeps,
> Its light breast heaving like the young pine tops.
> Some sink upon their pillow, tired of life,
> And heavily lie down to shut their eyes
> On earth's cold vanities; some, haunted by
> Fierce crimes, toss on a restless couch, and sigh
> For breaking morn; some, bless'd with virtue's meed,

A happy heart, close their soft lids, and dream
Of good deeds done and blessings yet in store.
   And is *crime* brooding now o'er that still scene,
Active and eager, in these tranquil hours?
Oh, may heaven shield thee, city of my heart—
Home of my household—where my dead repose!
God guard the *living*—would that I could hear
Their sleeping breath, and bless them as they lie!
The *dead* need not my blessing—safe are they.
   How *far* she seems, the city of my love!
The kindling spark might wrap her towers in flame,
And my weak voice sound faint as insect's wing
When thunder shakes the air !
                              My yearning soul
Looks towards her, as the fluttering bird that leaves
Its mother's nest too soon, and pants for home.
Oh, I am lonely in this midnight scene.
God guard the sleepers— I will go and pray.

A SOUTHERN SKETCH;

BY

MARY ELIZABETH LEE.

A SOUTHERN SKETCH.

The following lines from a delicate and favorite pen are so touchingly descriptive of a local scene of *actual occurrence*, as to seem happily adapted to the *Poetry of Travelling :*

A SOUTHERN SKETCH.

BY MARY E. LEE.

There was a hush of silence !—the lone room
Was darken'd to a soft and dreamy light ;
The morning beam look'd in, yet seem'd to shun
A spot so chill and noiseless : the Spring gale
Breath'd, as it pour'd its wealth of gather'd sweets,
A low and thrilling music ; and the flowers,
Fresh from Earth's sunny pastures, bloom'd around,
And shed a balmy fragrance o'er the scene.
The *dead* was there ! not in the sable pall
And stern and rigid aspect, that would haunt
In after-days the *living*, but the *dead*
So altogether lovely, that it seem'd
Clad in its spotless robes, as if just deck'd
To be the bride of Heaven.   Time had trac'd
No line upon her brow, and Death stood by
With weak and nerveless arm, as if he fear'd
To mar a thing so perfect.   There she lay—
She of the glossy locks and pale-rose cheek,
With lips half clos'd, and eyelids softly seal'd,
Like one, who in some blissful vision hears

22

A strain of seraph music.   On her breast
Her hands were meekly folded, while beneath,
The heart lay still, as if it joy'd to know
Its labours all were o'er.

A faltering step is heard ; and with his frame
Tottering 'neath weight of days, comes slowly on,
Leaning upon his staff, a dark-brow'd man,
Who counted more than fourscore years on earth.
Mysterious thoughts weigh on him ; and he moves
With wondering gaze, a trembling, awe-struck one,
Towards that fragile being.   They had sought
By gestures strong and oft-repeated words,
To nerve him for the conflict ; yet in vain—
In vain !   For to his lock'd and prison'd mind
The silvery key is broken ; age hath cast
A mildew o'er his senses.   There he stands
As if entranc'd.   Towards the flowers he turns ;
And now strong sympathies are waking up
In his benighted bosom.   He it was,
That long had rear'd and cherish'd them with care,
And hail'd the gladdening sunbeam, and the shower
That added to their beauty and their bloom.
And now he passes on with stealthy tread,
To gaze on that fair being, who was wont
To bid him always welcome ; and did look
So graceful and benign, when with meek smile
He tender'd the young blossoms, deeming well
That they shone *brighter* in her fairy hand.
He gazes on her with a vacant eye ;
Until at last the startling truth comes home
To his bewilder'd bosom ; then with brow
Knit to a fearful sternness, and his breast
Heaving and stirr'd with agony of thought,
He kneels in speechless wo. and seems to doubt
The hand that could have pluck'd a flower so bright
From Love's most cherish'd bower.   Now 't is past.
The fever-dream is gone !—he breathes again—

Each chilling doubt has vanish'd ; and a beam
Of Faith lights up the darkness of his soul.
He lifts his arms to Heaven, and kindling prayer
Lends a pure lustre to his ebon brow ;
Then humbly bows before *her*, as if mov'd
To do the pale dust homage ; then with look
More eloquent than words, he turns away ;
And leaves the peaceful sleeper with her God.

THE BLIND NEGRO COMMUNICANT.

A SKETCH FROM LIFE,

BY MARY E. LEE.

The Saviour's feast was spread.   Group after group
From Zion's scattering band, now silent throng'd
Around the sacred table, glad to pay
(As far as sinful, erring men can pay)
Their debt of gratitude, and share anew
The plain memorials of his dying love.
All ranks were gather'd there.   The rich and poor:
The ignorant and wise ; the tear-wet soul,
And the glad spirit yet in sunshine clad ;
All, with their many hopes, and cares and griefs,
Sought, quiet and unmarked, their 'customed place,
And still at the full banquet there was room.—
It was a solemn season ; and I sat
Wrapt in a cloud of thought, until a slow
And measured footstep fell upon my ear ;
And when I turned to look, an aged man
Of threescore years and ten appeared to view.
It was the blind Communicant !   He came,
Led by a friendly hand, and took his place
Nearest the table, with a reverent air,
As if he felt the spot was holy ground—
There was a perfect hush !—The hour was come !
The symbols were disclosed, and soon they rose

The sweet tones of the sheperd of the flock,
Telling once more the story of the Cross ;
And as he spoke, in sympathy I gazed
Upon the blind old pilgrim by my side.
The sight was touching!   As the Pastor taught,
In accents all subdued, how Jesus bore
The flight of friends, the stern denial-vow,
The spear, the thorns, the agonizing cross,
With want, shame, persecution, torture, death,
The old man shook, convulsed ; his ebon brow
Grew pallid in its hue ; a few big tears
Ran trickling down his cheek, and from his lip
Methought there came the words, " *Lord, is it I?*"
But when there stole upon each listening ear
And throbbing heart, that prayer of matchless love,
That type and watch-word for all after-prayer,
"Father, forgive them !" then he clasp'd his hands,
And bowing his hoar head upon his breast,
Wept, even as a weaned child might weep.
    There was a change !   The bread and wine were
        brought,
He wiped the gushing drops from his thin cheek,
Bowed solemnly—received them both—then paused—
Till, raising his dull eye-balls up to heaven,
As asking for God's blessing on the rite,
He broke the bread, received the goblet close
Within his wither'd hands ; restored it safe ;—
Then, while a peaceful smile illum'd his face,
Sank back as in an ecstacy of bliss.
The parting hymn was sung, and oft I paus'd
And stopped to listen, as the old man's voice,
Broken and shrill, sought too to mingle in
With modulated tones, and though his *lip*
Utter'd no music, yet I joyed to know
The *heart* was all link'd-melody within.
Christ's seal was stamp'd anew upon each soul ;
The solemn rite was finished, and the band,

Warmed to each kindly touch of human love,
Moved, full of thoughtful cheerfulness, along
The quiet church-yard, where gay sunbeams danced
On the white marble tombs, and bright flowers made
A pleasant home for Death; while 'mongst them all
The blind Communicant went groping on
Along his midnight path.   The sight was sad!
My heart yearn'd for him—and I longed for power
To say, as the disciples said of old,
" Blind man! receive thy sight,"—and in the might
Of strong compassion, I could e'en, methought,
Have entered his dark prison-house awhile
And let him gaze in turn, on the blue skies,
And the glad sunshine, and the laughing earth.
But soon I owned a sense of higher things,
And in the heart's soft dialect I said,
" Old soldier of the Cross, 'tis well with thee!
Thy warfare is nigh finished; and though Earth
Be but an utter blank, yet soon thou'lt gaze
On that bright country where thy God shall be
The never-setting Sun; and Christ, thy Lord,
Will lead thee through green pastures, where the still
And living waters play.   And though thou art
A creature lonely and unpriz'd by *men*,
Yet thou mayst stand a Prince 'mongst Princes, when
The King makes up his jewels!"

SOUTHERN LOCAL SKETCH.

ST. JOHN'S PARISH.

A young Greek remarked to me, on a recent drive
to this portion of the country, that he had seen nothing since he left his native land so beautiful and
affecting in natural scenery, as the gray moss waving in wild decoration on the trees near the old
church at Goose-Creek.   It is worth while for the

22*

traveller to turn aside and pause at this ruin, which was erected about 1707. The fences are broken down, the grave-stones defaced, and every object shows marks of decay ; still there are thoughts connected with St. James's Church in its romantic solitude and dilapidation, that many minds would not exchange for the trim finish of a city edifice. A friend entered the broken window, and opened the door for us.—There are four arched windows, two of them with a cherub in stucco on each key-stone. Over one door a Pelican is represented feeding her young. The Decalogue, Apostle's Creed, and Lord's Prayer, are carved on marble tables between Corinthian pillars. The following is the oldest epitaph :

Under this lyes the late John Gibbes,
Who deceased on the 7th August, 1711.
Aged 40.

The most curious object to an American is the Royal arms, which were formerly a fixture over the east window, but now, in their fallen and ruined state, are a striking emblem of the political change which has been wrought since they were placed there. I had the pleasure of hearing Lord Selkirk explain some points in this painting on his late visit to America ; but whether I was awed by listening to an Earl's son, or whether, as an American, I have a natural obtuseness on such points, I cannot say ; but I have entirely forgotten every thing he said on that subject. His simple, earnest, and unaffected manner, however, I vividly remember, as well as the interest he displayed in rice-culture and other local topics on Cooper river.

Sacred historical recollections are beginning to cluster over many a spot in our country, and the traveller will feel them in full force at the plantation of Henry Laurens, President of the first American Congress. It is a beautiful thought, that when domestic recollections begin to fade in the lapse of years, patriotism is twining its wreath to hang over the scenes where our country's saviours lived and trod. The avenue leading to the family burial-place is very extensive. It is shaded on one side by trees of luxuriant growth, and on the other a Cherokee rose hedge has grown beyond its original design, and throwing its arms around, gives a romantic wildness to the path. The burial-place is situated on a knoll of considerable elevation, just on a graceful sweep of the river. It is wooded to the base with a variety of forest growth, except where a stone wall encloses the remains of the dead. Without the wall, for a large space, are monuments with wooden crosses, indicating the spot where the negroes are laid, that numerous family over whom history declares he presided with such paternal kindness.

On returning to the avenue after having mused awhile over the tombs, and relieved the solemnity and awe of the scene by a glance at the shining waters of the Cooper, as it lay calmly in the noonday sun, my thoughts turned back to the past.—On this very path, I reflected, has one of our greatest patriots trod, perhaps in the bitterness of weeping affection, or in softened recollection wreathing the young vines, or planting those memorials which the busy heart loves to raise; or perhaps he stole to the seclusion of this avenue to muse alone, and plan great things for his country, and gird up his soul for his patriotic trials.

PRIVATE COLLECTION OF PAINTINGS.

This part of the country not only contains scenes of historical interest, but in the residence of H. S. Ball, Esq. affords a delightful treat to the lover of the fine arts. I have never experienced half the the delight in city exhibitions of pictures, however extensive, that I have felt in examining the paintings in this unbroken retirement. The tranquillity of the country seems peculiarly adapted to the chastened reflecting mood with which we pause over works of genius. The following list will show that the mind need not be idle here.

The first object to arrest the attention, and which is probably one of the greatest triumphs of the art, is *Spalatro's vision of the bloody hand, by Washington Allston.* Its exquisite finish as a painting seems to add, by contrast, to the fierce and hardy expression of the murderer. I have sitten silently before the picture, until I began to feel the wildness of that midnight scene over my whole spirit. This *chef d'œvre* was executed for Mr. Ball, and there is no other copy existing.

Second—*The Bride of Lammermoor, by Henry Inman.* This is in fine relief to the effort of Allston's, being purely a picture of the affections. Some critics have thought the figure of Lucy Ashton too *embonpoint* for the conception of the novelist. However this may be, the error is nobly compensated by the strange incertitude in the expression of her countenance, which wonderfully realizes the leading characteristics of the individual, filial awe and deep absording constancy in love. The clergyman, the mother with her iron obstinacy, the care-worn, heart-broken, yet noble lover, and all the minute points of the picture, are perfect. This also was painted for the present owner.

Third—*A portrait of Henry Inman.* Spirited.

Fourth—*A portrait of a child, by Stuart.* One of his most beautiful efforts.

Fifth—*Conrad and Gulnare, by J. B. White.* The dungeon and sleeping figure have Mr. White's peculiar merits, which consist in bold conceptions and strong contrasts.

Sixth—*A water-color drawing, by W. G. Wall.* A beautiful sketch.

Seventh—*Children playing, supposed to be of the School of Nicholas Poussin, by B. K.* These rogues are in the lovely freedom of youth, all grace and spirit.

Eighth—*Monkeys carousing, by David Teniers.* It is impossible not to sympathize with this odd group. The picture speaks its authorship.

Ninth—*A Madonna, by Carlo Maratti.* Exquisitely painted on amethyst; the effect is as if the figure were floating in clouds.

Tenth—*St. Ignatius, by Vandyck.* The attention is at once arrested by this bold and characteristic head, depressed in its broad margin of frame.

Eleventh—*Sheep, &c., by a French artist.*—Agreeable grouping and coloring.

Twelfth—*A sketch of the Aurora, from Guido's fresco in the palace at Rome.* This class of copies must always be less attractive than other pictures, from the crowding of objects in a small space. This is finished with great delicacy.

Thirteenth—*A view of Newport Harbor, R. I. in waters colors, by W. G. Wall.*

Fourteenth—*View of the entrance to Newport Harbor, W. G. Wall.* These bold rocks and smooth waters are among the finest of our local scenes as subjects for the artist.

Fifteenth—*The Shepherd, by Murillo.* This is a very peculiar picture. It represents a figure with a sheepskin thrown carelessly about him, and his fingers on his pipe, with an expression as if some pleasant note had just occurred to him. The open mouth gives at first an unpleasant effect, but a moment's observation shows its truth, while the eye rests unsated on the harmony of the coloring.

Sixteenth—*The Repast, by Terburgh.* A most finished work. The group consists of a lady elegantly attired, sitting at a table, a gentleman beside her, offering her refreshments, and two attendant females in graceful attitudes, and a boy selecting wine from a cooler. Every thing is in the highest style of elegance, and all graduated from her who seems to be the queen of this little festival.

Seventeenth—*Portrait of Rubens, by Ribeira, usually called Espagnoletto.* The shading of this artist well sets off the marked head of Rubens.

Eighteenth—*Lake Thrasymene, by J. Vernet.* This picture is peculiar for the cold gray tint of dawn, for which the artist is remarkable.

Nineteenth—*A charger, by Van Ayteman.*

Twentieth—*Lake Winnipiseogee, by C. Fraser.*

Twenty-first—*Squam Lake, by C. Fraser.* The coloring is so.true to nature as to seem cold, for that is the actual peculiarity of these scenes. The warmer pictures of this accomplished artist give me more pleasure, particularly his views of Niagara, which Allston once said looked like water rushing out of space. Mr. Ball has other pictures of Mr. Fraser's, not yet in this collection.

Twenty-second—*Copy from Jordan, by a young artist.*

Twenty-third—*Copy from Wouvermans, by a young artist.* Great promises, particularly the latter.

Twenty-fourth—*Landscape with Dogs, by W. G. Wall.*

Twenty-fifth—*Game, unknown.* And,

Twenty-sixth—*Fish, unknown.* Old paintings.

Twenty-seventh—*Ducks, unknown.* Do.

Twenty-eighth—*Landscape in water colors, by W. G. Wall.*

Twenty-ninth—*A Magdalen after Skalken.*—This wild and haggard looking being is a departure from the usual conception of artists, but the cave and the lurid light consort well with the idea of a penitent.

Thirtieth—*The Repose, by W. Page.* This luxurious picture is the antipodes of Skalken's Magdalen in all its bearings.

Mr. Weir, at West Point, is now painting a scene from Irving's Columbus, for Mr. Ball, which will probably add great value to his collection. Our artists will look up with hope when such a liberal example is imitated by men of taste. The following chaste and eloquent remarks of Professor Goddard may appropriately close this sketch :

" It may be well to inquire whether a more generous culture of a taste for Liberal Studies would not gratefully temper the elements of our present social character, and introduce higher and nobler interests into the whole of our social life. Would it not save us from an inordinate admiration of the least enviable distinctions of wealth ? Would it not impart to our manners more of variety, of grace, of dignity, and repose ; and to our morals, a more delicate discrimination and a loftier tone ?

" Liberal Studies are adapted not only to moderate an extravagant desire for wealth, but to aid in establishing the true principles upon which wealth should be expended. In a country like our own, these principles, if well understood, are apt to be very imperfectly applied. The primitive stages in the progress of refinement we have long since passed. Leaving far in the rear the cheap pleasures, the simple habits, and the unpretending hospitalities of our fore-

fathers, we have engaged, it is to be feared, somewhat too largely, in the career of ambitious splendour
and inappropriate magnificence.   Impelled too often
by the unworthy desire to surpass our neighbours in
some matter of mere external embellishment, we lavish thousands in multiplying around ourselves the
elements of an elegant and selfish voluptuousness.   I
am distressed by no morbid apprehensions concerning
the progress of luxury in our land.   I am terrified
by no apparition of monopoly.   I utter no response
to the vulture cry of the Radical, now heard in the
distance.   I am far from thinking that the opulent
ought to diminish their expenses.   I believe that,
with signal advantage, they might increase them.
But, in the selection of those objects of embellishment which it is in the power alone of abundant
wealth to command, I am not singular in contending
that the decisions of a simpler and better taste ought
not to be disregarded.   Is it not a matter of just re-
proach, that of all the apartments in our mansion
houses, the library is generally the most obscure,
and often the most ill-furnished; and that the fashionable upholsterer is allowed to absorb so much of
our surplus revenue, that hardly any is left for the
painter and the statuary ?   In all this there is
manifested a melancholy disproportion—an imperfect apprehension of some of the best uses to which
wealth can be applied.   In the spirit of an austere
philosophy, it is not required that we should dispense
with those costly ornaments which can boast no higher merit than their beauty ; but it would be hailed
23

as a most benignant reform, if, in the arrangements
of our domestic economy, there could be traced a
more distinct recognition of the capacities and destinies of man as an intellectual and moral being—as
a being endowed with Imagination and Taste—with
Reason and with Conscience. How few among us
culivate the Fine Arts! How few understand the
principles on which they are founded—the sensitve
part of our nature to which they are addressed! To
this remark, the imperfect knowledge of Music, which,
in obedience to the authority of fashion, is acquired
at the boarding-school, forms no exception. It may
still be affirmed, that we have among us no *class*
who delight in Music as one of their selectest pleasures; who gaze with untiring admiration upon the
miraculous triumphs of Painting; who are filled with
tranquil enthusiasm by the passionless and unearthly beauty of Sculpture. And is not this to be lamented? Do we not thus estrange ourselves from
sources of deep and quiet happiness, to which we
might often resort for solace, and refreshment, and
repose? To these sources of happiness there is nothing in the nature of our political institutions, or
of our domestic pursuits, which sternly forbids an
approach. We have, it is true, no titled aristocracy;
and property does not, as in the land of our forefathers, accumulate in large masses, and descend, un-
divided, through a long line of expectant proprietors.
But there is scarcely a city, a town, or a village in
this land, where some could not be found, blessed
with every requisite but the disposition, to acquire

a genuine relish for the Fine Arts.   Nay, more; in
our larger cities, all of which boast their commercial
prosperity, and some their Athenian refinement, why
should not the masters of the pencil and the chisel
be employed to furnish for the private mansion those
precious decorations, which alone are secure from
the capricious despotism of fashion?   By thus
expending some portion of their superabundant
wealth, the opulent would drink deeply of those
finer joys which are perversely left unapproached by
the indolent, the voluptuous, and the profligate.
Thus, too, would they gather around themselves almost inexhaustible means of winning others from
sordid pursuits, to a contemplation of the imperish-
able glories of Genius and of Art."

SKETCHES FROM

BUNCOMBE, N. C.

BY

ANNA MARIA WELLS.

23*

BUNCOMBE, N. C.

The following prose extracts from private letters afford too interesting an addition to the other effusions from the same pen, to pass without a record in the Poetry of Travelling. The poems seem now like pearls arranged on their appropriate string.

I am enveloped in mountains. In no direction can I turn without seeing them, piles on piles—one behind another, of a fainter and fainter grey as they vanish in the distance. We had a thunder-storm this evening. Never speak of thunder in Charleston. "Not from one lone cloud; but every mountain." Poor weak mortality must needs quail to hear it.

I could not help admiring the beauty and freshness of the woods, at the early hour of morning, as we flew by them in the car; and I felt ashamed of being any part or portion of that noisy boisterous thing, that with such bustle and uproar was disturbing their majestic solitude. I was vexed at being whisked by so many beautiful wild flowers, with a mere glance at their splendid colour, and not the faintest notion of their form. We were soon beyond all traces of the Magnolia, the beds of water lilies were left far behind, and I saw no more of a splendid swamp flower, which had caught my eye by its rich dress of scarlet, bordering on crimson. I inquired its name ; but the object was mistaken by my neighbour, who answered, " That is the Magnolia Gander Flower ! you've nothin like that at the North, I reckon !" " I *guess* we hav'n't"—I wanted to say, but I was afraid of getting too well acquainted.

We were hurried through our breakfast at Woodstock, yet so great in *man*kind is that wicked organ of destructiveness, that we not only stopped, but returned on our way to effect the destruction of an Alligator. All the passengers alighted to see the unfortunate mother and her young ones (" all my pretty chickens and their dam") dragged from their retreat and killed. I was very glad when we arrived at Augusta. Though I had railed at rail-roads all day, I began to think it a " ra-al clever contrivance," as my new acquantance would have called it, when I rested, after a journey of 136 miles, with less fatigue than one of 40 has often given me. I christened my fellow-traveller Jonathan Wildfire, he reminded me so much of Hackett's celebrated representation, the *truth* of which, but for him, I should never have known.

We left Edgefield the third morning at dawn of day, and such a stage as we were packed in ! " This ere stage has had a heap of upsets I reckon," said Jonathan, pointing out the various broken and mended places, " no small number any how !" There was no help for it—the roads before us were the worst on the route, and at such a break-neck rate as we drove ! Up hill and down—horses at full gallop, and coachman whipping them on—stumps and stones in the way, and a broken carriage to boot.   On we went—

" We stopped not for *break*, and we stopped not for stone,
And we dashed thro' the rivers where bridge there was none."

I could not help contrasting, in this situation, the Northern and Southern character.   Crossing the mountains in Vermont, I have observed, how the passengers would all spring to one side, to preserve the balance and prevent an overturn ; how they would get out and walk at dangerous places, and how the coachman would hold in his reins in going down hill, and even chain the wheels—while here, all is neck or nothing—driver and passengers—all seem reckless of danger, and so infectious is the spirit, that even I, with all my constitutional timidity, began to feel as if my neck might be broken to be sure, but that it might be *mended somehow*.   The only indication of caution that I noticed was in Jonathan himself, who, after riding one morning on the box, came suddenly, feet first, through the carriage window, exclaiming, " I'm no way particular, but I can't keep my seat with that ere fellow any longer ; he's as bad a hand at his trade as ever I see." " I'll pester ye for a little of that water," said he, as the driver stopped to water his horse at a brook.   " Its powerful bad water, but (with a grin) not worse than your *drivin* I recon."   " Well, the truth ont is," said the driver, " I never was no sort of a hand at *steerin*, but my *team* is mortal feard on me, any how."

With this candid and comforting confession, we were obliged to content ourselves till the next stage, when, to my great relief, we changed driver, carriage and horses, and arrived here safely.

*   *   *   *   *   *

L—— proposed a ride on horseback this afternoon, and we followed a winding path through the woods, which suddenly brought us before a little building, formed, in the usual manner, of rough logs, and standing in the middle of a small cleared spot, surrounded by the lofty trees and thick under-brush of the forest.

"It is a church," said L——; "the country people assemble here every other Sabbath, and when the weather is fine, the services are performed in the open air; but otherwise, within the building."

I was ready to smile at its rudeness and insignificance, but a sudden feeling of awe came over me: I remembered it was God's Temple, and that the glow of devotion might be kindled as warmly here as at a prouder shrine.   Amid the stillness, the beauty, and grandeur of such scenery, the presence of the Deity must be deeply, strongly felt.

My horse's foot stumbled over some obstruction. I looked—it was a decayed wooden tomb-stone. I gazed around, and for the first time discovered that I was within the sacred pecincts of the dead. Some few of the graves were surrounded with little wooden palings, but most of them were open to the passing footstep.

How peacefully they sleep here, thought I.   No

sound to disturb the deep repose, but the gentle stirring of the leaves, the plaintive moan of the wood
pigeon, or occasionally the hymn of devotion, arising
from that consecrated building.

As we returned by a little broken by-path, we
passed two superb azalias. What a contrast was
their vigour, and beauty, and freshness to the train
of thought I had been pursuing! My feelings resolved themselves into the following strain:

THE MOUNTAIN CHURCH.

As one without a friend, one summer eve
I walked among the solemn woods alone.
The boughs hung lovely, and the gentle winds
Whispered a song monotonous and low,
That soothed my mind even while it made me sad.
  The path I followed, by a turn abrupt,
Brought me to stand beside that humble roof,
Where the few scattered families that dwell
Among these mountains and deep forest shades
Meet weekly, to uplift the soul in prayer.
A few rude logs up-piled were all the walls,—
There were four windows and a door, not e'en
Adorn'd with rudest art; and in the midst
A pulpit,—cushioned not, nor overhung
With crimson folds of fringed drapery,
Nor graced with gilded volumes richly bound.
Amid the mountain pines the low roof stood,
And mountain hands had reared it; but it wore
An air of reverence.
                    Few paces onward,
O'ershadowed more by the green underwood,
Some slight raised mounds showed where the dead
          were laid.
No gravestone told who slept beneath the turf.

(Perchance the heart that deeply mourns, needs not
Such poor remembrancer.)   The forest flowers
Themselves had fondly clustered there,—and white
Azalias with sweet breath stood round about,
Like fair young maidens mourning o'er their dead.
In some sweet solitude like this I would
That I might sleep my last long dreamless sleep!
Oh quiet resting place! Divine repose!
Let not my voice, I whispered, oh let not
My heedless step profane thy sanctity!
Still shall sweet summer smiling, linger here,
And wasteful winter lightly o'er thee pass;
Bright dews of morning jewel thee! and all
The silent stars watch over thee at night;
The mountains clasp thee lovingly within
Their giant arms, and ever round thee bow
The everlasting forests; for thou art
In thy simplicity a holy spot
And not unmeet for heavenly worshipper.

*   *   *   *   *   *

In our ride this afternoon we passed along the
banks of *Cooper's Creek*, a miserable little, muddy,
sluggish stream, which nevertheless awakened a feeling of interest when Mr. —— said, " Do you know
these are the waters of the Mississippi ?"

Through the woods our road was narrow and
winding, and the boughs came so closely together
from either side, that we lost sight of each other continually, and were obliged to bend quite down to avoid
being knocked. off our saddles as we passed under
the hanging branches.   There was excitement and
pleasure in it, and, more than all—health!

We rode to the summit of a hill to see the sun set
behind the mountains : it was misty, however, in the

distance, and the Day-God departed not with his usual splendour. How well are these heights named the BLUE RIDGE! Their colour is beautiful: the more distant ones to-night were almost of the hue of the violet; and along their bold outlines was a continuous thread of light that looked like a golden rim crowning their majestic heads. Mount Pisgah seemed to tower higher than ever, though S—— declares that "none of these mountains are as high as they were eight years ago!"

We returned home slowly; there was a quiet solemnity in the twilight that sobered us all. Even little A—— hushed her song and her prattle as it grew dark, and seemed to feel with me how deep was the power of solitude. The mountains seemed to be closing us in. The trees whispered to us as we passed by them, and the whippoorwill sang unanswered. Silence was about us and in our hearts, and I went to my own room and wrote the following stanzas, under impressions of melancholy that I like not often to indulge in.

TO THE WHIPPOORWILL.

The shades of eve are gathering slowly round,
   And silence hangs o'er meadow, grove, and hill,
Save one lone voice, that, with continuous sound,
   Calls thro' the deep'ning twilight— *Whippoorwill.*

Faintly is heard the whispering mountain breeze;
   Faintly the rushing brook that turn'd the mill:
Hush'd is the song of birds—the hum of bees;—
   The hour is all thine own, sad *Whippoorwill!*

24

No more the woodman's axe is heard to fall:
   No more the ploughman sings with rustic skill.
As if earth's echoes woke no other call,
   Again, and yet again, comes *Whippoorwill!*

Alas! enough; before, my heart was sad;
   Sweet bird! thou makest it sadder, sadder still.
Enough of mourning has my spirit had;
   I would not hear *thee* mourn, poor *Whippoorwill.*

Thoughts of my distant home upon me press,
   And thronging doubts, and fears of coming ill;
My lone heart feels a deeper loneliness,
   Touch'd with that plaintive burthen— *Whippoorwil..*

Sing to the village lass, whose happy home
   Lies in yon quiet vale, behind the hill;
But, doom'd far, far from all I love to roam,
   Sing not to me, oh gentle *Whippoorwill.*

Lov'd ones! my children! Ah, they cannot hear
   My voice that calls to them!   An answer shrill,
A shrill, unconscious answer rises near,
   Repeating, still repeating, *Whippoorwill!*

Another name my lips would breathe;—but then
   Such tender memories all my bosom fill,
Back to my sorrowing breast it sinks again!
   Hush, or thou'lt break my heart, sad *Whippoorwill.*

   *   *   *   *   *   *

The face of nature is beginning to change; the
foliage of the mountains is already touched with
orange, crimson, and brown; and the meadow-pinks
and honeysuckles and azalias, which have made the
woods so beautiful all summer, are beginning to give
way to the various shades of blue, purple, and yellow,
that seem to be the prevailing colours of the autumn-

al flowers. Now, too, for the first time, I see the lilies of the field " and how they grow,"—the woods are full of them, arrayed in gold and scarlet, with spots and streaks of the darkest crimson, and bending close to the earth, as if to hide their glory. I had seen them before in our gardens at the North, but here, in their wild state, they assume a different character. The scenery along the banks of the French Broad is very lovely ; but my feelings have been most excited and elevated by views from the summits of the high mountains. I am astonished to find myself so embosomed among them. As I look down and afar off, for miles and miles distant, still they are rising, wave on wave, blue and misty like those of the ocean, and giving me the sensation of dizziness which we feel at sea. Below me, as I stand upon these giddy heights, lie the everlasting forests, with here and there a cleared spot, in the midst of which I can discern the tiny farm-houses and the long winding mazes of the French Broad, twining like a silver thread among the harvest fields. The air on these mountains is so bracing and sweet, as amply to repay the heat and fatigue of the ascent. The following lines will tell the rest :

LET US GO TO THE WOODS.

Let us go to the woods—'tis a bright sunny day :
They are mowing the grass, and at work with the hay.
Come over the meadow and scent the fresh air,
For the pure mountain breezes are every where.
We'll follow this winding path up to the hills,
And spring with a lightsome foot over the rills.

Up—up—it grows sweeter the higher we get,
With the flowers of the season that linger here yet:
Nay—pause not to gaze at the landscape now;
It is finer when seen from the high hill's brow.
We will gather all curious flowers as we go;
The sweet and the scentless, and those that bend low;
The pale and the gaudy, the tiny, the tall,
From the vine, from the shrub, we will gather them all.

Now here's the *clematis* all graceful and fair;
You may set it like pearls in the folds of your hair.
And if for your bosom you'd have a bouquet,
Here's the *Meadow-pink*, sweet, and the *Touch-me-not* gay.
Here's the full-blown *Azalia*, perfuming the air,
Here's the *Cardinal-flower*, that a princess might wear.
And the wild mountain *Phlox*, pink and purple and blue,
And *Star-flowers*, both white and of golden hue.
And here's a bright blossom, a gay one indeed,
Our mountain-maids name it the *Butterfly-weed*.
So gorgeous its colours, one scarcely can tell
If the flower or the insect in beauty excel.

Here's the low dwarf *Acacia*, that droops as it grows,
And its leaves, as you gather them, tremble and close.
And near us, I know by her breath on the gale,
Is the tall yellow *Primrose* so pretty and pale.

Here's the *Pigeon-Pea*, fit for a fairy's bowers,—
And the purple *Thrift*, straightest and primmest of flowers.
Here is *Privet;* no prettier shrub have we met,
And the *Midsummer Daisy* is hiding here yet.

But stay—We are now on the high hill's brow!
How bright lie the fields in the sun light below!
Do you see those white chimneys that peep o'er the grove?
'Tis you own little cottage, the home that you love—
Let us go by the fields where the *chinquapins* are,
And through the long lane where the *Chesnuts* hang fair,

They are scarcely yet ripe, but their tender green
Looks lovely the dark clustering foliage between:—
And we'll stop at the nest that we found in the wood,
And see if the *black-bird* hath flown with her brood :
And we'll list to the *mocking-bird*, wondering thereat,
Till he pauses, as if to ask ' who can do that ? '
We will listen and gaze; for the lowliest thing
Some lesson of worth to the mind can bring.
If we read nature's book with a serious eye,
Not a leaf, but some precious thought on it doth lie:
And 'tis good to go forth among scenes like these,
Amid music and sunshine, and flowers and trees,
If 'twere only to waken the deep love that springs
At the sight of all lovely and innocent things.

MOUNTAIN LODGE.

We arrived here yesterday about sunset.   The
evening was gloomy and wet, but even storms cannot quite obscure the beauty of this place ; and this
morning the sun has come forth again—

"·Laughing the clouds away as if in scorn."

The house stands unusually high, and never did
my eye rest upon a more lovely scene than that
which lay outstretched before me when I threw up
the chamber window.   The mists were just curling
down the sides of the distant mountains ; and the
wide extent of forest which lies beneath them, seemed
in the distance more like fields of verdure than the
disconnected foliage of lofty trees.   Within this green
amphitheatre my eye reposes upon sunny hills and
cultivated plains.   In yonder dewy pastures I see
the quiet sheep, and hear their pleasant bleating min-
24*

gling with the incessant warbling of the birds.   To
the left lies the little field of the Turkey-minder ; and
there, these two hours, has stood the untiring girl,
beneath the spreading oak, with her feathered flock
about her, by no means the least striking object
in the picture.   Just beside this pretty rural group
stands a grove of maples, and beyond them lies the
artificial lake, which Mrs. ——, with her unrivalled
energy, has brought up to increase the picturesque
beauty of the scene, and supply its only deficiency.

Further to the right, seen through an opening in
the trees, stands the little Gothic church, the result
of the same creative taste and liberal spirit ; and
within all this are the large and richly cultivated
gardens immediately surrounding the house, where
no weeds are permitted to encumber the rich and varied *parterre,* where the shaven turf seems tempting
the feet to try its softness.   Yellow butterflies are
chasing each other from bank to bower ; and the delicious fragrance of the sweet-briar, the mignionette,
and the honey-suckle, are rising up like incense.
Yonder pathway leads to the little vine-shaded stone
dairy-house, at the door of which a fountain, surrounded by shells, throws out incessantly its fresh
and sparkling waters ; and that other winds up the hill
behind it, whither, with all expedition, I mean now to
follow, that I may have one wide look over the whole
landscape before the sun steals away all its jewelry.
Well ! and what effect had the Buncombe scenery
upon your mind ? you may ask.

Like almost every thing else I have seen since I left New England, it served only to bear me *home*, and leave my thoughts where my heart is :

SONG.

New-England, New-England, my home o'er the sea!
My heart, as I wander, turns fondly to thee ;
For bright rests the sun on thy clear winding streams,
And soft o'er thy meadows the moon pours her beams.
   New-England, New-England, my home o'er the sea !
   The wanderer's heart turns in fondness to thee.

Thy breezes are healthful, and clear are thy rills,
And the harvest waves proudly and rich on thy hills.
Thy maidens are fair, and thy yeomen are strong,
And thy rivers run blithely thy valleys among.
   New-England, New-England, my home o'er the sea !
   The wanderer's heart turns in fondness to thee.

There's home in New-England, where dear ones of mine
Are thinking of me and the days of lang syne,
And blest be the hour when, my pilgrimage o'er,
I shall sit by that hearth-stone and leave it no more.
   New-England, New-England, my home o'er the sea !
   My heart, as I wander, turns fondly to thee.

LETTERS FROM GEORGIA:

THE

GOLD MINES.

LETTERS FROM GEORGIA.

The Gold Mines.

C. H. Geo. Jan. 1835.

My Dear Friend.

You ask me for a more particular account of the visit I made two years since to the Georgia Gold Region. I do not wonder that the interesting novel of " Guy Rivers" should have awakened your curiosity to know more of the remarkable tract of country in which its scene is laid. I hasten to gratify your wish, so far as may be at present in my power ; and promise as faithful a description as my memory will enable me to give.

I first entered the Northern part of Georgia, not, like the hero of " Guy Rivers," on horseback, with pistols at my saddle-bow, though I have no doubt the description of young Colleton's equipage accurately delineates that of many travellers in that section. I however came more peaceably along, in a clumsy stage, rumbling and jolting over intolerable roads. Both roads and stages, I presume, have since improved. From Athens, the seat of the State University, where I had attended a very creditable Commencement, I directed my course towards Clarks-

ville. This village, the seat of justice for Haber-
sham County, is beautifully situated, in a most healthful and temperate region, near the mountains, whose
blue summits rise in full view around it. The village itself is very pretty, with numerous well-built
frame houses, and a brick court-house in the middle
of its square, according to the invariable plan of
county towns in Georgia. I arrived about noon on
Sunday, and had the satisfaction of attending service in a building, comfortable and neat, though plain,
belonging, I believe, to the Methodist denomination,
though on this occasion its pulpit was occupied by
a clergyman of other sentiments. The next morning found me on my way to the mines, on horseback,
and in agreeable company. We crossed the beautiful valley of Naucoochy, a spot which had been
under cultivation long before the whites became pos-
sessors of the soil, and probably even before it was
occupied by the Cherokees. A small conical hill
was pointed out to me, rising from the level of the
valley, and supposed, with great probability, to be a
work of art, and to contain the bones of some Indians
of an earlier race. In another portion of this valley, the miners, last summer, while digging for gold,
encountered beneath the soil unexpected vestiges of
the hand of man. They disinterred a number of
huts, constructed in the usual manner of log-houses,
but with the remarkable circumstance that they were
without doors or windows. These apertures are, in
building log-huts, generally sawn out after the logs
have been secured in their places; so the natural

conclusion is, that this cantonment, commenced by some party, was, from some cause unknown, hastily abandoned before it was completed. But who were the builders? The most probable conjecture, perhaps, is that they were Spaniards, by whom, it is well known, under the command of De Soto and others, Georgia was partially explored.

After being deserted by their builders, it seems probable that these half-finished huts were for a time under water, and that Naucoochy valley was temporarily a lake, among the accumulating alluvium of which the huts were at last buried. The lake at length forced its way through its bank, and left, as at present, the valley intersected by a small stream.

But I must leave Naucoochy, and turning to the left, cross a branch of the Chatahoochee, and make my way along the side of Mount Yonah,—now no longer inhabited by the *bears* from which it derives its name.[*] It was my object to spend a few days with a friend who had made his home in this region; and with him and his acquaintances I learned that warm hearts and cultivated minds can live in log cabins and deal in gold. It was not long after arriving at my place of destination, before I walked forth to visit a gold mine. The first which I saw was one of the alluvial or deposite mines. These are found along the banks of the rivulets or " branches," and the gold is separated by the simple process of

[*] Yonah, in Cherokee, signifies *bear*.

25

washing. For my gratification, a workman went through this process in its simplest form, that of "panning." This is merely to fill an iron pan with the gravel among which the gold is found, and to stir the pan about with the hands for some time, under water, throwing out the gravel from time to time. The metal, by this process, sinks to the bottom of the vessel, and the workman comes to you at last with nothing in his pan visible at first sight except a little black sand. On narrowly inspecting this sand, however, you discover here and there a bright yellow speck, which is pure gold.

This process of panning is of course slow and laborious; very little of the gravel can thus be washed at a time. But in this manner the gold-diggers at first laboured, and it is thus that you may suppose Guy Rivers, Forester, and their companions, to have been employed. To expedite the business, however, a machine is now commonly used, called a rocker. One of these machines finds employment for ten or twelve men, who are commonly negroes. You see three or four at work in digging out the gravel, which lies commonly about two feet below the surface, and composes, itself, a stratum of the same thickness. Two or three are employed in carrying the gravel in wheelbarrows to the rocker. One is occupied in shovelling it from the barrows to the machine, others keep the machine in motion, and another, with a large rake, distributes the gravel over its surface. The upper part of the rocker is like a very coarse sieve, and the gravel being thrown on it, and washed with

water from the stream, which continually runs upon
it, the smaller particles, among which is the gold,
fall through the sieve into a box, where they are still
further washed until the water runs out. This lower box contains a quantity of quicksilver, which, as
you well know, attracts other metals and combines
with them. This quicksilver therefore seizes the
small particles of gold from among the sand and
water with which it is still mingled ; and at night
the owner of the mine finds in his machine a mass
of amalgamated quicksilver and gold. He may then
have the metal in a pure state by exposing the whole
to a strong heat.

But it is time for me to close this letter. At another opportunity I will continue the subject, and may
perhaps in future attempt to describe something of
a different character from gold mines,—the noble
works of nature, which I witnessed in all their primitive wildness, amidst the deep forests of my adopted state. Till then adieu.

S. G. B.

My Dear Friend,

According to promise, I proceed with the history
of my first excursion to the northern part of this
State. At the conclusion of my last, you recollect
I had just visited a deposite or surface mine, and
witnessed the process of separating the gold from its
accompanying gravel. By far the greater number
of mines at present wrought in Georgia are of this
description : since the hill or vein mines, though
richer in the precious metal, require more machine-

ry than most gold seekers can command.   In these
latter, the metal exists not interspersed among gravel, but deeply imbedded in rock ; and in order to obtain it, the rock must be broken out and reduced to
powder before the process of washing can be commenced.   I have not yet seen any works in full
operation for the performance of this process.   I visited, however, a few days after the time mentioned
in my last, a lot where extensive and very costly preparations were making for the purpose.   A small hill
had been pierced with holes from above, and in various directions around its base, till it looked like a
colander ; but this part of the work had been abandoned for another attempt.

I entered one of the openings, with a guide who
carried a torch.   On each side of me were deep pits,
full to the top with water.   Quantities of rock, however, had been cut out, from which perhaps, before
this, gold had been procured.   The workmen were
at the time engaged on another and larger opening,
—a shaft, about twelve feet square, and, at the time
I saw it, perhaps forty feet deep.   This was half full
of water, which the " hands" were baling out by the
barrel-full, with the aid of machinery.   I was told
that the owner expected to penetrate about a hundred feet deeper before he touched the wealthy vein,
but that when that had been reached, its profits
would be incalculable.

When I looked into the yawning gulf before me,
where the flow of water suspended the possibility of
further excavation, I did not envy him his pros-

pect. The same morning I visited a rich deposite mine, belonging to the same gentleman. Here I was shown some very beautiful and valuable specimens of virgin gold, by which term the metal is designated when found pure, and in pieces of sufficient size to secure it without the use of quicksilver. A steam machine had been erected here, for effecting more rapidly the process of washing; but it had been found on trial, inferior to the rockers, and it now lay useless and motionless, like the carcase of a slain mammoth.

Another method of obtaining gold has been resorted to by some enterprising men. This is, to search, for the precious metal, the sands of the rivers and smaller streams. In some instances the course of the water has been turned, and its ancient channel laid bare to the eye of industry; elsewhere machines are employed to draw up from the bottom of the river the precious deposite. The Chestatee and Cane Creek especially appear to rival the ancient Pactolus, to which, according to the fable, king Midas, by bathing in its waters, imparted his own power of making gold. I hope Georgia is not destined to exemplify in some other respects the truth of that most ingenious and instructive fiction. May she never, like Midas, find her wealth a curse, and, losing the habits of regular productive industry, starve in the midst of uncounted riches, like the unhappy king who could not touch an article of food without turning it into gold.

The danger, however, which existed, of such a re-

25*

sult, is, I trust, decreasing. The mode adopted by
Georgia, of disposing of the lately acquired territory
by lottery, gave, it is to be feared, too great encouragement to unprincipled speculators; and among
the population who first crowded in upon that region, there were many who would scarcely have
been tolerated any where else. With them, however,
were others of correct principles and unexception-
able conduct; and as the wildness of a new settlement gradually wears away, the Gold Region assumes and maintains more and more the aspect of
an orderly, moral, and religious community. The
first excitement which attended the discovery of the
metallic treasures in our country has worn off; and
it is perceived, that with a few remarkable exceptions
both on the favorable and on the unfavorable side,
gold-mining is like any other form of honest labour;
he who works hard, may expect moderate prosperity;
he who is idle, will fail of success. I may add, however, that to the lover of nature the view is more
agreeable, of a field of waving grain or flowering
cotton, than of turbid streams, muddy ditches, and
exhausted, squalid, and sickly negroes. Whatever
evils, however, attend this branch of industry, will
gradually give way. The deposite mines will, before
many years, be exhausted; and in the vein mines,
which may be regarded as the permanent wealth of
that section, the use of machinery will probably su-
persede the cause which renders mining at present
unhealthy. This cause I consider to be the necessity of working much in water. But the miners

have at present a free circulation of air and a fine
climate. They are not pent up within the walls of a
factory, nor are they exposed to the dangerous va-
pours of a level soil. Thus Providence apportions
among different climes and occupations the advantages and disadvantages of life. I will not tire you
with longer reflections, but promising soon to repeat
my communications, remain affectionately yours,

                                    S. G. B.

TALLULAH FALLS.

My Dear Friend,

Mount that steed which imagination will bridle
and saddle for you in a moment, and clearing at a
bound a few hundred miles of sand and pine-trees,
join me, as I am about to set out from our friend
V——'s log-hut, for a ramble among the hills.
Little need be said of our losing our way. We
cross-questioned every stupid boy and deaf old woman to know whether we were going right or wrong.
Those whom we addressed had generally "hear'n
tell of Terrora Falls;" but here their knowledge ter-
minated, though the remarkable scene of which we
were in search was but a few miles from them, and
constantly visited by travellers from every section
of the State. After going twice as far as we needed, we at length found ourselves near the object of
our journey. My companion informed me, to my
no small gratification, that another mile would bring
us to the house where we could lodge during the
approaching night, and from which to the Falls

would be but a brief ride for the following morning. Our path here led up the ascent of a hill. On gaining the summit, we turned to gaze over the more level country of the South. It was a magnificent spectacle,—magnificent in its unbounded wildness. Below, all around, as far as the eye could reach, were forests, whose shades appeared as unbroken as if they had never been penetrated by man. It was difficult to conceive that a population of active human beings existed among those interminable woods; for from the eminence we had attained, not a cultivated field, not a dwelling, could be discerned. We knew that rivers flowed below, but the thick woods shut them from our view. We knew that villages and plantations were scattered around, but the mighty forest seemed to have engulphed them. The sun, about to set, glanced over an ocean of foliage. This resemblance struck the eye and the mind in an instant. In the distance, the greenness of the woods faded into that uncertain colour which marks the remoter portions in a sea view, till, as in such a view, the last tints blended with those of the sky above. The Currahee mountain rose like a gigantic island amid the waves of oak and pine. Distance had softened down all its irregularities of form, and as I gazed on it, a perfectly symmetrical cone, I could scarce believe it was the broken and forest-clad hill which, a few days before, I had wandered over.

Mr. Taylor's biscuits and his beds were highly acceptable to way-worn travellers; and in the morning we renewed our course to the Falls, or, I should rather say, the Ravine of Tallulah. The name, I believe, signifies in Cherokee, *terrible*. The country people have half translated and half corrupted the name into Terrora, or Terroree, as I find it spelt on a map of Georgia.

Fastening our horses to the trees, we advance a few paces, and stand on the brink of an awful gulph. Deep, deep is the descent—here perpendicular, there broken, with old black and gray rocks every where lying in gigantic masses. Whether it be six hundred feet, or double that distance, to the bottom of this tremendous ravine, I do not remember. It might well be either, for the emotion produced at the time, and the lasting impression of the scene upon the memory. Take care where you tread. A false step precipitates you where those birds of prey, that now are wheeling far *beneath* you, will alone be able to find your quivering remains. Look beyond. Had ever kingly castle a battlement like that which frowns upon you from the distant side? On that height the rocks have piled themselves in the form of a rude hermitage; but no foot of man ever entered that door. The eagle is the only dweller there. A wood grows between—far, far beneath you, but through it you may see a river, here wildly dashing, and there gliding quietly along. You hear the distant sound of a waterfall. Look as far as the eye can reach towards the left. You see it there. In one spot the river leaps forward in a single mighty bound; there again it slides over a smooth rock, then dashes, broken, into an abyss that foams up again to receive it. Haste thither. It is a mile or two further from your present point of sight; but before you go, take a last look at this tremendous ravine. Here! Stand on this projecting rock, the " Devil's Pulpit," and creep on your hands and knees, till you can look over, and again see the river sparkling, the grey rocks, the waving woods, and those eagles wheeling about beneath you. Now away! " The voice of many waters" calls us to the higher part of the stream.

And here keep a sure footing,—for we must descend to the very brink, that we may stand near the torrent in its leap. Hold by that sapling,—now by this. Well! we have gained this rock; but we must go lower yet. In passing here, however, a slide may precipitate you where the waters will be your grave and their eternal music your dirge. They who venture here must put the shoes from off their feet, and trust in the surer tread of unassisted nature. The scene is worth the toil encountered in placing it within our view. We stand side by side with the river in its might. Look behind;—it is there bursting from above. Look before;—it is there breaking, foaming, and at last sinking exhausted, and gliding thence in peace. But the cataract itself is as nothing compared with the savage grandeur of the scenery around. Look along that ravine. There is the spot where you lately stood;—there, still proudly eminent on the other side, that hermitage, whose secrets man has never explored. And now away! but not without—

A HYMN OF PRAISE TO THE GOD OF THE FOREST AND THE FLOOD.

The forest, Lord, is thine;
Thy quickening voice calls forth its buds to light,
Its thousand leaflets shine,
Bathed in thy dews and in thy sunbeams bright.
Thy voice is on the air,
Where breezes murmur through the pathless shades ;
Thy universal care,
These awful deserts, as a spell, pervades.
Father! these rocks are thine,
Of thee the everlasting monument,
Since, at thy glance divine,
Earth trembled, and her solid hills were rent.
Thine is the flashing wave,
Poured forth by thee from its rude mountain urn;
And thine yon secret cave,
Where haply gems of orient lustre burn.
I hear the eagle scream;
And not in vain his cry! Amid the wild
Thou hearest.   Can I deem
Thou wilt not listen to thy human child?
God of the rock and flood!
In this deep solitude I feel Thee nigh.
Almighty, wise and good,
Turn on thy suppliant child a parent's eye!
Guide through *life's* vale of fear
My placid current, from defilement free,
Till, seen no longer here,
It finds the ocean of its rest in thee!

S. G. B.

FALLS OF TOCCOA.

My Dear Friend,

It was a matter of doubt to me, whether, in returning from the mountainous region, it would be worth my

while to deviate from the direct road for the few miles which intervened between it and the falls of Toccoa. The stream, I was told, was so scanty, that the scene was not worthy of comparison with what I had already visited. I concluded, however, to direct my course thither,—carefully preparing myself not to expect too much. I travelled alone, and on horseback, a mode of journeying by no means disagreeable to one who can find company in his own thoughts. Are there clouds in the sky? Their forms supply fancy with materials for her transient but pleasing structures. Is the sun bright and the sky clear? Then, if one's own heart is at ease, sunshine is happiness in itself. I love, too, to ride among woods. I have a cause of sympathy with them, which is not shared by all. Call me fanciful or superstitious if you will, but

> "——— 'tis my faith, that every flower
> Enjoys the air it breathes."

Why should we not admit that the inferior species of life, which exists in the vegetable world, is accompanied by an inferior species of sensation,—of susceptibility to pleasure or pain? To me it is a sufficient argument for such a faith, that it honors the Creator, by increasing the amount of enjoyment in his creation. What to most spectators is yonder tree? A beautiful object indeed, but utterly lifeless in any proper sense of the word life. Its existence adds no more to the amount of enjoyment in the universe, than if it were made of stone. To me, on the contrary, it seems, as the wind waves its branches, to feel in every leaf the same delightful coolness that fans so gratefully my own brow.   Life, enjoyment, darts from spray to spray, and penetrates to the very centre of the aged trunk.   Conceive, then, of a forest of such *beings*.   How different is the belief which represents every leaf and flower through the boundless woods, as instinct with pleasure, from the cheerless imagination that—here is much good timber!   There are many things, too, which to my mind confirm this faith.   The tendency of leaves to turn towards the sun, of roots to penetrate in the direction most favorable for obtaining moisture, of climbing plants to turn with so much seeming ingenuity, first one way, then another, in search of a support, and the phenomena of sensitive plants,—these things confirm the existence, in the vegetable world, of something approaching to animal instinct, and which may therefore be combined with something approaching to animal feeling.

Such thoughts, be they well or ill founded, were in my mind, when a gentle murmur struck my ear, and glancing upward, I saw, above the tops of the trees, the object of my curiosity,—the glassy, transparent stream, rippling and sparkling over the projecting brow of a rock, then falling, without other interruption, in a pellucid curtain.   In an instant I dismounted, and penetrating the wood which intervened, stood amid a scene of Nature's calmest, purest loveliness.   Before me rocks were piled in savage majesty ; but their wildness served but to render

26

more beautiful by contrast the lovely stream which descended so constant, so mighty, yet so gentle. The height of the fall is a hundred and eighty feet, and as the rock bends slightly forward, the stream, except at either edge, is almost unbroken. Here and there, however, shrubs, which have grown in the interstices of the rocks, extended themselves to catch that increasing shower, and broke for an instant the glassy curtain, which would reunite directly below them. A beautiful effect is produced by the scantiness of the stream in comparison with the great height from which it falls. From its own tenuity and the resistance of the air, it is divided before it reaches the basin below, and descends in rain-like drops. The spray that rises to meet it, sometimes assumes the tints of the rainbow, but none was visible when I was there. Here and there, where a bush or a rocky point had checked the current, white foam gleamed in the sun. Before me, at the foot of the rock, was the basin which the waters had scooped out, and from which, toward one side, the stream pursued its way. The woods formed the other side of the amphitheatre. Rocks were scattered in the centre. There was a voice from the waters, powerful enough, as sad experience proves, to render inaudible even the cry of a perishing victim. But so steady, so calm was that voice, and so softened was its influence by that of surrounding objects and associations, that the impression of stillness prevailed amid the unceasing roar of the cataract. I sat on a rocky fragment, and gazed in ecstacy.   After the first moments of admiration that left room for no other thought, a desire arose to retain some memorial of the impressions then received ; and with my pencil, and using the rock for a table, I sketched a few verses, which, with slight alterations, I enclose :

THE FALLS OF TOCCOA.

Hail loveliest, purest scene!
How brightly mingling with the clear, blue sky,
Thy glancing wave arrests the upward eye,
    Through thy grove's leafy screen.

Through thy transparent veil,
And wide around thee, Nature's grandest forms,
Rocks, built for ages to abide the storms,
    Frown on the subject dale.

Fed by the rapid stream,
In every crevice of that savage pile,
The living herbs, as with a quiet smile,
    Repay the gladdening beam.

And over all, that gush
Of rain-drops, sparkling to the noon-day sun !
While ages round thee on their course have run,
    Ceaseless thy waters rush.

I would not that the bow,
With gorgeous hues should light thy virgin stream,
Better thy white and sun-lit foam should gleam
    Thus, like unsullied snow.

Yes ! thou hast seen the woods
Around, for centuries rise, decay, and die,
While thou hast poured thy endless current by
    To join the eternal floods.

The ages pass away,
Successive nations rise, and are forgot,
But on thy brilliant course thou pausest not
    Mid thine unchanging spray.

When I have sunk to rest,
Thus wilt thou pass, in calm sublimity.
Then be thy power to others, as to me
    On the deep soul impressed.

Here does a spirit dwell
Of gratitude, and contemplation high,
Holding deep union with eternity.—
    O loveliest scene, farewell!

Connected with the fall of Toccoa, is a wild and
melancholy tradition. During some hostilities, many
years ago, between the Indians and the whites, a
small party of the latter were in a situation of some
peril in the vicinity of these falls. The Indians
obliged a white woman, who was their prisoner, by
threats of torture and death, to co-operate with them
for the destruction of her countrymen. On pretence
of leading them to a safer position, she induced them
to trust themselves to her guidance, but insisted on
the condition that they should blindfold themselves.
The reason she assigned for this was, that the
path by which she was to lead them was a secret,
which she could not permit them to discover without endangering her own life. She directed them
to follow her footsteps in single files, and thus proceeded with them to the brow of the hill. Here she
turned aside, but the blinded victims, supposing her
to be still before them, passed on, and one after an-

other fell, and perished on the rocks and in the water
below,—the roar of the cataract preventing those
that followed from hearing the cries of those who
had preceded them. But those cries were heard in
the imagination of their wicked betrayer. She lived many years, but never knew happiness again. "I
tell the tale as 'twas told to me." How much of it
is probably true, you can judge as well as I. But
the story, and the scene to which it is ascribed, present a forcible illustration of the contrast between
the changeless purity of God's fair creation, and the
dark crimes which man has committed to desecrate
it ; but, notwithstanding which,

"Nature still is fair."

COWETA FALLS, GEORGIA.

Immediately opposite the beautiful and flourishing
town of Columbus, in the State of Georgia, on its
western side, are the Coweta Falls, extending in full
length across the bold and rapid Chattahouchee.
which at this place is about one quarter of a mile in
width. There is no part of the shoal where the water descends more than ten or twelve feet perpendicular, as discernible to the eye, though the actual fall
of water, as measured from its level above and below
the cataract, is fifteen feet. This happens at various
places, and in detached shoals, forming to the spectator, viewing it from either shore, a wide and irregular heap of billows, apparently chasing each other
down the tremendous ledge of rocks, over which they

dash their snow-crested foam. But when viewed
from below, there seems to be a beautiful and regular fall of water, extending the whole width of the
stream without the slightest variation in height or
appearance, save an occasional bulge formed by the
obstruction of some elevated rock.   Immediately
above the eastern side of the cataract is a fine oval
basin, completely girt round by a fall of water above
and below it, as well as on its western side, while the
shore terminates it on the eastern.   This is used by
the citizens as a place of bathing during the beautiful summer nights of our Southern climate.   There
have been several instances of adventurous, or at
least unfortunate persons being carried so far out
towards the rush of waters which skirts the basin
on the west, as not to be able to regain their balance ;
in consequence of which they have been swept down
the watery precipice, swift as an arrow, and in most
cases never seen or heard of more.   Hence the Indian tradition of the " watery spirit," who, they say,
seduces those unfortunate victims over the cataract,
and bears them away to its own rocky dell, where
they live in an entirely altered state of existence
from our own, never being permitted to return to their
friends on earth again.   Notwithstanding this dreaded demon, however, there have been instances of
Indian canoes passing over in safety, as well as one
of a white man, who, slipping from a place called
" fisherman's rock," while numerous individuals were
standing around, was never expected to be heard of
more, when he arose several hundred feet down the

river, amid the acclamations and congratulations of
his friends, and was safely borne to land by a canoe
which happened to be near him, although completely exhausted and almost lifeless.

To one who has gazed upon and admired the stupendous cataract of Niagara, the Coweta Fall may
not possess much of grandeur; though it certainly
cannot be made to lose its beauty in comparison with
any spot on earth.   I am convinced that a more
picturesque scene could not be invented by the most
fertile fancy than this cascade as viewed from the
white bridge situated about a quarter of a mile below it, and taken in conjunction with the romantic
town on its right.   All that the mind can conceive
of beauty is here depicted in the sight of the setting
sun, on a calm lovely evening in summer.   I once
participated in the enjoyment of such a scene, when
the fine promenade, which ran along the banks of the
river adjacent to the Falls, seemed literally thronged with people of both sexes, enjoying the pleasant
and refreshing breeze from the cascade in the mild
brilliant sunset.   The old grove of oaks, that rose majestically above the heads of the promenaders, seemed to smile propitiously upon the scene, and bright-
en up as the breeze played laughingly among their
full-grown boughs ; while the brushwood underneath
them, forming a more useful and shadowy bower immediately over their heads, reminded me of those
sweet Arcadian groves where the ancient poets delighted to court their muses.   Gradually peering
above the latter, and beautifully interspersed among

the branches of the former, lay the northern precincts
of the town, in which may be seen some as stately
edifices, and built with as good taste, as in many of
our larger cities.   Still further to the right, the widely scattered houses, intermingled as yet with many
of the old forest trees, stretched themselves along,
till the dense wood arrested their progress, and seemed as if bidding defiance to the farther progress of
civilization.   In the back-ground the same line of
tall old oaks and towering pines, forming the same
" vast contiguity of shade," arrests the attention of
the spectator, gradually lowering as the eye turns to
the left, until at length there is a complete indenta-
tion formed where the bed of the river interposes itself in the distant view of the horizon.   Here I
paused for a moment in admiration of the scene, and
then, as if led by the lulling sound which issued so
musically from beneath my gaze, I cast my eyes downward, and beheld the bright sheet of smooth uninterrupted water, as it moved gently but steadily onward, to the daring acclivity, over which it was soon
destined to plunge, and mingle with the foam that
looked like " snowy hillocks on the dappled stream,"
or turn to the spray which rose so beautifully to the
evening clouds, on which the colours of the rainbow
were reflected with prismatic beauty by the brilliant
light of the setting sun.   A few flats and airy skiffs,
with some dusky forms seated in them, were dashing
across the stream below the Fall, and here and there
a fisherman might be seen along the margin of the
river, intently gazing on his line, while a few strag-

gling swallows occasionally dipped their wings in the broad stream before me, and then flitted again gaily above the invigorating element.

I gazed on the scene till the spirit of romance gently descended and enshrouded all my mental faculties. Nor did I awake from my reverie till the nightfall had gradually mingled the picturesque scene which lay before me, in such a confused mass, as to permit me only to behold the grey outline of what had seemed before so passingly beautiful. The shrill whoop of the Indian hunter on the same side of the river which I occupied, and the broad flash of his lighted torch across the stream, soon aroused me to a sense of my situation, and informed me of the lateness of the hour. Accordingly I re-crossed the beautiful bridge which led to the town, wondering in my mind whether the scene I had beheld was real, or only the freak of an over-excited imagination. Mingling with the few lingering amateurs of the retiring crowd, I soon found myself dispossessed of the mantle of romance, and comfortably seated at my hotel, surrounded by a circle of friends, whom the force of circumstances had given me within the limited period of a short month. But the impression of that beautiful scene still lingers in my memory, after an absence of two years, as fresh as though I stood upon the same spot, and witnessed anew that vivid and inimitable picture of romantic scenery.

                                        P.

Scenery on the Chattahouchie, Georgia.

The scenery of the Hudson has been extolled as being the most sublime and picturesque to be found in the wide-extended continent of America, and comparable to the most beautiful specimens even on the banks of the Rhine. But I doubt not, however, that in many of the wilder and less frequented portions of the States, there may be found scenery, which, if but seen as often by persons of taste, and panegyrised by as able pens, would rival the far-famed Hudson. A day's ramble on the river Chattahouchie has confirmed me in the above opinion, and I am convinced, that to one of a poetic fancy, no place is better calculated to call forth those high and ecstatic feelings which none but poets know, than a visit to its wild and uncultivated banks. Not only has Nature, with an unsparing hand, been lavish to this spot, in elevating the towering hill, inserting the craggy rock, and placing the bold and beautiful river to meander beneath them; but here is also to be seen the flowery vale, interspersed with numerous specimens from Flora's hand. Specimens of unparalleled beauty overhang the mossy banks of the river, and skirt the brow of the rugged bluff. While, waving over them in monarch-like majesty, the elegant magnolia, shadowy oak, and loftier and more desolate pine, seem to protect them from the blasts of the hurricane, and promise succour and shelter from the ever-returning frosts of October.

Through such an Eden as this, our little party

had wended their way from the environs of Columbus for the distance of several miles.   We were all
pedestrians, inasmuch as the river is entirely unna-
vigable, from the frequency and elevation of its falls,
which last for more than twenty miles; and the high
bluffs and deep ravines are equally unsurmountable
to horsemen; from which cause, I doubt not, that
many, even of the citizens, more especially ladies,
have been deprived of the pleasure of beholding this
earthly paradise.

Till now, each heart had throbbed with the sweetest emotions, for we had been walking through the
dominions of Flora, where all her woodland delicacies
were scattered in rich profusion.   The beautiful
ivy, mellifluent honey-suckle, and clambering wood-
bine, greeted our vision with their varied colors,
while their odours made us feel and enjoy the sentiment,

"That hill, and dale, and mossy bank, seemed filled
   With the delightsome flowers of spring, which bloom
   With such superior charms of loveliness
   On the wild margin of the forest lakes,
   And scatter perfume on the desert wind."

The Goddess of flowers may be worshipped with
great justness in her artificial temples when she
adorns the gardens of the rich, but I am better pleased to offer up my devotions to nature in her wildest
simplicity, where the workmanship of the hands
seems to be purer and more beautiful.

After admiring this delightful land of birds and
flowers, we continued to wind our way up the river,

crossing such little streamlets as came in our way,
and clambering over hill and craggy rock, until our
course was obstructed by an almost perpendicular
acclivity, which appeared to be several hundred feet
in length. It did not form an entirely impassable
barrier to our further progress up the immediate
bank of the river; but, being directed by our guide,
we began to ascend the hill, which we effected by
pulling up ourselves by the shrubs and undergrowth
which grew on its sides. When we arrived at the
summit, the scene which presented itself to our view,
with the dashing of the rushing waters beneath us,
and the deep ravine which separated us from the
mountain on the opposite side of the river, was only
surpassed by that which we were soon after permitted to behold, and to which we directed our footsteps.

The high knoll of land on which we now found
ourselves, proved to be a kind of promontory, which
projected for some distance into the course of the
river, and caused it to wind around its base in a ser-
pentine manner. We had but a half mile to go to
complete our intended visit to the Lover's Leap,
which was situated at the extremity of this promontory. On our way thither we passed through an
old Indian field, where once the native sons of the
forest had tilled the land in imitation of the more
artful and scientific white man. As we cast our
eyes on this scene of desolation, and then to the Indian forests, from which we were only separated by
a river, and thought that ere long those too must be
given up for other houses and other forests in the

wilds of the West, we could but sympathize with them, and feel that they were a hunted and oppressed race of men. While at the same time we admired the wise dispensations of Providence, which had instituted the noble principles of Christianity where so lately savages and beasts of prey had reigned in universal dominion.

I shall not attempt to describe my own feelings, or the feelings of my companions, on arriving at the rocky tower called the Lover's Leap, inasmuch as I conceive myself entirely inadequate to the task. The simultaneous burst from every bosom was, "grand! beautiful! inimitable!" Let your readers bring to remembrance the effect the painting of Geneva had upon their minds when first the optical illusion came over them, and the lake, and river, and city were all magnified to their natural sizes, and seemed to swim off to their respective distances; and they may, in some degree, imagine our feelings on first beholding one of the most magnificent displays of scenery which Nature or Art had ever presented to our vision.

We stood on the Lover's Leap,—a high and craggy rock, which fretted over the river Chattahouchie, forming the termination of the lofty knoll we had just ascended. It takes its name from the tradition of one of the early frontier settlers, who, despairing of obtaining the affections of one he loved, cast himself from the lofty summit of this craggy height into the dismal depth beneath, where he perished, a victim of suicide. We stood on the same

27

spot, and cast our eyes far beneath us, where the bold and beautiful river, which washes its base, rushed forward down a ledge of rocks, and sent up to our ears the hollow sound of the distant waterfall, which one might imagine proceeded from the gloomy Styx or Acheron, from its deep bellowing sound, the echoes of which seemed to reverberate from rock to rock and from mountain to mountain. A natural dome of firm granite, apparently hewn into the most exact proportions, as if measured by the line and plummet of the artist, extends from the base of the Lover's Leap some hundred feet into the river, around which it is forced to wind its way through a narrow defile, with an almost unparalleled swiftness, forming, at the same time, a beautiful curve in the river, which, from the continued shoals over which it dashes, and the white foam they create, resembled, when viewed from our lofty elevation, a streak of snow lying in a deep forest of trees, with occasional interception of sable spots, apparently thawed by the influences of the burning sun. In front, the noble brow of a lofty hill rose up majestically to the clouds, which by some shock of nature had seemingly been separated for some hundred feet into its bosom, from whence sprang a large fountain of water, dashing with majestic strides down its side, over rocks and every interposing obstacle, until it reached the vale beneath, where, collecting together, the waters ran off in a beautiful and placid brook to the bed of the river. I cannot imagine a more picturesque scene than this cascade, appearing above the very tops of the

trees of the valley, leaping and skipping with playful agility down the craggy precipice. To the left,
the eye views the downward progress of the Chattahouchie, whither its waters move onward to the great
gulf of Mexico. Nor here is the scenery less poetical, or filled with less to entertain the spectator. In
this direction the stream is as straight as it is rapid,
and allows the vision to penetrate through the deep
ravine which follows its course without any obstruction, while the towering bluffs, which arise on either
side with all their forest pride, were seen in majesty
far above. In the dim distance, and through the
spray and fog which rises from the Coweta Falls,
the eye can distinguish the beautiful white bridge
that crosses the river at Columbus, as well as the
fine steamers which rest upon its bosom, and which
serve to bear the produce of the country to the great
waters of the ocean. While to the left some of the
more elevated and imposing buildings of the town
itself add not a little to the beauty of the scene; all
of which tended to impress upon our mind the much
admired sentiment of Campbell,

" Why do those cliffs of shadowy tint appear
  More sweet than all the landscape smiling near ?
  'Tis distance lends enchantment to the view,
  And robes the mountain in its azure hue."

P.

THE SOLDIERS' MOUND,

On the Eastern branch of the Oakmulgee, Georgia.

Among the many vestiges which the aborigines of our country have left behind them, to preserve the remembrance that such beings once existed, none seems more properly adapted to the purpose than the numerous tumuli, or mounds of earth which rise up in almost every forest, and say in a language not to be misunderstood, " here lie the fathers of a once powerful, but now almost extinguished race of men." These tumuli, however, do not seem to be dedicated to the relics of departed spirits, nor do they all contain the bones of human beings. On the contrary, many of the largest seem to have been erected for a different purpose, if not by a different race of men. The smaller ones, however, appear to have been used as cemetries for the dead, and contain not only the bones of human skeletons, but also numerous specimens of Indian idolatry, as beautiful ruby coloured stones, and such like trifling gewgaws, with which their more degenerate sons seem so excessively delighted at the present day. The larger mounds are much fewer in number, at great distances apart, and seem better calculated for the purposes of war than the less pompous and more solemn obsequies of burial. Of this class we have a fine specimen about one mile and a half south-east of the city of Macon, Georgia, on the eastern branch of the Oakmulgee river, significantly called the " Soldiers' Mound."

Like most curiosities, it has been suffered to lie almost unnoticed by persons living in its immediate vicinity, though it affords matter of considerable interest to almost every traveller. Under this prevailing feeling of apathy, it is enclosed in such a manner by fencing as to prevent any person on horseback approaching very near it. Consequently our visiting party were under the necessity of turning pedestrians before they could experience the pleasure of beholding it. After crossing the elegant bridge which leads from the main town to East Macon, we entered a blind and thickly overshadowed pathway, which led us immediately down the banks of the deep, still Oakmulgee; and after crossing various ditches and fences, and brushing the dew from numerous leaves and spires of grass, we found ourselves emerging from the depth of the dark wood in an oblique direction from the banks of the deep river into an open field, at the end of which the tumulus rears its ancient brow,—a truly isolated spectacle when contrasted with the appearance of the flat alluvial country which surrounds it. At the first view of the mound I could not conceive for what purpose so enormous a mass of earth could ever have been gathered together: yet that it was done by human power, the proofs appeared too evident and convincing to admit of a well-grounded doubt. Its studied situation and exact proportions are not the least among these proofs, though it must have been the work of years, and reared many years ago. In fact, while standing upon its lofty summit, and view-

27*

ing the surrounding country, one is almost ready to imagine it another Babel, the design of whose elevation was no less than to pierce the very skies. On the ground, however, of some faint historical reminiscences and slight circumstantial evidences, men of extensive knowledge and good judgment have been led to conjecture the probability of there once existing in this Southern clime a half-civilized race of men, whose greater ingenuity had prompted them to further advances in the arts and sciences than the neighbouring tribes of Indians. In fact, we have some striking evidences of such a state of things in the erection of the "Temple of the Sun" in Mexico. That such a race existed, we have but little doubt : that they are now extinct, and have been so for years, appears to be equally evident. The ultimate conclusion appears then to be, that they were destroyed by some hostile, designing foes. Probably the envious spirit of the barbarians of the north prompted them to bear down upon them like a rushing torrent from the mountains in the cessation of winter and the melting of the snow, verifying, in our western and less antiquated world, a similar state of things to that which once transpired in the east. Hence the erection of the larger tumulus of earth for the purpose of protecting and defending the builders from the invasions of their enemies, and of the smaller ones, for the purpose of interring their fallen soldiery with the honors of war. The Soldiers' Mound, as I before stated, must have been reared ages ago, inasmuch as there are to be seen growing on its sides and its summit, very large towering oaks, several feet in diameter, which look as if they had stood the shock of earthquakes, as well as the tempest's rage, for days innumerous as the leaves that flutter on their boughs. The mound itself is several hundred feet in diameter at its base, and more than a hundred feet in elevation, being nearly as many across the flat surface of its summit. It is built in a perfectly pyramidal form, being gradually tapered upward from its base in exact proportions throughout its circumference. Some individual of a lofty imagination once planted a garden on its summit, which, however, has recently gone into utter decay. From this height, the view of the surrounding country is pleasing and sublime. To the south, a large forest of pine, intermingled with occasional patches of oak and hickory, is to be seen, through whose dense body the sluggish Oakmulgee winds its way with slow, but steady pace. On the north, old Fort Hill rises majestically upwards in gradual ascension from the bed of the river, and maintains an elevated station among the hillocks which surround it, overlooking the village of East Macon, which lies at its foot, and bearing on its sloping sides the scattered and newly formed village of Troy. On its summit, Fort Hawkins rears her ancient watch towers, some distance above her more impregnable walls of defence. It, however, at present exhibits quite a dilapidated condition, much of its wooden structure having gone to decay, and many of the bricks being thrown down. The beautiful grove of native forest growth, so elegantly pruned by the soldiers more than twenty years ago, which covers its brow, is too exquisitely romantic to escape the glance of the most careless traveller who passes it in the stage.   Farther to the left, the infant city of Macon* rears its spires and elegantly built houses high in air; while the lofty hills which surround it on the west, with their fine and numerous edifices, add much to the sublimity of the scene.   A little to the right of these, the beautiful village of Pineville may be partially seen through the academic grove, which contains a noble edifice sacred to the cause of education and science.

As all absorbing as the surrounding scenery might have been to us, there was an object in our immediate vicinity which attracted much of our attention. This was a small mound of earth, with a rough stone at its head, bearing the inscription of some almost illegible letters upon its face concerning the interment of two soldiers,† who were also brothers. Their name has entirely escaped my memory, though it was rudely carved upon the stone which marked their resting place.   Their history is short, as told me by a young lady of M——.   During the late war with Great Britain and the Indians, a soldier belonging to the American camp, at that time stationed at Fort Hawkins, which lies about one mile north of the mound, was seen to retire to this spot

---

* Macon has been incorporated as a city by the Legislature of Georgia. It was founded in 1823, and at present contains about five thousand inhabitants.

† Hence the title of the mound.

in the shades of the evening, and kneel in lonely, silent devotion. His piety soon became proverbial, and his brother, who first discovered him, was much affected by it, and afterwards joined him in his vesper oblations to heaven. Ere the removal of the army from this station, it was the unfortunate lot of the two brothers to fall victims to some epidemical disease, as they were both foreigners. In just remembrance of their virtues, their fellow-soldiers buried them at the very spot where they had offered their daily devotions.

P.

EXTRACTS FROM A PRIVATE JOURNAL

KEPT ON A TOUR

FROM CHARLESTON TO NEW-YORK;

BY FOUR FRIENDS.

[The following Journal is valuable as furnishing an account of one of the land routes from Charleston to New-York. It is written with the familiarity of private correspondence, and was a *jeu d'esprit* of four travellers, who threw out their thoughts on the same sheets as inclination prompted. This circumstance will account for any apparent difference in the style of various parts.

There are exhibited on these sheets many points of useful information for general readers, and to a large private circle these sketches will afford a deep though mournful interest, since one of the brightest and purest spirits which animated that group has gone to her final rest,—has accomplished her brief but lovely pilgrimage of life.

The following lines, written a year or two before her death, will show her preparation for intercourse with immortals :]

DIALOGUE BETWEEN THE BODY AND SPIRIT.

Body.—Spirit! I feel that thou
    Wilt soon depart.
    This body is too weak longer to hold
    The *immortal* part.
    The ties of earth are loosening—
      They will break ;
    And thou—even as a joyous bird,
      Thy flight will take
        To the eternal world.
    Say, spirit! say !
    Wilt thou return again? once more illume
      My house of clay ?

28

Or must this body, which has been to thee
A temple and a dwelling-place,
Perish forever—and forgotten be?

Spirit.—Yes! I must leave thee.
I am longing
For the communion of those blessed ones
Within the courts of heaven,
Who tune their golden harps
To the eternal praise of Him, who gives
   That home above—
Which *they* have gained, and which I would attain,
Through Him who came to prove
   That *God is Love:*
And by Him too, I know that *thou,*
   My earthly tenement,
Within the dust must lie,
And there, turn to corruption,
Even as the seed doth die,
   To be revived again.
Death hath no power o'er the *soul,*
For Christ hath conquered—
The grave cannot retain its victims
When *He* cries—come forth!
   Then I return to *thee*—
The victory is gained—
For " *Christ hath made us free.*"

EXTRACTS FROM A JOURNAL.

The Private Conveyance.

How shall we get from Charleston to Columbia? This was a question that was seriously discussed by our little party, just setting out on a journey. We had planned the after-part of our tour, deciding that we would waltz our way northward, avoiding a straight line as far as was consistent with some sort of tendency to a fixed point. But how were we to go from Charleston to Columbia? There was a river and a steam-boat, but the water was low, and the boat was sometimes detained for several days among the swamps and rice-grounds, where we should be sure to take the country-fever. There was a rail-road, not exactly to Columbia, but to another place that would answer our purpose as well, and we might be whirled there in the space of marvellously few hours. But some of us loved our lives too well to risk them on a structure so frail, that it seemed a mere " tempting of Providence."*

* If our tourists *had* chosen the quiet, easy whirl of the rail car, we should have been deprived of the lively narrative of their broken wheel and foundered horses.

At last it was all arranged, and one clear and
cloudless Monday morning we set out with fair pro-
spects.   We were four—two ladies, two gentlemen
—all equable, amiable, just the sort of people nature
formed for travellers.   We just filled a commodious
carriage, and our effects perfectly and harmoniously
fitted into the external space.   Two horses, strong
and steady, were our moving principle; and to *per-
petualize* the motion, two others had preceded them
the day before, and waited for us at a suitable distance.   Our driver was trusty Joe, a discreet and
respectable old negro.   As he figures in our story, it
may be well to individualize him to inquirers into our
adventures.   He was short and thick, with a curve
of the lower limbs that would have been ludicrous, if
the effect had not been counteracted by an awfully
sedate expression of countenance.   His face was a
labyrinth of wrinkles, in which, not age, but a sense
of responsibility, had bewildered and lost itself; and
yet it seemed alert, as if it was looking for the way
out.   Honest Joe! how we enjoyed the look of
careful satisfaction with which he took his seat after all was rightly disposed; it augured well for the
journey, that we resigned ourselves to pleasant cer-
tainty that all would go right.   It was not dusty, it
was not uncomfortably warm, it was early; we
should be forty miles before sunset, far among the
hills, and elevated above all swamps, bogs, and dread
of low-land fevers.   The early sunbeams lay in lines
of ruddy splendour on our path, as we parted from
our last friend, who had accompanied us ten miles on

our road. We rode on ; tall trees cast their shadows over us, and the long grey moss swung in the plea-sant breeze. Hour after hour we passed over miles after miles—slowly, for we rode over a sand-bed, but ·surely, oh full surely.

Ah! Ah! what was that? Was it? Why yes, it was a little slipping of the tire of the wheel, and we had no hammer and nails to fix it all right, but a wedge would do ; it would hold till we could reach a house. We rode on, but with a new feeling—a slight sense of care. There was another crack, and we concluded to walk to the house which was in sight. The road was bordered by Swamp magnolia and Honey-Suckles, but a deep ditch of stagnant water lay between, and none of our little party seemed in spirits to leap the ditch, and gather them. We reached the house, and there it was decided that our case required a smith ; but as none was to be had just there, we must move on carefully till we found one.

As our gentlemen and Joe were operating upon the wheel to the best of their abilities, M. and J. en-tered into conversation with the landlady. She was a long, lank, sallow body, the image of despair. She said the country about was dreadfully sickly ; she had lost one husband, all her children, and did not think she could live long herself. This was cheering, supposing the wheel could not be mended. At last we were called out to take our seats. The wheel was bandaged with a leather-strap round and round. Joe shut the door after us, looking at the wheel as he did so. The wrinkles were deep, and his whole face contracted; but he mounted the box and drove on, only very slowly. Round and round it went, like the other wheels. We began to feel better, it would do till we could reach the blacksmith's, and then we should be another hour or two later in reaching our lodging-place, but that would be all. It was twelve o'clock, the sun powerful, the sand deep, the shade that had bordered the roadside gone, —a crack! stop! stop! Joe! and stop he did; but not a moment too soon, for the spokes had parted, and in another moment we should all have been upset. Here was perplexity! After a little consultation the horses were taken out, one was tied to the carriage behind, and Joe was mounted on the other, and sent for assistance. We propped up the carriage, and resigned ourselves to sit in it, and wait for deliverance. An hour passed on! The heat was overpowering! We said little, but every eye was strained in the direction from which we hoped for aid. At last a cloud of dust was seen. A figure, which we knew for Joe, first emerged, and something seemed to be following him. We gazed earnestly, until it took the shape of a wagon, and came rattling and lumbering towards us. It was a farcical conveyance!—A rough, loosely-put-together road wagon, long, and covered at the sides to meet a very high back and front, with half a dozen chairs dancing about in its immensity of space. The harness was indescribable, being composed partly of rattling chains, and partly of knotted ropes. And then the steeds!— One was a tall wreck of a bay horse, on which a ragged, dirty negro was mounted ; and one was a small, active mule, tied on to help as much as he could. The negro held him by a bridle, and he came jumping on to keep up with the tall horse's strides. It halted ; three trunks, four carpet bags, two ladies, were transferred into its expanse ; and the two gentlemen seated themselves with open umbrellas, and gave the signal for motion. We cast a look behind ; a supernumerary chair, and the broken wheel, hung swinging at the back of our vehicle. There stood our carriage, resting in quiet magnificence on a crutch ; while three negroes rode abreast of us, raising a cloud of dust behind them. These were Joe, and two assistants, riding on the carriage horses, and one of our relays. After two or three miles, we drew up at a house of entertainment. The wheel was despatched to a blacksmith's a mile further, and we alighted. We found ourselves in the very palace of intemperance and unthrift,—an idle landlord—a silly, lazy landlady—stupid servants. But then it was not of much consequence, as it was only for an hour or two ; when the wheel was mended we should push on rapidly with our fresh horses, that were here waiting for us. We had some dinner. We grew impatient, for Dr. —— had charged us, as we valued our lives, to go forty miles from Charleston that night ; and here we were, many miles short. The sun went down! the twilight deepened into night, and still the wheel came not !

Mr. A—— went to investigate, and we had then a cause of anxiety in his exposure to the noxious night air. A servant came to light a fire on the hearth, a precaution that plainly contradicted the assurance that every body considered the place perfectly healthy. The frogs sent up loud and shrill croaks all about us, a sure proof that we were surrounded by swamps. The windows were broken, the dim flame of the candle flickered, and we fancied we felt the malaria and breathed infection. Oh what an hour ! Some fine black-berries were on the table ; we tried to taste them, we tried to look cheerful, and to talk. At last Mr. A—— came in. The wheel was mended, but we must resign ourselves to our fate for the night, and if all were well in the morning, we would proceed ; that some one would be ill, we expected, for we had decided that it would be almost a miracle if all should escape. Let no one ridicule our fears ; there was ground for apprehension. We had been told to flee as if the pestilence were behind us. No wonder that we lay down to sleep with heavy hearts. B—— said he would sit up all night, having heard that the only danger was in sleeping. M—— and I suffocated ourselves with a roaring fire to purify our portion of the atmosphere. Morning came, and we looked on ourselves and each other, to be sure that all was as well as it seemed. We waited awhile for the fogs to disperse, and set off. George, a more comely but equally sedate negro, was our driver now ; and Joe followed us a few miles with the extra horses. At the breakfast house we exchanged the animals, and bade honest Joe farewell. It would have done any heart good to see how the wrinkles had been

slackened since the accident.   His eyes actually
glistened with animation as he looked his last on us,
and felt the responsibility of our safe conveyance
lifted off *his* shoulders.   Though the weather was
warm, and our ride about twice the length we originally intended, that day passed pleasantly, the wheel
seemed strong.   Night came on, and brought us to
a certain Mr. ——'s, a great barn of a house, the mistress absent, and he idle and moody in his " solitude."
He was a youth, and perhaps longed for some better
companion than his absent mother.   Let silence and
oblivion cast a veil over the wretchedness of our entertainment; the sour bread, the sour milk, the broken
tea-cups, the leaden spoons.   Let forgetfulness take
into her keeping the long dark chambers to which
we were consigned for the night!   Let the reports
of country fever, and all manner of diseases, even to
the measles, that excited anew our scarcely laid apprehensions, never be recalled.

What cheering intelligence greeted us next morning, as we appeared with our bonnets on, all ready
to ride!   One of our horses was foundered; he had
met with his misfortune some years before, but had
been considered good enough for our purpose, and
his exertions of the day before had brought on a
second attack.   What was to be done?   Our host
at length consented to lend us a horse for the next
ten miles, and we started.   On we went, stopping at
every house to try for a horse, admonished thereto
by the little boy sitting beside George on the box,
ready to take the other back as soon as his place

should be supplied.   We found only women and children in every house; the men were in the fields. This betokened industry, and we should have commended it at any other time; but now we wanted to hire a horse, and no woman could venture to accommodate us.   We stopped at the end of the ten miles, mounted our retainer, despatched him home and considered.———— The stage would leave Columbia the next morning, and not again for several days.   On we must go.   We stated our case to "mine host," he stated it to his neighbors, and at last, after prolonged preliminaries, and solemn injunctions to take care of him, a horse was procured.   On we went till noon, more at ease, and remarking the beauty of the country, and the improved appearance of cultivation.   Cotton fields and corn fields, hills and running streams, spoke of health and comfort.   About noon we apprehended a thunder shower, and moreover held a consultation over the wheel, which showed incipient symptoms of a relapse.   But we went on, kept in advance of the rain, and at last lost all trace of it.   As the sun began to decline, and the miles to grow fewer, our spirits rose.   The Oak, Hickory, Chesnut, and Chinkapen trees never looked so fresh and lovely,—the fields of grain were never so vividly green as in the level rays of that sunset; and when from a high hill we caught a distant view of Columbia, we drew a long breath of perfect satisfaction. We rolled slowly over the covered bridge that crosses the Congaree at this place, turning our heads every moment to enjoy from the windows on both sides the picture of a rapid foaming river, wooded islands, and green banks, feeling as light of heart as if we had never known care.   We were soon set down at Clark's, and George and the carriage left us to return no more.

The Stage Coach.

How glad we were, when on the 20th of May we seated ourselves in the leathern convenience which was to convey us on the rest of our journey.——— The feeling of responsibility belonging to the care of the private conveyance was at an end ; horses, driver, and carriage were no longer our concern ; and with a feeling of satisfaction we took our places, gave a parting glance at Columbia, that we might say we had seen it, and at five o'clock in the morning drove off at a rapid rate, greatly enjoying the elastic motion given by four brisk horses.   We found a new companion, a foreigner, very polite and agreeable, who reported himself from Amsterdam, travelling for pleasure ; evidently taking, with great good nature, things as they came, careless of trouble where information or amusement was to be gained, and well acquainted with various countries of Europe which he had visited.

We had much pleasant conversation, during which we found he had travelled much in our country, and knew it well.   Dined at a log-house, the external appearance of which promised little, but the two rooms which composed the dwelling were neat and clean.   Books, papers, hunting implements, and a fine, fat, rosy baby, laughing good-humouredly in its cradle, told us, as plainly as such things could, that the master and mistress had enjoyments beyond the daily drudgery of life. They were a good-looking couple, and gave us a plain but decent dinner, much better got up than usual; which we all attributed to the personal exertions of the hostess, who did not leave us to the care of servants, but attended to the management of the establishment herself. Had a pleasant drive that day—"pottered" a good deal, and read Fanny Kemble—reached Newberry about 5 P. M.

*　　*　　*　　*　　*　　*　　*

The Blue Ridge.

Enlivened by the clear and full-toned notes of the stage-horn, and assured that our driver was a first-rate whip, we left Greenville in full spirits, anticipating a day of much interest and amusement. The glories of the Blue Ridge had been vividly depicted to us, and in faith that all would be right, we commenced the first of June. There were various reasons, too, for satisfaction; we were alone in the stage, and whether or not the feeling be selfish, yet true it is that we cared not for any addition to our numbers. We had a self-satisfied feeling, which, as the poet hath it,

> " Cared not for the world without,
> Knowing it had its world within."

Moreover, our effects, baskets, books, port-folios,

&c., were all snugly deposited. Their fair proportions were not diminished in any way, and if they
could have spoken, they would doubtless have expressed their comfort, and protested against any innova-
tion. Merrily went we on, the lamps attached to the
carriage cast a flickering light on the passing objects; and once, when we stopped to water the horses,
threw their glare on the face of our driver, displaying a good-natured rosy rotundity of *Phiz*, which
told more of the roguish boy than the age and so-
briety desirable in one holding so responsible a station. But our landlord said he was a " first-rate
whip,"—so we went on in faith.

Day dawned, and the long line of mountains
stretched on our right its dark outline, coldly contrasted with the fair blue sky, from which, serene
and bright in its silver beauty, shone out the morning star. Nature was scarce awakened into consciousness, the giant of the course had not yet put
on his robes of glory, and this fair herald of the
morn sat quietly watching for his appearance, before whose more effulgent beams she retired in maid-
en modesty.—

———————" And see,
On wings of glory, up the east he shines,"

giving, as it were, a renewed energy to our Jehu's
whip; for rapidly and more rapid went our steeds,
while we rode up to the humble door of the widow
F****'s. Here we were to breakfast; and the externals, though plain, promised fairly. There was an air
29

of neatness about the premises, and on a chair at the door lay a large old Bible, which looked as if it had not been opened for the first time that morning. The widow was a trig old lady, who gave us a good breakfast; she had lived there, she told us, thirty-nine years, had lost her companion many years since, but she had much to be thankful for in her solitude.

But ladies, said she, how do you like your driver?

Oh exceedingly, we answered; he is a first-rate whip.

Well, exclaimed she, I'm glad on't; it's only the second time he ever drove.

There was a discovery! we gazed upon the widow, and upon each other, and internally congratulated ourselves upon our safety, and rejoiced in the possession of an all-confiding faith.

Another driver and fresh horses waited the conclusion of our meal, which was rapidly discussed, and, much strengthened by the creature-comforts we had appropriated, we took our seats; and having exchanged adieus with our good-humored and reckless boy driver, went on our way on a very rough road, over the very stony parts of which our driver would "*tote*" us to the sound of his whip. Merritsville was down on the map; of course it must be a place of more or less consequence, and we looked out for Merritsville. Eighteen miles were gone over, and *a house* by the way-side proved *the place* so noticed on the map and so desired by us.

We began to ascend the Saluda Mountain; the road was very rough and winding, and our horses gave evident symptoms of weariness. The thick woods on either side were dressed in their light and dark shades of green interspersed with the wild yellow honey-suckle, displaying its rich blossoms in every direction, and discovering here and there many a humble flower half hidden by the grass, or peeping out as if in wonder at the sounds which distracted its tranquillity. The giant of the heavens was putting forth his strength, and we were drooping beneath his power, when lo! water in the wilderness, clear and sparkling, cold and pure from its granite basin, gave life to our failing energies, and told that some philanthropic spirit had, in kindness to the way-faring, furnished this blessed beverage to recruit the fainting traveller.

The water of this spring is brought through pipes a short distance down the hill, and spouting through a stop in its granite slab, falls into a basin of the same material. On the slab is the simple and modest inscription, " J. R. P. 1823." For this conveyance and luxury, travellers are indebted to Joel R. Poinsett, Esq. of Charleston, who, being a commissioner for making the road, erected this fountain at his private expense. Much refreshed, we continued our drive, the road becoming every moment more rough and difficult of ascent. The scenery was as wild and beautiful as imagination could picture ; hill and valley lay before us ; the sparkling waters of the Saluda river, which takes its rise in this mountain, were rushing past like a silver stream, now wider, now narrower, and dashing in foam over the rocks which intercepted its passage. Above, the heavy clouds were slowly and awfully gathering in their strength, and nature around lay in that stillness which awaits some dreadful event. There was a corresponding silence within the coach, except when it gave a heavy lurch to one side, warning us to hold up on the other. This revolution was not unfrequent, and we were being well drilled into the exercise, when a sudden plunge towards the horses, set them off, and down the mountain they tore. Forgetful of their weariness, careless alike of their own, or the necks of those who came after them, they pitched us about without mercy; and with a precipice on one side of the narrow road, our visions were not of the most elevated nature, but, like other visions, they passed rapidly, and we were soon after brought up at Flat Rock, where we had a good dinner and a pretty woman in our hostess. This is a pleasant, retired, cool looking place; and in its immediate neighbourhood are several handsome houses, the retreat of Charlestonians, who come here in the summer to rusticate.

Among others, we passed the residence of Mr. Baring; saw the house in the distance, extensive grounds handsomely laid out, and on an eminence near the road a pretty church of the Episcopal order, erected by Mrs. Baring. We stopped to water the horses, all feeling weary, and little able to encounter the storm which was encompassing us; and sure enough it came an "even down power" of rain, accompanied with thunder and lightning, and such hail stones!

Night approached ; our best light was from the flashes lent by the heavens, and yet we had to plod on.
Thus we went for several miles, when the rain (from
which the cloaks and coats in which we were enshrouded, scarcely protected us) abated, and, after
dragging on some distance further, we arrived at
Ashville.

French Broad River.—Paint Rock.

We had heard of the French Broad River, a tributary of the Tennessee, as singularly romantic in
its passage among the Alleghany Mountains ; and the
ride along its banks had been represented to us very
fatiguing and somewhat dangerous ; so that, when
summoned to take our places in the stage-coach, we
felt an unusual degree of excitement. It was two in
the morning, very dark, and the coach crowded.

As day approached, I perceived that beyond the
row of trees and shrubs that bordered my side of the
road, there seemed a deep precipice, and the murmur
that had for an hour risen from behind this thick hedge,
began to deepen into the dash and roar of waters.
On turning an angle of the road, we had our first view
of the river, and for an hour I saw nothing but the
river, for I felt that I could never be satisfied with
watching its endless variety of motion. The whole
course of the French Broad is over a bed of rocks,
and there is a body of water sufficient to give grandeur to the rapidity of its descent. During the thir-
ty-six miles we followed it, the fall is 1300 feet, and
its whole surface is a sheet of foam, from its impe-

29*

tuosity, and the obstacles it meets. Masses of white and pale gray rock, in every variety of form, stand up in the channel, and brave the angry dashing of the waters they oppose. Here, after one leap of ten or twelve feet, the river keeps a comparatively tranquil course, over hidden rocks, till a group of green islands parts it into as many channels, and then suddenly re-uniting the whole combined force, it is bent upon a ledge of rocks that extends half way from shore to shore. Here an elevation from one side turns the current into a curve, and the next moment we have a dashing wave breaking beside us. I fixed my eyes on a little flake of foam that was pursuing its course alone. I followed it as it was borne along by the winding current. I saw it safely carried down the rapids, around high rocks, till it danced round and round the verge of a whirlpool, and left it there at play with a withered leaf and a broken twig. Was it not like the beings who forget the urgent errand of their immortality among the trifles of time? I saw a fallen tree, that maintained its place by a hold on the bank, and amid this rush and confusion lay tranquilly intent on collecting what it might ; straws, leaves, and even drifted blossoms had fallen into its toils, and it would not let them go. Are there not beings, who, like the tree, are intent only on accumulating, and indifferent to the chances and changes of time, except as they add to their stores? I saw one long, low, and fairy island, so covered with laurel flowers, mingled with green graceful foliage, that I could have fancied one huge bouquet bound up and cast here to float along the tide. But my fancies and moralizings were interrupted by exclamations from my companions, and my own awakened sense, that in seeing all this beauty we were encountering some peril. The road we were passing over was entirely artificial—a wall of broken rocks lightly covered with earth, so very narrow that our wheels almost dipped in the water, and often carried so high from the river, that a deviation of a foot from the path would have been destruction. M——, and all on her side of the coach, were exclaiming about the immense rocks that overhung the other side of the road, and my glimpses of them through the window realized something of their fearful grandeur; but after I was fully awake to the danger of the path, I could not keep my eyes from the brink. Our stranger ladies were groaning and expressing their fears, and one gentleman was holding forth on all that might happen. I questioned him about the road, and learned, that until the last eight years, there had been no outlet for the produce of East Tennessee, or inlet for the good things from abroad, to the unhappy people imprisoned there; that a passage over the mountain was sometimes attempted, but it was death to men and horses. Under this state of things, a company was incorporated to construct a road over a certain mountain, and along the French Broad River, and succeeded, after several years' labour and immense expenditure. Most of the foundation of the river-road had been forced from the cliffs above by blasting, and that in places where the task seem-

ed hopeless.   He said it was already a very profit-
able undertaking, for the number of wagons passing
over this turnpike every year was immense, and that
without this road he would not give one cent for East
Tennessee.   He seemed a very sensible sort of man,
but he ought not to have enlarged so on our danger,
and pointed out every rock that stood loosely over
our heads, and might fall very easily.   We all tried
to forget our fears, and there was enough of interest
to help us.   The water's edge was bordered with
young willows, oaks, and tall trees of laurel in full
bloom.   The Rhododendron was not yet in flower,
but it stood in heavy masses of green-pointed leaves.
I had no idea of such quantities, or of the height to
which it grew.   Many of the trees were fifteen or
twenty feet in length.

The wet leaves often dashed in our faces, but we
rather welcomed them, for we felt that the trees
would be a slight barrier to our fall in case we should
be jolted off the edge.   The extreme loneliness of the
road struck me as singular.   Now and then an over-
grown toad hobbled off at the rattling of our wheels,
and once we saw a solitary fisherman, seated on a
log, so intent on his occupation that he did not raise
his head to look at us.   It did not surprise me to
find no inhabitants where there was not a level spot
for a house, but I was expecting and dreading an encounter with other travellers.   I do not know what
can be done in that case, for the road is too narrow
to admit of vehicles passing, or even turning about.
At last we came to the breakfast house, which stood

in a niche apparently forced out of the rock. And here, owing to an important change in my situation to the opposite window of the coach, an entire revolution in my train of ideas commenced. The scene of danger from below was no longer forced upon me, and if I might have apprehended a greater danger from above, the fear was lost in the grandeur of the objects I beheld—rocks, massive ancient rocks, in every variety of form, and hue, and position. Here they towered hundreds of feet above our heads, with their grey severity unrelieved by even a twig or a leaf. Here was a vast rock, worn smooth, and rounded by its descent from some high point above, resting now on some slight obstruction, ready to move on without a moment's warning. Here was a mass of rock, worn into little fragments by the action of the elements, still retaining its show of solidity, but falling in a shower of pebbles at every touch. The arrangement of the strata of rocks varied at every step. Here stood a range, which was almost as regularly perpendicular as columns, or as the volumes on the shelves of a library. Here they lay, like the books that have fallen when two or three have been removed; and here again they were piled one above another, like the same books reposing on a table. Under some of the largest rocks, and where they seemed to need the strongest support, yawned cavities large enough to have received stage and horses. Often the eye was refreshed by the rich green of the shrubbery, covering all the ruggedness of the cliffs, and waving from the top. Bright wild flowers peeped from the rugged crevices, and laughed at their security from all our attempts. One little crimson flower attracted our particular admiration, and for want of a better name we called it the scarlet lichen. There were many beautiful little streams that came leaping from the rocks above, and dashed over the narrow road into the river. In one spot we traced the little stream from its first trickling descent, down five or six successive falls, till it was received in a natural basin, and afforded a delicious draught for us and the horses. I must not forget one or two attempts to take agricultural advantage of a little softening down of ruggedness of the mountain side. The scattered grain stood up among young oaks and cedars, as if it was frightened at its own temerity. At last, after being successively delighted and alarmed for many hours, we crossed the roaring river on a frail bridge, to look for a few moments at the warm spring, which is remarkable for nothing but its temperature. We recrossed the river, and took the narrow path once more; but, instead of being simply as dangerous as it was before, it now began to ascend the cliff only wide enough for the wheels, so that a foot of deviation would have carried us over the brink. The road rose gradually till the cliff above diminished into nothing compared with the precipice below, and our hearts seemed for a few moments to stop beating. We were moving along the verge of a precipice of more than 300 feet. The river was roaring and foaming at its foot. To add to the terrors of the place, the road had been much washed, and shelved fearfully. In one spot the outer wheel entered a deep rut : the whole body of the coach hung over the precipice, the inner wheels were raised from the ground ; one inch more of elevation, and we were gone. But the dangerous pass was soon accomplished, and we rode on in comparative tranquillity. We went on following the river till nearly sunset, when we came under the walls of the celebrated Paint Rock. We had heard of the singular appearance of this rock, from several marks of a deep orange colour, so artificial as to seem the work of man, and yet in such places as seemed inacccessible. But we were not prepared for the imposing effect of the vast pile under which we found ourselves. For nearly a quarter of a mile it rose above us a perpendicular wall of 250 feet in height. The solid unbroken surface was yet so checkered by apparent fissures, that it seemed hewn and heaped up by human labor ; and it needed but little effort of the imagination to see in it a frowning Gothic castle, with battlements and arched door-way. In one spot, under a projection of the rock, the wagoners had fitted a temporary shelter ; and the smoke of their frequent fires had blackened over the whole line of upward surface. We turned the corner of this vast monument, and bade farewell to the river, and moved and breathed in Tennessee.

The Red Sulphur, the Salt Sulphur, and the White Sulphur Springs.

About 6 o'clock in the evening we had the satisfaction of seeing below us the white cottages and green lawns which fill up the little sequestered valley of the Red Sulphur Springs. In a quarter of an hour we were dashing round the circle before the hotel, and in a few minutes more took possession of quarters in " Philadelphia Row."

What deepest green valley the wide earth knows,
Once offered four wearied wanderers repose,
Where o'er a cool fount a white temple rose?
      'Twas the Red Sulphur Springs.

Fair white buildings are ranged round the green,
Clean gravel walks run these buildings between,
Groups of gay people around are seen,
      Oh! the Red Sulphur Springs.

Buxom blithe health flies to sip at the fount,
Sickness so feebly comes down from the mount,
The grave and the gay, quite too many to count,
      Meet to drink at the Springs.

Here are belles from the city, with beaux in their train,
Here are dowager dames, here are pretty and plain,
Health, pleasure, or fortune, each one tries to gain,
      So they come to the Springs.

Whatever the motive of feeling, which brings
To this spot all these bipeds, you'd think they had wings,
For they fly the moment the dinner bell rings,
      Fast away from the Springs.

And dressed in their gayest, as quick as they're able,
They seek for their names or their plates at the table,
And make such a racket you'd think 'twas a Babel
    Rose anew at the Springs.

Do but see that thin lady, what mouthfuls she takes;—
And waiter! stop, waiter, some more batter-cakes,
Some cream, and the butter, those venison steaks
    I must eat at the Springs.

Who would think of their ailments when luxury lies
So temptingly near us, just under our eyes?
Oh waiter, those batter-cakes;—how the man flies,
    They're all mad at the Springs.

But avaunt, creature comforts! we'll turn now from you,
To the joys of the mind, which in visits we knew,
And which over our mornings and afternoons threw
    A delight at the Springs.

Then we sat in our room ; we worked, talked, and read,
Our table with books and with needle-work spread;
It was yet in more style that withal was a bed,—
    'Twas the way at the Springs.

We trod the piazza both early and late,
But 'tis useless on joys that are past to dilate,
Since too soon came the day on which 'twas our fate
    To leave the Red Springs.

Let all who seek health, with comfort and quiet,
Let the gay who love pleasure without any riot,
Come down this steep mountain, and hasten to try it,
    They'll like the Red Springs.

We left the Red Sulphur at 6 o'clock on Thursday morning, after enjoying a comfortable little breakfast sent to us in our own room ; we were the only passen-

gers, and set off with an agreeable prospect of reaching Fincastle by Sunday. We rode on, passing
over rough roads and dangerous places that would
have frightened us before we had passed over worse.
We stopped at the Salt Sulphur Springs, seventeen
miles from the Red, tasted the water, but were not
in suitable trim to test the grounds of the reputation
this house enjoyed. Ranges of white-washed log
cabins are scattered over a bright green enclosure,
but the natual beauties of the situation are far inferior to those of the Red Spring. We dined at a
thorough temperance house, with a smiling landlord;
and after passing over seven miles of noted rough
road, found ourselves on the five miles of smooth
turnpike, near the White Sulphur Springs. The
inferiority of accommodation at this fashionable
watering-place had been fully set before us, and we
had no intention of staying longer than till the first
stage-coach should depart for Fincastle. Contrary to the positive assurance of the Agent, we found
we should be detained till Monday, and in utter despair we resigned ourselves to all the ills of our situation.
We were a spectacle, from the mud which pelted us
in great balls all day, and we were ushered into a
drawing-room in which the ladies were collected preparatory to a rush into the tea room, and were kept
two hours waiting for rooms to be arranged.
There we had the mortification of being recognized by some of our fashionable acquaintance. We
returned to the drawing-room after tea, and witnessed a display of dress and airs much after the

fashion of Saratoga, and saw the company scatter over the grounds for an evening walk. The extensive rows of low white buildings in every direction, and the rich green of the trees and grass, make the view pleasant, though there is not much wildness of scenery. After waiting till candle-light, word was sent us that our cabin was not ready, but we could go over if we chose; we sat a short time on the piazza, until the window sashes could be put into their places, and many preliminaries could be settled about bedsteads and bedding; and at last, after five hours waiting for a room, composed ourselves for the night, heedless of the attractions of the gay saloon. It rained powerfully the next morning; we ladies breakfasted in our own room, and dined there also, not liking to walk through the long wet grass. We passed the day quietly, sewing and writing, as if we were any where but in the midst of the gaieties of a celebrated watering-place.

Owing to the numerous visiters at the White Sulphur Springs, and our consequent scanty accommodations, we gladly accepted a proposal that we should depart sooner than we had expected, in a new and very elegant coach, running for the first time to Lexington. We proceeded as far as Callahan's, fifteen miles, to pass the first night. We sat down at a plentiful table, and feasted to our hearts' content. At breakfast, a party of travellers entertained us with an account of a recent upset; they soon drove off, and our coach came to the door. We were going to take our seats, when the horses gave a sudden whirl, which would have overturned the coach, but for the presence of mind of the driver, and set off at full speed. All was confusion; some of the by-standers shouted, one man ran after them, and caught one of the horses by the reins, and hung on for some distance, but failed to stop them. They were out of sight in a moment; the agent mounted a horse, and set out to see what had become of them. We four, and two other passengers, stood looking at each other in silence. We were soon told that the horses had never been put together before, and that one of them had never been in harness till now in his life, but great confidence was expressed in the skill of the driver; and it was moreover suggested, that if the coach should be in a condition to proceed, the horses would be probably all the better for this previous exercise. We left the gentlemen discussing probabilities, and walked forward, determined to be guided by appearances. We had gone nearly two miles, when our fellow-travellers overtook us, two walking and one on horseback. They brought word that all was safe, that the wayward horse was undergoing some additional equipment of bit and bridle; and that the agent, a very skilful driver, was to ride on the box to assist. The vehicle soon appeared; we saw it pass a bridge, where the horses might have been frightened if they had chosen. We took our seats, but not without some misgivings. The person on the horse, who, we found, had negotiated an exchange of seats with the agent, cast back some

pitying looks at us, and one old man had walked still
furthur on, to be more sure that all would go right
before he included himself in the risk ; but he consented to ride after another mile.   We soon became
quite interested in him ; he was a plain farmer, dressed in homespun, and said he had determined to walk
to Covington, five miles, and try to get a horse there,
for he must confess he was afraid.   We went on so
safely two or three hours, that we had almost forgotten our dangerous horses, when they took a second
fright at a long beam drawn past us on wheels.
The leaders attempted to turn, the agent sprang off
and caught them, we threw open the door, and were
on the ground in an instant.   It was some time before we could summon courage to take our places
again, but there was no help in our case.

Our next adventure was in fashion as follows : we
we were riding along the edge of a steep brink,
where the perpendicular descent was from 12 to 15
feet ; when the agent again sprang from the box, and
screamed to us to get out.   The two doors were
opened in an instant, and the coach empty before we
had time to think.   There stood our leaders, with
their feet over the precipice, and the wheel-horse,
lying on the edge, struggling with one foot over the
pole and the other entangled in the harness.   If he
had not fallen, there had been no escape for us.   As
soon as we women could recover from the fright, and
stand without trembling, we walked on in a state of
mind not to be envied, leaving half a dozen men, who
had run from a neighboring field, to assist in setting
30*

the horse on his feet, and repair damages. Our drive for the rest of the day was any thing but agreeable. We were forced to retain our dangerous horses, as no arrangement could be made for a change on the road. The turnpike was smooth and hard, but it was very narrow, and in many places carried so high that it was fearful to look over; and remember, we were in the power of animals which had once manifested an inclination to try the plunge. Even Mr. S. who had in the morning protested against jumping out, under any circumstances, sat with his hand on the door, and frequently tried it, to be sure that it could be opened at any sudden emergency. We soon lost our old farmer, after he had earnestly hoped we might be under the protection of Providence, and, moreover, pointed out his beautiful farm to our admiring eyes.

In the course of the afternoon we made an exchange of passengers, taking in the equestrian, whom we found very intelligent and agreeable. Right glad were we to see before us the Dutch place of entertainment kept by Mynheer Armitrout, where we were to rest till morning. It was an abode of industry and comfort; the spinning wheel stood on the floor, the walls were garnished with skeins of colored yarn, and the shelves on the sides of the room were loaded with blankets and homespun counterpanes in every variety of pattern and fringe. We all sallied into a garden, and finding ripe raspberries in abundance, sent a petition to our hostess that we might be permitted to gather some for our supper.

This was readily granted, and in a few moments, the travellers, some of whom had never met in their lives till that morning, were scattered over the garden earnestly engaged in the common enterprise, and heaping in one bowl the common store.

The next incident met us in the morning in the form of a foundered horse. To fill his place, one of the wayward team of yesterday was pressed into the service, and we set off to cross a very considerable mountain. The passage over the " North Mountain" deserves a whole chapter instead of a passing notice. The firm, level road which leads over it, has immortalized Col. Jordon, who undertook and executed it after it had been pronounced impossible by an experienced engineer. It is, indeed, a triumph of art, much of it being based upon an artificial wall from ten to twenty feet high. After riding for two hours, with the path winding far above us, we reached the summit, and immediately commenced our descent, but not before we had paused awhile to view a prospect such as none of us had ever beheld before. We stood at a point where a parapet wall guarded a narrow turn of the road, and looked far down a rocky precipice ; while vallies, rich with harvest, intersected by roads and rivers, and adorned with villages, filled all the spaces of mountain ranges, in all their possible varieties of form, and colour, and position. It was a sea of mountains, with glimmerings of comfort and happiness from a thousand islands of plenty. With feelings of superiority to persons who had only seen Catskill and Holyoke, we commenced our rapid descent, and were safe in the valley in half an hour. And here we could not help congratulating ourselves that we had seen so many mountains, and that we had crossed the last. We found the country below washed and confused from a recent freshet; the waters had subsided, leaving the harvest prostrate—bridges borne away, and roads to be cleared of stones and drift wood. As the new line was not expected, a bridge was wanting for its accommodation, but a passage was accomplished by fording for some distance, and we reached Lexington safely at last, on the 30th June, in time for dinner.

NOTE. On the Jackson river (which, a few miles lower than where we crossed it yesterday, becomes the James) we saw one of those wonders that puzzle geologists. On each mountain bank of the stream is an arch of rock, so distinctly marked out, and so perfectly corresponding, that the union of both at some former period cannot be doubted. The alum rock on this river is also a great curiosity. The rock is composed of lime-stone and iron ore; and pieces of sand stone, round and smooth, are found embedded. The alum, which gives the rock its name, is found there in a pure state, and a spring is strongly impregnated with it.

Lexington, Virginia.

Our first inquiries, on entering the hotel at Lexington, were for a vehicle to take us to the Natural Bridge that afternoon, that we might return in the stage the next morning, proceed to Staunton, and thus avoid further loss of time. To our surprise and mortification, not a carriage of any kind was to be had ; what was to be done ? Our appetites for dinner were gone, and, after a silent meal, we repaired to the parlor for consultation—what was to be done ? The stages only passed three times in the week. Should we miss the one in the morning, we might be detained several days : but *then* to go without visiting the Bridge, for a sight of which we had encountered so many hardships and come such a distance, it was not to be thought of; so we diverged to other subjects, wishing, like all the world, to keep the unpleasant point out of view until the last moment left for decision. After tea, Col. D. paid us a visit, with whom we had some pleasant conversation, and from whom we learned that Lexington was possessed of one of the oldest colleges in the state ; founded by Gen. Washington, from whom it took its name. Washington consented to receive a certain sum as a compliment from the State, provided he might be permitted to appropriate it to some public institution ; which being agreed to, he endowed " Washington College " with $100,000. The sum of $50;000 has been since added, but at present the institution is neglected, owing to the want of professors, who, however, are shortly expected, when it will, no doubt, return to its former rank in the State. Various matters were discussed, and at last the all-important one of the Bridge was brought forward. Our griefs were stated, and our kind friend the Colonel declaring it would be a disgrace to Lexington if we could not gain a conveyance to the Bridge, sent to a friend for his carriage ; this failed, and, after deploring our unfortunate case, he bade us good-night, giving hope, however, that there was one chance more, and if successful, we should know early in the morning. Daylight came, and with it the pleasing intelligence that Major A.'s carriage was ready for us. This was owing to the colonel's influence ; so with a bright sun and light hearts we commenced our drive to the Bridge, distant fourteen miles, the first seven of which were rough enough to shake dyspepsia from the most confirmed invalid. But the Bridge was beyond, and we cared not for the ups and downs which intervened. At length the road improved, the country became flat and less romantic than it had been, so that we could scarcely credit all we had heard of the wildness and romance of the Bridge scenery. Having been told, too, that we might pass it without being aware of the fact, we were now every moment on the lookout. But hearing at last that the hotel was before, we were satisfied that no trick was intended, and therefore turned our eyes to the dwelling ; at the door of which, to our surprise and pleasure, stood Mrs. D. and her party, who had just arrived before us. Warm were the greetings on either side, and many the details of accidents, hopes, and fears, past, present, and to come. After a short rest, we proceeded to the top of the bridge. But who can describe

The Natural Bridge?

After all that has been said and written, after the
various engravings, and the vivid imaginings on all
the aforesaid efforts to enlighten the public, and give
a correct idea of this most magnificent of nature's
works—*after all these* have failed, as most assuredly
they have, why should I attempt to describe *that,*
which, having seen, I feel it utterly impossible to dwell
on without a sense of mental and physical weak-
ness, which makes all I have ever known dwindle
into insignificance, and my very frame tremble, as
beneath the power of some mighty invisible agent
just about to crush me into nothing? It is vain, utterly vain! I can tell the length, and breadth, and
height of this stupendous structure;* but to bring
it in all its mighty grandeur, in all its *overpowering*
wildness, in all that vastness which causes the mind
almost to lose itself, to bring it in its sublime reality before the imagination of any one, is *impossible.*
To each and all, who have the power of locomotion,
I would say, " Go, and see for yourselves."

But perhaps, for the amusement or benefit of those
who may read this journal, I should detail our own
movements on this never-to-be-forgotten day. To
begin then:—Having rested ourselves, we proceeded
to the top of the Bridge, over which the road runs
so naturally, and the trees and shrubbery on either
side grow in such wildness, that few persons, unpre-

---

* Height, 215 feet, span of arch, 90 feet, breadth of arch, 75
feet, thickness of bridge, 55 feet.

pared for the scene, would imagine they were in the vicinity of this miracle of nature. We wound through a little narrow path, from the edge of which we gazed into the abyss below; at its bottom a narrow stream threads its way under the arch, the span of which met our view from our present position. But we looked from a dizzy height; an awful chasm yawned beneath, and we drew back with that sort of feeling which induces a long breath; the sensation experienced on a sudden relief from danger or fatigue. Having taken a few moments' rest and thought, and being joined by Mrs. D., we proceeded down the hill along a winding path under the bridge. It is from the first view which here presents itself that the engraving is taken, and though to one who has never been here, it can give no idea of the original, yet it may serve as a memorial to those who have. We stood in silent admiration, and slowly and by degrees took our way under the Bridge, on the face of which, and as if drawn by a skilful artist, is the form of a spread eagle. Under its left wing is the perfect representation of a lion's head, the eyes and mouth being distinctly visible: and, singular as it may seem, both these animals present the same appearance from either side of the Bridge. They are delineated by a darker colouring of the rock, and at a little distance beyond is the figure of a bat. Strange it is that the spread eagle, the national emblem of our country, with the lion of England under its wing, should be supporting, as it were, this most stupendous of nature's arches! What does it mean? Surely it would seem as if the hand of the Divinity had imprinted on tables of stone this emblem of our country's independence and future supremacy. My sight failed, and my neck ached with looking up towards these curious and mighty workings of nature. Seating ourselves on the rocks, we closed our eyes, to realize that we had the scene imprinted on the memory, and then taking our way up the hill, stopping at intervals to cast a long lingering look behind, we bade farewell to the Natural Bridge.

Dined at the house where we left our friends, and after a pleasant drive, reached Lexington just before dark, where Colonel D. received us, together with our tribute of gratitude for the enjoyment which his exertions had been the means of our attaining.

Wyer's Cave.

We awoke refreshed after the fatigue of our visit to the Natural Bridge, and ready to continue our pilgrimage to the shrine of all-wonderful nature. Our drive to Staunton was without incident, and early the next day we took a comfortable carriage for the cavern ten miles from that place. Nothing on the way indicated the existence of such a place, and when we reached the little inn kept by the guide, I could have found it in my heart to doubt. We made our toilet for the occasion, and proceeded along the side of a steep hill, climbing nearly to the top, where a bench stands in the shade before a door

31

in the rock. We sat down to become perfectly cool before entering, while the guide unlocked the door, produced candles and matches, and made his preparations, and here our party completed their equipments; M. and I laid aside our bonnets, and Mr. S. gallantly made turbans for our heads of colored handkerchiefs. R. tied his handkerchief over his shoulders in the fashion of a cloak. The guide gave each a candlestick formed of a curved sheet of tin to protect the eyes from the light. We surveyed ourselves in the polished mirrors they afforded, and then entered one by one. I cannot follow our course, for we went up and down, through a narrow, slippery passage, our over-shoes often adhering to the clay of the floor. We passed through openings just large enough to admit us stooping to the very earth, and then stood in halls more than 50 feet high. Now we descended on narrow steep ladders, and then climbed piles of rocks, or made a circuit to avoid falling into some deep pit. A map of the cave resembles somewhat the chain of lakes on our northern boundary, repeated several times. But let me try to systematize. The first object that attracted our attention was the wall of the passage set thick with rugged stalactites. It was a close, heavy fringe, covering roof and sides like long icicles; and here let me remark that these formations have not the brilliancy usually ascribed to them except when examined closely with candles. When the light is held behind them, they seen to be transparent, and of a rich flame color. As we passed on, we found

the shapes and dispositions of these formations infinitely varied ; sometimes they hung in long pointed
leaves, depending to the floor, and sometimes in
graceful folds like drapery. Our guide conducted
us into an opening called the music room, and striking the columns, drew from one spot the sound of a
heavy drum, from another that of a tambourine, and
from some small tubes an excellent imitation of the
Pandean pipes. Further on he struck the rocks
with a staff, and the whole apartment vibrated under
the heavy gong ; the sound was so deafening that
we held our hands over our ears for pain. We next
entered what is called the ball-room from having
been occasionally used for that purpose ; it is wide
and high, and the dim light of our scattered candles
made it seem vast. As we passed out of it and groped
our way onward, sweet distant sounds seemed to
glide before us, sometimes distinct, and again seemingly lost in some deep cavern beneath, or floating
through the arches above us. It was our guide's
companion, who had preceded us with a flute. We
descended a natural stair called Jacob's ladder ; this
and many other passes are narrow and difficult, and
all who attempt them must depend entirely on their
own exertions and strength, as no one can assist another. The gallantry of our gentlemen was severely
tried, as they could do nothing for us but hold our
candles occasionally, that we might use our hands
to cling to the rocks. It is vain to attempt describing each of the apartments to which a name has
been given. Some have been named from a real or

fancied resemblance of objects, and others from patriotic feeling, without much regard to propriety.
Here, in odd conjunction with the Leaning Tower
of Pisa and Cleopatra's Needle, are Jefferson's Hall,
Congress Hall, and Washington Hall. This last apartment filled me with awe from the vastness which belonged to it in that imperfect light. It rises far above
the rays of the candles, and is lost in black obscurity.
The candle of the guide at the opposite end of it
seemed to us a mere point of light.   Near the centre
stands a colossal stalagmite, so like a statue wrapped
in drapery, that one can hardly dispel the illusion ;
this is Washington at a distance ; approach it, and
it becomes a shapeless mass of stone, dripping muddy water.   Lady Washington's apartment boasts a
mirror, fringed hangings, and countless folds of drapery.   The guide placed his light behind these stone
curtains, and showed us, as he said, " not only a hem
but a border."   The Tower of Babel is a large circular rock, with a fluted surface, looking like columns bound together.   Solomon's Throne is a lofty
chair with steps and a cushion, though I must confess it needs something from the fancy.   Objects of
interest are found at every step—figures of animals,
birds, human features, and even profiles, stand as
memorials of nature's freakish moods, and the grotesque shapes in which no resemblance to particular
things may be traced, are found hanging and standing, and lying about in wild gracefulness, like the
tracery of frost executed in stone.   We had a delicious draught of cool water, which falls in drops from

the rock; some thoughtful mortal has placed beneath it a vessel fashioned in the world above, that wearied pilgrims may be refreshed. But the darkness, the stillness, and the echo that every sound calls forth in this subterraneous world, were to us most striking; they give the scene its sublimity, though the impression is strangely at variance with the minute examination of perpetually changing objects, and the frequent discovery of ludicrous caricatures. Our guide awakened the echoes by a song, to which his fine voice gave full effect, and —— stunned us by firing the pistol. *The* pistol! if this companion of our journey has not before received its due notice, let it be here recorded that its one effort was now to die away *in sound*. We were tired enough when our guide announced the end; but all our steps were to be retraced before we could rest. Our candles were burned low, and the fearful thought of being left in darkness in such a place, suggested itself, not as a thing to be apprehended, for we knew that our guide had provided against such misfortune, but as the climax of all possible horrors. To increase the effect, we were listening to a tale from the guide, of a foreigner to whom it once happened, and whose guide found the way out after hours of peril. At last we saw gleams of pale light beginning to contend with the red glare. The effect of suddenly emerging into daylight after three hours in the cave, was strange enough, and resuming the temperature of the world without was as uncomfortable as singular. Worn out as we were, we could

31*

not avoid laughing at our plight, covered as we stood
with a plaster of red mud over our strange attire.
But water and brushes and a change of dress soon
restored us, and after the refreshment of dinner, we
pursued our journey to Harrisonburgh, talking over
our exploits, and the wonders we had encountered.

The Valley.

We were roused from our slumbers, at 2 o'clock
A. M. by the firing of guns and beat of drum under
our windows. At first we could not imagine what
it meant, but recollection came, and with it the
memory of the 4th of July. It was rather hard to
be disturbed in this style, and kept awake until day-
light by such a racket; but the spirit of patriotism
rendered it endurable, and we arose to breakfast with
feelings and appetites quite American. At nine
o'clock we saw the Harrisonburgh Rangers in review before us, and soon after, taking the stage
which came up with five passengers, we continued
our journey through the valley of Virginia, which
we entered at Lexington. This valley is as celebrated for the beauty of its scenery as for its high state
of cultivation and the badness of its roads. We
reached Newmarket to dinner, and had the satisfaction of viewing the troops in parade celebrating, to
the best of their ability, the glorious Fourth, and truly
the assemblage was grotesque enough. Three officers in uniform were in command, about twenty men
were in hats and feathers, the rest, I suppose fifty,
of every age and size, were in citizen's dress, with

sticks over their shoulders instead of guns, and the music consisted of two violins, flutes, and pipes : it was ludicrous enough; but the spirit, which in this little place prompted this exhibition of public feeling, was beautiful, and to be commended. Every little village through which we passed, showed some sign of respect for the day ; and after a pleasant drive we arrived at Woodstock. Our hotel was filthy, and after a miserable night, we gladly took the stage at 1 o'clock, A. M., reached Winchester to breakfast, and spent the Sabbath there ; left it on Monday morning, 6th July. The country was beautiful, and our road ran along the line of the great Ohio Rail Road, which is finished as far as Harper's Ferry, where we arrived about 11 o'clock, A. M. This beautiful place is as wild and romantic as the most fanciful mind can picture, and here is the meeting of the Potomac and Shenandoah rivers, which after their junction seem to have forced their passage, and caused a separation of the mountain. Here we dined, and at 1 o'clock took the rail road for Baltimore. The scenery, just after leaving the ferry, is wild beyond any description. The canal runs along the road on one side, and immensely high rocks are piled up on the other; while at little distance the Potomac runs in a line with the canal, and winding among the hills, gives life and spirit to a scene of exquisite romance. These piles of rock continue for a distance of several miles, and afterward the road runs through a cultivated and beautiful country. We travelled most of the way by horse-power, though we had the locomotive for 16 miles.   About 7 o'clock we stopped at Sykesville for supper, and then proceeded by a fine moonlight, passing some beautiful country-seats, and about 9 o'clock reached Ellicott's Mills, situated on the Patapsco, which had been sparkling in its silver beauty, reflecting the moonlight, for many miles of our course.   These mills are very extensive, comprising cotton and flour mills—iron works, &c. &c.   They are in fine order, and most picturesque in their situation and appearance.   Here, too, are several fine bridges, particularly one, which, crossing the stream at this place, unites with the road which branches off to Washington City.   Reached Baltimore at half past 10 o'clock, paid an hour's visit to Mrs. M., passed the night at Barnum's very comfortably, and took the boat at 6 A. M. for Philadelphia, where we occupied the afternoon in a visit to the Water Works and our friends in Walnut Street.   The next morning saw us in the boat for New-York, which city we reached at 3 in the afternoon, in good health and spirits, thankful for our preservation through a journey so long and so full of perils, and happy in meeting our friends after so long absence.

We have wandered far and wide
By the graceful streamlet's side ;
Over mountain, through the glen,
In the valley we have roved—
Countless scenes, where nature proved
The magic wonders of her pen.

She has written on each heart
Things which may not soon depart,
Of each bright and troubled scene.
And although, of this Quartette,
None remain together,—yet
All shall keep its memory green.

Though our pilgrimage is o'er,
And we daily meet no more,
In our bosoms still shall glow
Friendship's lustre ever bright,
Yielding unalloyed delight,
Till to our final bourne we go.

A WEEK AMONG AUTOGRAPHS.

BY

S. GILMAN.

A WEEK AMONG AUTOGRAPHS.

A RECENT visit to the mansion of I. K. Tefft, Esq. of Savannah, furnished me with an unaccustomed entertainment, in describing which, I may hope to impart it, in a faint degree, to others. This gentleman has devoted a portion of his leisure for several years to the collection of *autographs,* or specimens of original hand-writing by eminent persons of various ages and countries. If it were not otherwise known that his literary taste and habits had peculiarly fitted him for such an occupation, the fact would be sufficiently evident from the actual fruits of his researches. His compilation of manuscripts, by different writers, nearly all of whom have been persons, in some way or other, of considerable distinction, amounts to about five thousand articles. They thus constitute a very rare curiosity, or rather assemblage of curiosities, which few can even partially inspect without strong feelings of surprise and gratification. They present, too, a striking testimony of the extraordinary results that may be achieved by directing one's attention and energies to a particular pursuit, whatever it may be.

Nor can such a collection be simply regarded
32

as a curiosity. It deserves, in many respects, the
higher praise of usefulness. The inquiries and exertions necessary to its formation, must often bring
to light some valuable literary or historical document. It is not mere signatures, or scraps of hand-
writing, that Mr. Tefft has been so sedulously collecting. He has intended that each specimen should
consist, if possible, of an interesting letter, or some
important instrument. Must it not be readily allowed, that a series of only single letters from all the
eminent men, who were active, both in a civil and
military capacity, throughout our revolutionary war,
would of itself constitute an interesting volume, and
throw a desirable light on the history of that period?
Yet such a series might be culled with great ease
from the collection we are now contemplating.

Very few large autographic collections are known
to exist. They are among the last intellectual luxuries grafted on a high growth of refinement and civilization. Here and there some peculiar taste or
bias determines an individual to the pursuit, and he
experiences the innocent delight of beholding his
treasures rapidly increase, while his friends and
acquaintances, in the mean time, are permitted to
enjoy many an hour of deep interest and pleasure
in reviewing the proceeds of his quiet yet enthusiastic
labors. In our own country, besides Mr. Tefft,
there are but two very extensive collectors, the Rev.
Dr. Sprague, of Albany, and Robert Gilmor, Esq.
of Baltimore. Dr. Sprague's collection has attained considerable celebrity, and amounts to more than

twenty thousand articles. Mr. Gilmor's, also, is particularly valuable; and a printed list of the most important articles has been circulated by him for the convenience of himself and his friends. His American is separated from his Foreign collection, and is thus classed: Civil and military officers before the revolution—military officers of the revolutionary war—military officers since the revolution—naval officers—signers of the declaration of independence —worthies of the revolution—signers of the constitution of the United States—presidents and vice-presidents—secretaries of state—secretaries of the treasury—secretaries of war—secretaries of the navy—attorneys general—post-office department—governors of states and territories—members of congress—diplomatic—law— divinity—physic— literary—scientific—artists—miscellaneous, which includes all that cannot properly be placed under one of the other heads. The foreign autographs in the same collection are subjected to a similar arrangement. The accomplished Grimke, during the last few years of his life, paid much attention to this subject, and has left a considerable collection of autographs, which, had he been longer spared, would soon undoubtedly have been greatly enlarged. Among the most distinguished collectors abroad, are, Rev. Dr. Raffles, of Liverpool, the well-known author of the "Life of Spencer," and Rev. Mr. Bolton, of Henly-upon-Thames. It would thus appear that clergymen have a particular partiality for this pursuit; though by what affinity, I presume not to determine.

Few autographs, comparatively, have reached our country from the continent of Europe, nor is Mr. Tefft acquainted with any collector in that part of the world. That there must be such, however, is highly probable, particularly in France, Germany, Holland, and Italy. The Enyclopædias contain no information on the subject, though it would seem to deserve a place in their miscellaneous records. The Encyclopædia Americana, which is mainly a translation from the German, dismisses the article with the tantalizing remark, that "some collections of autographs of famous men are very interesting." I should apprehend that there is a sufficient number of autograph-collectors in the world to justify and support an annual publication on the subject. Such a work would be invaluable to the fraternity. It should contain catalogues of all existing collections. It should give an account of new and interesting discoveries. It should present fac similes of the rarest and most valuable subjects. By this means, every collector might compare his own deficiencies with the redundances of others, and an equilibrium be everywhere maintained at much less trouble and expense than are incurred at present.

Mr. Tefft has succeeded in forming his large compilation without incurring any direct expense. Through the liberality of many persons in our country who have held choice autographs in their possession, he has always on hand duplicates of considerable worth, by the exchange of which with persons either at home or abroad, he has been enabled to con

fer so peculiar a value and extent on his collection.
Having amassed five thousand specimens, it may be
supposed that he has nearly exhausted the range of
distinguished names; and accordingly, when some
obliging friend from a distance sends him a parcel,
he finds, on looking it over, that it scarcely contri-
butes a single new name to his collection, though the
whole may be otherwise valuable and interesting.
Some of his most curious specimens he has received
gratuitously from friends in Great Britain, although,
as might be expected, in a very artificial state of society, they would often command considerable prices
in that country. The poet Campbell raised forty-
five guineas for the Poles by autographs; and, visiting a lady who had notes from distinguished people
on her table, he advised her to conceal them, or they
would be stolen. Brougham's autograph was valued
at five guineas. Distant, undoubtedly, is the day,
when the casual holder of a few bits of paper in
America will think of extorting a compensation
from the gentle and devoted collector of autographs.

One of the most interesting features of this occupation consists in the personal correspondence between the autograph-collector and individuals who
are in possession of the desired articles. Between
the collectors themselves, not only an acquaintance
is formed, but often a warm and substantial friendship. If one could imagine the mutual regard entertained between two persons who are in the habit
of interchanging a few Birds of Paradise, or a real
Phœnix, or a consignment of the most delicious

32*

tropical fruits, or a goodly specimen of Georgia gold, one might understand the emotions derived from the reception of a long-sought-for scrap by one of the signers of the Declaration, or perchance the veritable signature of some foriegn name,

"Wherewith all Europe rings from side to side."

Again : nothing can exceed the obliging and courteous language and actions of several distinguished men, who have been applied to for autographs within their control.   My Savannah friend has rarely, if ever, had the misfortune to be met with neglect in answer to applications of this kind.   His letters from such men as ex-Presidents Madison and Adams, Prof. Silliman, Gen. La Fayette, Washington Irving, Duponceau, Joseph Buonaparte, Dr. Mitchell, Mr. Grimke, Basil Hall, Dr. Raffles, and many others, exhibit their private characters in a truly amiable light.   When thus not merely the nature of this occupation, but its external circumstances are of so agreeable a description, we cannot wonder at the zeal with which it is pursued.

The science of the autograph-collector is not without its higher and peculiar mysteries.   By much experience and exercise he acquires a skilful discernment, which belongs not to common eyes.   He will tell you of correspondences between the hand-writing and the mental disposition of individuals, about which he is rarely, if ever, mistaken.   He will speak of immediately discerning, amidst a hundred new specimens, and before inspecting the signatures,

those which have been written by the most eminent
persons. And why should it not be so? Perhaps
it will be found more philosophical to credit such
pretensions, than to ridicule or distrust them. For
if we often judge of a character, with no little precision, by a single tone of the voice, by a single motion of the body, by an instantaneous glance at the
physiognomy ; and if, which is yet more to the point,
a *nation* has its peculiar style of writing, so that a
French manuscript is as easily discernible from an
English one as are the respective dialects of the
two countries ; if the manuscripts of the *same* nation
at different eras are also perceptibly different, so
that a writing of the sixteenth century is no more
like one of the eighteenth than are the dresses of
those two periods like each other ; if the chirogra-
phies of the two sexes are almost always immediately distinguishable, so that a brother and sister, educated under the same circumstances, and taught by
the same writing-master, shall yet unavoidably re-
veal their respective styles ; and if, lastly, different
classes of persons shall be known by their different
hand-writings, so that a mere child could pronounce
which is the mercantile clerk's, which the lawyer's,
and which the leisurely gentleman's, let us beware
how we rashly discredit the experienced inspector
of autographs, who deduces from the signature of an
individual the qualities of his mind.

The occupation we are describing is sometimes
enlivened by moving adventures, hair-breadth rescues,
and joy-inspiring discoveries, which the uninitiated

world knows nothing of; and sometimes it is damp-
ed by the most cruel disappointments. A manuscript
is often sought for with anxious diligence for years;
and when perhaps all hope is abandoned, and something like acquiescence or resignation is beginning to
compose the spirits of the baffled inquirer, not only
the desired signature, but (precious and ample reward
for all past labors and regrets) a .whole letter by the
same hand, is sent in from some unexpected quarter.
Mr. Tefft was long in pursuit of an autograph of
Kosciusko. He received from a northern friend a
scrap of paper containing the simple signature of
that warrior's name, with an expression of regret
that nothing more under his hand could be found.
Some time afterwards, he received from another
friend an entire letter of Kosciusko, with the exception of the signature. On comparing the two papers, with trembling anxiety, it was found that they
both originally constituted one and the same letter.
Sometimes an ignorant descendant of renowned ancestors will be unwilling to part with any of their
manuscripts, through an inability to comprehend the
collector's object; sometimes a heaping trunk is
committed by a vandal hand to the flames, or, if rescued, its contents are perhaps found to be ruined by
the moulds and damps of age.

But we have perhaps been too long detained from
examining the valuable collection which has occasioned these preliminary remarks. We find the
manuscripts in excellent perservation, being arranged and classed in six volumes, after the man-

ner of Mr. Gilmor's collection already described. There is, besides, a box of miscellaneous autographs. Let us first open this. A very courteous letter from Capt. Hall lies on the top, inclosing an engraved fac simile of the letter written to him by Sir Walter Scott when detained at Portsmouth by the wind in 1831, and giving some account of Sir Walter's own favourite production, "The Antiquary." This letter has been already published in several American newspapers, and we will dismiss it by simply remarking that Sir Walter's first sentence has been erroneously deciphered and printed. He does not say, "My dear Captain Hall, as the wind seems *determinately* inflexible," but he says "As the wind seems *determinedly* inflexible."

We have next, a letter, dated in 1833, from an eminent law-editor of Edinburgh, who states that he has declined autograph-collecting on account of the expense attending it. "It is now," he continues, "a favorite hobby with the *ladies* as well as gentlemen, which makes it doubly difficult to procure a tolerable set of autographs—for even parliamentary franks on the backs of letters from members of both houses are kidnapped from all the public offices and private desks, here and in London, for wives, daughters, and sweethearts."

Next is an invaluable document. It is a communication from the son of Dr. Currie, of Liverpool, the biographer of Burns, covering a long and interesting letter from that immortal poet to the celebrated Dugald Stewart. It is written in a large, bold, perpendicular, and slightly angular hand, not unworthy the author of " Tam O'Shanter."

A distinguished Professor of a northern institution, in a very kind letter, thus writes : " We have in Yale College a very remarkable autograph, or rather auto-delineation : it is a sketch of himself with a pen, made by Major André a few hours before his execution. There is also a lock of his hair taken from his grave. In the sketch, he is represented as sitting at a table ; the portrait is full length, and about the size of the palm of your hand. It came into the possession of Lieut. Nathan Beers of the Connecticut Line, then on duty, and who stood near to André, as a member of the guard, at the moment of execution. Lieut. Beers is my near neighbor, and at eighty years of age enjoys his faculties perfectly, except hearing. Col. Talmadge, a very gallant and distinguished cavalry officer, was charged with the immediate custody of André's person, and upon his arm the unfortunate man was leaning, on his way to execution, when he first saw the preparation for what he deemed a dishonorable death ; he recoiled a moment at the sight, and asked with emotion if he must die in that manner. Col. Talmadge is still living, and cannot, even now, relate that tragedy without tears."

We have next a letter from an eminent clergyman in England. The following extract will touch a sensitive chord in every American bosom :—" I now possess every signer of the Declaration of Independence, save one, viz. George Taylor. By the

kindness of a friend in Liverpool, a countryman of
yours, I have been presented with a proof-impression
of Trumbull's picture of the Signing of the Declaration, which I purpose binding with the volume
which the signers are designated to form, and which,
when so bound and illustrated, will constitute not
only one of the most interesting articles in my collection, but, I apprehend, to posterity at least one of
the most interesting volumes in the world."

As a happy pendant to the foregoing, we have
next a letter from our Lafayette, dated in 1832,
saying, "With much pleasure I would gratify your
autographic inclinations, but have for the present
no European writings to offer, excepting a note
from the King of the French, which I inclose. As
for this letter of mine, which you are pleased to
call for, I hope it will be placed in the *American*
part of your collection. I beg you to remind me to
my friends in Savannah, and to believe me most sincerely yours.   LAFAYETTE."

There is next an affectionate letter to a young
friend at St. Mary's College, Baltimore, dated Washington, 1827, written in a very elegant hand, and
signed J. R. of Roanoke. It may be remembered
that Mr. Randolph in early life wrote in a wretched
hand, and was induced to alter it on his first visit
to England, by seeing some specimens of the writing of Mr. Pitt, whose manuscript was remarkably
fair. The effect of this characteristic emulation
evidently continued with him to the last.

A business letter by a celebrated senator from

Massachusetts soon follows, and is remarkable for being written very much in the manner of Walter Scott.

Not far from this, is the letter of a distinguished citizen of Philadelphia to the late Dr. Samuel Mitchell, of New-York, introducing a friend to his acquaintance. Dr. Mitchell himself sent this autograph, on which is endorsed in his own hand, " Received 20th March, 1823. Answered by Tea-party, 29th."

We soon take up a letter, apparently from a London merchant or banker, dated 6th April, 1676, to his friends in the country. It is curious in mentioning that King Charles II. was then at New-Market, " and 'tis said," continues the letter, " his Majesty in Counsell did on Sunday was seavenight past order that the chimney money should be assigned for payment of the bankers." This chimney money probably coresponded to the house-duty of modern times. It is sometimes called *hearth-money* by the historians. The same letter contains the following passing touch of private life :—" Matt. H. and little Kitt were both invited through Easter to Sir Wm. Bucknall. The hinmost was not there, but the foremost was, and questionless the orange was well squeezed."

Another document is an order, dated in 1724, for the payment of a dividend on the South Sea Stock, celebrated in history as the cause of such widely-extended ruin.

There is also an original letter, written by Miss

Elizabeth Scott to her father. The greatest curiosity about it is, that Dr. Doddridge once tried to marry Miss Scott, but without success. She was a lady of great talents and accomplishments, and the authoress of some poems. The letter before us is only remarkable for a deep tone of piety and filial affection. The writer seems to have been a great bodily sufferer. One little thing about the exterior of her letter bespeaks its feminine authorship, and carries us back, as by a magic power, through a hundred years. Some thirty or forty *pin-holes* are stuck into the wafer of the letter, the fair and worthy writer apparently not having a seal at hand. The privilege of seeing pin-holes, made in a wafer by the fingers of a lady to whom Dr. Doddridge was attached, is one of no small value. If she could have found it in her heart to favour the fond divine more indulgently, doubtless she would have been able, instead of a pin, to have used a seal, with the device of a blazing heart, and the initials of **P. D.** beneath it. As to the superscription, directed upside down, we know not what to say.

Turning over a number of interesting articles, which we cannot possibly specify, we come to a MS. sermon of Cotton Mather. It is written half unintelligibly in the finest and closest hand, on three very small leaves, the latter part of it seeming to be only notes or hints for extemporaneous enlargement. The text consists of the words, " Blessed be God." An instance of Mather's bold and poetic imagination occurs near the middle of the discourse. Des-

cribing the life and character of the Apostle Paul,
who had such valid reasons to bless God for his
conversion, he says, "a vile sinner *against* God
may become a high servant of God. As they said,
Is Saul among the prophets? thus they could say of
another Saul, Is he among the Apostles? A fierce
persecutor of our Lord Jesus Christ may become a
rare ambassador for him." At this point he inserts
in the margin, as an after-thought, which he felt
necessary to crown his climax of antitheses, " and a
fire-brand of hell may become a bright star of
heaven."

As this autograph of Mather is among the oldest
in the collection, I may here mention that the *very*
oldest is dated in 1665, and that on one sheet of paper
are fastened four small documents, written in New-
England between the years 1665 and 1689. Thus
the Collection is not yet peculiarly rich in antiqui-
ties.

We now turn over a considerable number of articles, consisting of letters, dinner-notes, orders, and
signatures, from the most conspicuous Americans
of past and present times. However *piquant* it may
be to the curious in such matters to inspect the hasty undress and confidential billets of Presidents and
Ex-Presidents, Members of Cabinets and Congress,
and various others eminent characters, the laws of
decorum must not be violated by transcribing and
blazoning them here. But see! we arrive at a
mutilated letter from Benedict Arnold. It is written in a large, clear, bold, regular hand, and contains a

complaint of his character having been cruelly and unjustly aspersed; concluding thus—"I have the honour to be, with the greatest respect, (here some one has written in pencil, *a Traitor*) Your Excellency's most obedient and very humble servant,

"B. Arnold."

Soon following this, is the rough draft of an animated Address to the young men of Boston, dated Philadelphia, 1798, by the elder President Adams. It begins thus: "Gentlemen, it is impossible for you to enter your own Fanueil Hall, or to throw your eyes on the variegated mountains and elegant islands around you, without recollecting the principles and actions of your fathers, and feeling what is due to their example." After alluding to the dangers of the country, he writes, "To arms, then, my young friends; to arms!"—and concludes in an equally characteristic strain. Some sheets after, we find a letter from the same pen, written from Philadelphia to Boston as early as 1776. It is addressed to a certain Miss Polly Palmer, in a style of playful gallantry. The whole of it is so interesting, that it shall be extracted here entire:

Philadelphia, *July* 5, 1776.

Miss Polly.—Your favour of June 15, 1776, was handed to me by the last post.—I hold myself much obliged to you for your attention to me, at this distance from those scenes, in which, although I feel myself deeply interested, yet I can neither be an actor nor spectator.

You have given me (notwithstanding all your modest apologies) with a great deal of real elegance and perspicuity, a minute and circumstantial narrative of the whole expedition to the lower harbour, against the men of war. It is lawful, you know, to flatter the ladies a little, at least if custom can make a thing lawful : but, without availing myself in the least degree of this license, I can safely say, that from your letter, and another from Miss Paine to her brother, I was enabled to form a more adequate idea of that whole transaction, than from all the other accounts of it, both in the newspapers and private letters which have come to my hands.

In times as turbulent as these, commend me to the ladies for historiographers; the gentlemen are too much engaged in action,—the ladies are cooler spectators.—There is a lady at the foot of Pens-Hill, who obliges me from time to time, with clearer and fuller intelligence than I can get from a whole committee of gentlemen.

I was a little mortified at the unlucky calm which retarded the militia from Braintree, Weymouth, and Hingham.—I wished that they might have had more than half the glory of the enterprize ; however, it satisfies me to reflect, that it was not their fault, but the fault of the wind they had not.

I will enclose to you a DECLARATION, in which all America is remarkably united. It completes a revolution, which makes as great a figure in the history of mankind as any that has preceded it:—provided always that the ladies take care to record the circumstances of it, for by the experience I have had of the other sex, they are either to lazy, or too active, to commemorate them.

A continuance of your correspondence, Miss Polly, would much oblige me.—Compliments to Papa and Mamma, and the whole family.—I begin now to flatter myself, however, that you are situated in the safest place upon the continent.

Howe's army and fleet are at Staten Island—But there is a very numerous army at New-York and New-Jersey, to oppose them.—Like Noah's Dove, without its innocence, they can find no rest.

I am with much respect, esteem, and gratitude, your friend and humble servant,

JOHN ADAMS.

A letter from the unhappy Zubly lies side by side with several from John Houston. They were both members, from Georgia, of that Congress which signed the Declaration of Independence. Zubly was charged, in Congress, with holding a treasonable correspondence with Sir James Wright, then British governor of Georgia. He fled homewards. Houston was ordered to follow him, and counteract his influence, and thus was deprived of the distinguished honour of adding his signature to the Declaration. Zubly, it appears, continued to live and to preach in Savannah; for in the letter above-mentioned, written in 1779, he says to his friend, " I

33*

preached yesterday to a few people, among whom many were very rude. A critical day seems to be drawing near." I saw also his grave and monument during my recent visit at Savannah.

The autograph-inspector must not, however, flatter himself he can always find a very interesting document, apart from the mere signature or hand-writing of the eminent individual to whom it belonged. The every-day correspondence, even of heroes themselves, is not particularly heroic. You will turn over many a precious relic of the officers engaged in our revolutionary war, and find perhaps nothing more important than an order upon a Quarter-Master-General, or the detail of accidents unworthy of a permanent record. Yet sometimes a few hastily written lines will transport you in imagination to the heat and bustle of the contest; as, where Lord Stirling enjoins Col. Dayton, "besides watching the motions of the enemy along the Sound, to get some certain intelligence from Staten Island and New-York of their preparations or intentions; and I will be with you in the morning, but say nothing of that;"—or, where Archibald Bullock, the first republican governor of Georgia, begs Col. M'Intosh, Commander of the Continental Battalion, in a letter which is quoted by M'Call, the historian, immediately to withdraw a sentinel from his door ; "since," he continues, "I act for a free people, in whom I have an entire confidence and dependence, and would wish upon all occasions to avoid ostentation ;" or where Thomas Cushing of Boston, in 1773, invites

Elbridge Gerry to a meeting of the Committee of
Correspondence, to prepare for the possibility of approaching war; and says in a postscript, "It is
thought it will not be best to mention abroad the
particular occasion of this meeting;"—or when
M'Henry writes to Governor Hawley, that he had sitten up two nights to produce two numbers of some
address to the people, and adds, " We go against
Arnold, but let us not be too sanguine.   He is covered by entrenchments.   War is full of disappointments," &c.; or where Rawlins Lowndes writes
to Governor Houston of Georgia, "I hope you will
be able to keep off the enemy until succours arrive
to your assistance.   General Lincoln set off this
morning, and the troops are on their march."

It is curious, however, to observe the turn taken
by the correspondence of the same class of men as
soon as the great struggle for independence was
over.   They enter now upon the field of local or
general politics; or they look after their private affairs, which have evidently been deranged by their
long devotion to public service; or they order from
an artist, an eagle, the badge of the Cincinnati; or
they inquire into the value of grants of land voted
them by legislatures; or they solicit the office of
sheriff; or they take measures to establish academies,
and improve society around them.

We now open the box lettered Distinguished Foreigners.   And first greets the eye a precious parcel containing several autographs of Sir Walter
Scott.   We have this note to his favourite publisher

and friend Jas. Ballantyne :—"Dear James, You
have had two blank days, I send you copy from
fifty-two to sixty-four, thirteen pages." We have
an entire and closely-written leaf of the History of
France in Tales of a Grandfather. We have a
billet without direction, sent probably to some one
waiting at the gate of Abbotsford, and couched in
these terms : "Sir Walter is particularly engaged
just now. Andrew Scott is welcome to look at the
arms, and Sir Walter encloses a trifle to help out
the harvest wages." We have an order on a bookseller in this fashion :—"Mr. Scott will be obliged
to Mr. Laing to send him from his catalogue

9373 Life of J. C. Pitkington,
9378 Life of Letitia Pitkington ;"

and lastly, we have the solitary signature, Walter
Scott, which will no doubt be worth its full guinea
before many years. One peculiarity distinguishes
the manuscripts of this author from all others. It
is, that he never dots an i, or crosses a t, or employs
punctuation of any kind, except, now and then, a
solitary period. In this respect his writing strongly resembles the inscriptions of the ancients. On
comparing the sheet of copy which he furnished for
the printer, with the published History of France, I
find a number of essential variations. The probability is, that James Ballantyne, who was an accomplished scholar, or perhaps the press-corrector, who, in
Europe, is often possessed of no mean acquirements,
treated Sir Walter's manuscripts pretty much after
their own pleasure. The magic weaver had dis-

missed his fabric, wrought indeed in the firmest texture and the most beautiful figures and colours. But
the *finisher* went carefully over the whole, adjusted
the irregular threads, removed the unsightly knots,
stretched out every part to an agreeable smooth-
ness, and thus rendered the wonderful commodity
fit for the general market.

Reluctantly laying aside these memorials of the
Great Enchanter, we take up a very polite letter
from Joseph Buonaparte, enclosing the autograph of
his far more renowned brother.   It is on the outside
of a note addressed by Napoleon to Joseph, when
the latter was a member of the Council of Five
Hundred. It is written on a thick, firm piece of
paper, which has been clumsily and hastily sealed
with red sealing-wax. The seal is inscribed with
the name of Buonaparte, in the French, not the Italian mode of spelling it ; and bears the device of a
female figure leaning on a lictor's axe and rods.
The superscription is this :

> " Concityen
> Joseph Buonaparte
> deputé au conseil
> des 500
> *Paris.*"

Thus the autograph fixes its own date before 1800,
the Council of Five Hundred having been dissolved
on the 9th Nov. 1799. In fact, it is not at all impossible that this very *envelope* covered a note from
Napoleon to his brother, penned during that agitat-
ing week which preceded the death-blow of his
country's liberties.

If ever hand-writing was characteristic, this little superscription is decidedly so. Were a painter of genius employed to represent a field of battle by a few lines and dashes of a pen, he could not execute a closer resemblance than this. It is difficult to inspect it without being almost induced to stop one's ears. The i's and j's indeed, unlike those of Scott, are dotted; but the dots look exactly like flying bombs. The t's are all duly crossed; but they are crossed as was the bridge of Lodi; and that imagination must be slow indeed, which does not perceive that the hand which produced even this little specimen, was guided by a soul, whose congenial elements were power, rapidity, confusion, victory.

A singular juxta-position has brought near this autograph of Buonaparte the original copy of several stanzas of Delta, the peace-loving poet, published in Blackwood, and entitled, *I'll think of thee.*

What next has found its way to this little world of Autographs?

Lafayette's toast.

"The Holy Alliance of Nations is the cause of equal rights and universal freedom." Then follows the same in French, all in his own hand-writing.

About twenty specimens onwards, all of them very interesting, but out of the question to be noticed here, occures the skeleton of a sermon by the late Rev. Thos. Spencer.

Next, is an order of Southey the poet, on a bookseller, for Aretino and Strabo.

Next, a note from Wordsworth, but who will credit its being entirely concerned with the letting of land, the laying down of crops, and the productiveness of a certain blacksmith's shop?

There is a characteristic scrap from John Wesley, though a few of the words are unintelligible. The readable part of it is this:—"Within a few months I am brought much forward. A few more, and I shall be no more seen. May I * * *

Your affectionate friend and brother,

J. WESLEY."

Two sonnets by Bowles, in his own hand-writing, will gratify the lover of poetry, and remind him of the high testimony of Coleridge to the merits of that elegant bard.

Next, a manuscript of two pages by William Cobbett, which appears to be a diatribe against the English government for its conduct towards America during the last war.

Next, the beautiful lines of John Bowring, entitled, " Whither shall my spirit fly ?" written in his own hand, and marked by his own signature.

Next, a note from Lady Byron to her bookseller, ordering a number of theological works.

Next, a letter from Adam Clarke, inviting a distinguished clergyman of our own State, who was then in London, to visit him.

Next, a long and interesting letter from Whitefield on the subject of his school for orphans.

Dr. Franklin, in a letter lying near, says of Mr. Whitefield himself, " I knew him intimately upwards of thirty years. His integrity, disinterestedness, and indefatigable zeal in prosecuting every good work, I have never seen equalled, I shall never see excelled."

In turning to a large parcel of American autographs, I observed the following profound and valuable remark in a letter of Gouverneur Morris. Speaking of a distinguished Southern politician, he says, "He seems to me one of the best of men, who, even if they begin life wrong, soon get right ; and let me tell you, this thing is much more rare than experienced men suppose."

A letter from Bartram, the celebrated botanist, now attracts the eye. It is dated Charleston, So. Ca., April, 1775. To what friend it is addressed, does not appear ; but it is evidently dictated by a heart in which the love of goodness and of botany are both prevalent. "I wrote yesterday," he says, "to your son John, at Jamaica. I begged him to associate with the best characters, and at the same time I begged of him to take notice of the plants and other national productions of the island, and to send you the seeds and fruits. I am resolved to take another scout in the Indian countries. Believe I shall go among the Cherokees ; thence through the Creek nation to West Florida. I want to see the Western and mountainous parts of these colonies, where I hope I shall pick up some new things. It's look'd upon as hazardous, but I think there's a probability of accomplishing it."

Of Spurzheim, all that could be obtained was one

of his printed lecture tickets, on which he wrote the date, and on which he also stamped his favourite seal, " *Res, non verba quæso.*" Every relic of this distinguished individual has been in great demand ; and unfortunately the supply was diminished by the application of his heirs for every scrap on which he had written.

The autographs of *divines* form one of Mr. Tefft's divisions. And in this department he has the signature of every American Bishop since the Revolution.

Among the foreign autographs is a conspicuous list of the Ministers of France for several years after the restoration of the Bourbon dynasty. Some of the names are those of Baron Portalis, Duc de Broglie, Duc de Cadore, Serrurier, Menou, Duc de Bauzun, D'Hauterive, Talleyrand, Neuville, Pelletier, La Febvre, Dessoles, Choiseul, Deffands, Rayneval, Fouché, Clermont de Tonnerre, Molé, Polignac, Montmorenci, Decrés, Marshal Jourdain, Richelieu, Sebastiani, &c. &c. which are generally subscribed to foreign consular papers. There are also a few French Revolutionary documents.

Despairing, however, to present any thing approaching an adequate idea, or even complete catalogue, of the various treasures of this collection, I will only further remark, that the curious in these matters may here inspect entire letters or notes of James Hogg, Alexander Munro the anatomist, Gen. Braddock, Rev. Andrew Fuller, a celebrated Baptist clergyman, Haydon, the distinguished painter and

writer, Lord Brougham, of whom there are two specimens, Tennant, author of Anster Fair, Dr. Chal-
mers, John Galt, Lucy Aiken, Dr. Parr, John Wilson's note to William Blackwood, Granville Sharp,
Clarkson to Joseph Lancaster, Duke of Bedford to
the same, Rev. Dr. Rippon, Thomas Campbell, Wm.
Jay the preacher, Shee the poet and artist, Rogers
the poet, Martin the painter, Mrs. Grant of Laggan,
J. R. M'Culloch, Murray the publisher, Mrs. M'Le-
hon the Clarinda of Robert Burns, Dibdin the Bio-
grapher, Principal Baird of Edinburgh, Wilberforce,
Du Portail the French minister, Atherton the poet,
Dr. Wardlaw, Dr. Currie of Liverpool, Rev. Row-
land Hill, Wiffen, the excellent translator of Tasso,
Count Ney, the Rev. Matthew Wilks, William
Godwin, Miss Jewsbury, the late Mrs. Fletcher,
Godoy the Prince of Peace, Miss Francis Wright,
Rev. Matthew Henry the Bible Commentator, the
Duke of Wellington, Thomas Hartwell Horne, Sir
John Sinclair, Archdeacon Wrangham, Matthews
the Comedian, Francis Jeffrey, Mr. Alison of Edin-
burgh, Leigh Hunt, Prof. Jamieson of Edinburgh,
Scoresby the Artic Navigator, Robert Owen, But-
ton the antiquary to the Duke of Bedford, William
Roscoe, Rev. Prof. Lee of Cambridge, with mottoes
in Hebrew, Arabic, Persian, and English, Lord Gren-
ville, (an order for some plants,) Mrs. Hemans to a
friend on songs and song-writing, Lockhart, Napier,
present editor E. R., Thomas Coke the celebrated
Methodist, Dr. Lettsom, an elegant letter of introduction from Baron Humboldt to the late Stephen

Elliott, written in French, Geo. Canning, Gen. Oglethorpe when in Georgia, Dr. Fothergill to John Bartram, De Quincy the Opium-eater, James the Novelist, Ryder, Bishop of Litchfield and Coventry, Gen. Moreau, Miss Edgeworth, and Miss Martineau.

Of *simple signatures*, we have those of Chateaubriand, Bishop Watson to a College bill of the late Judge Grimké when at the University of Cambridge, Sir Robert Peel, Miss Benger, Lord Sidmouth, Lord Lauderdale, William Howitt, Sir A. Cooper, Earl Grey, Sir Jas. M'Intosh, Helen Maria Williams, Lord Castlereagh, Lord Eldon, Lord Erskine, two of Louis the Sixteenth, one of Lord Melbourne, the Marchioness of Wellesley, Marshal Davoust, Leigh Richmond, Joseph Hume, Geo. Thomson the friend of Burns, William Pitt, the present Duke of Grafton, the present King of England when Duke of Clarence, being the address and franking of a letter from him to Prof. Lee of Cambridge, Lord John Russel, Duke of Devonshire, franks of a large number of members of Parliament, Lord Liverpool, Countess of Huntingdon, Whitfield's friend; Talleyrand, an almost impenetrable signature; Buckingham the traveller and writer, Lord Hill, and Sismondi.

The collection which I now have attempted to describe is liberally open to the inspection of every respectable inquirer. Any important contribution to it is received with gratitude by the proprietor. Should the present essay awaken attention to the subject, the writer will recur with increased pleasure to his *week spent among autographs.*

ANOTHER WEEK AMONG THE AUTOGRAPHS.

A number of valuable acquisitions has been made to the collection of T. K. Tefft, Esq. and his kindness permits the following notices of them to be communicated to the public.

We have, first, a letter from John Pynchon to his son in London, dated Boston, May 18, 1672. This was forty-two years after the settlement of Boston. The sight of this manuscript carries us back to "the day of small things" in that now populous and extended city. We see in imagination its three or four churches scattered among the three hills of the place. We see its few crooked streets (a quality which they still possess,) winding about to accommodate the gathering settlers. Boston at this period contained probably three thousand inhabitants. Even then they were a noble set of men. Only eleven years after the date of this letter, when the colony of Massachusetts fell under the displeasure of Charles II. who issued a decree against its charter, a legal town-meeting of the freemen was held, and the question was put to vote, whether it was their wish that the general court should resign the charter and the privileges therein granted, and it was resolved in the negative unanimously. Soon after, Sir Edward Andros was appointed the first royal governor, and his administration proving arbitrary and oppressive, the people took forcible possession of the fort in Boston, and of the castle in the harbor, turned the guns upon the frigate Rose, and compelled her to surrender, seized the governor, and held him a close prisoner under guard in the castle.   These were evidently the true progenitors of those sons, who, in 1765, resisted the Stamp Act, and in 1773 emptied the tea chests into the dock.

The letter before us, however, which begins with " Son Joseph," is only an effusion of anxiety and complaint from a loving father, who had heard no tidings from his son for a long time.   He seems to have resided at Springfield, Mass., and to have made a journey all the way to Boston to hear something of his son.   Though short, the letter is full of religious expressions.   How different in this respect from most letters in modern days.   The writer prays that his son may be delivered from the tempest of the times, and so with his earnest-prayers he leaves him to the Lord.

The next specimen (we take them promiscuously, without classification,) is worth more than its weight in gold.   It is no less than a long letter from the celebrated poet Wieland, author of Oberon, and numerous other works of the rarest merit.   It is addressed to Pfeffel, himself a jurist and diplomatist of considerable eminence.   Many an enthusiastic German would cheerfully give a small bit of his little finger to be possessed of this treasure.   It is observed by Menzel, one of the ablest living German critics, that " it was Wieland who first restored to German poetry the free and fearless glance of a child

34*

of the world; a natural grace, a taste for cheerful
merriment, and the power of affording it. The
cheerful, amiable, refined Wieland, he continues, a
genius exhaustless in grace and lightness, in wit and
jest, banished the unnatural from German poetry,
discovered nature in the world as it is, and taught
the national mind to move easily, firmly, and in harmony." From this description, we may suppose
that a German would value an autograph of Wieland as highly as an Englishman would prize one
of Pope or Addison, or an American, one of Irving.
It does not diminish, but rather enhances the value
of the specimen before us that it was written when
Wieland was quite a young man—only about seventeen years old; for we have examples enough of his
composition at more advanced periods, and our curiosity is particularly gratified by seeing how the youthful poet and scholar expressed himself, so long before
he felt the public eyes of admiration and criticism fastened upon him. The letter itself is of sufficient interest to be extracted entire. We make use, with a
few immaterial alterations, of a translation furnished Mr. Tefft by some German friend:

"GOETTINGEN, April 16, 1750.

" *Dearest and best Aulic Counsellor :**

"I have been waiting three or four days for the
departure of the mail, to give you some accounts of

* An Aulic Counsellor was one of the judges of the Supreme
Court of the German empire.

my journey and happy arrival at Goettingen. Our fate, as far down as Durlach, you have learned from Mr. Wild. I arrived safely at Frankfort, where I stayed the greatest part of the time with Mr. Sarasin, and after three days went to Cassel, where I experienced a kind reception from the Countess. She desired me to let the mail-coach proceed, and promised to procure me a private conveyance for Goettingen. An acquaintance of hers conducted me through the whole town, and gave me a sight of every thing remarkable. I had her invitation for supper, breakfast, and dinner. I related to her the conduct of her son,—his faults—his indolence— without the least reserve. She was much pleased when she heard that, notwithstanding all of them, he still retained the affection of yourself and Mr. Lerfe. She promises to aid you in some suitable method to effect his correction. Full confidence is placed in your skill and experience in education, and she will shortly write to Colmar. The letter I received at Frankfort from the Count, gave her a great deal of uneasiness, as it spoke of a rising upon his right shoulder. It was her wish that he should drink beer in lieu of wine at his meals. May I beseech you, my dearest Mr. Pfeffel, to console her on these two points in your next monthly letter. She truly deserves all the attention and pains that you can take on her account. She is the noblest woman—the best mother—so without all pretension, and full of kindness. Never have I seen so many good qualities united in one woman. Do not consider this a blind judgment of mine ; on the contrary, I was fully prejudiced against her ere I knew her so completely, and I feel persuaded, that after the visit she intends paying you, you will be of the same opinion with me. The Count, as much as I esteem his good heart, is not worthy of such a mother. May you soon be able to give her better news of him. She expects none before the expiration of three months, but flatters herself that her contemplated measures, together with his governors, will produce a change of mind. She gave me a letter of introduction to Pastor Feder, and desired me to write to her from time to time.

"Monday the 10th, I arrived here at Goettingen. Your son is perfectly well. We board together with young Stonar, (an excellent youth,) Escher from Zurich, and Zwickig ; and as our chambers are close together, we can always be in company. He has given me his entire confidence, and I think we shall continue in the closest harmony. How great is my good fortune to cultivate that friendship with the son which his noblest father has honored me with ! To-morrow our lectures commence, four of which we have in common, and we can repeat together.

"I cannot express my thanks for your letters of introduction to Mr. and Mrs. Less, and the kindness and indulgence you have favoured me with. It is my daily wish that an opportunity may occur to enable me by deeds to show that I am not ungrateful.

"I am much pleased with this city and its establishments, but never walked a more costly pavement.

The purse must be continually in hand, and every thing is paid for fourfold.

"May you, my dearest and best Aulic Counsellor, continue in uninterrupted health. Remember me in the circles of your amiable friends, your dearest consort, Mr. Lerfe, Luce and his worthy companion, the country counsellor, most kindly ; and accept assurances of my everlasting attachment and regard Your obedient friend and servant,   WIELAND."

The document receives an additional value by being endorsed in the hand-writing of Pfeffel himself —" Wieland, ce 24 April, 1750." Thus we have a a double autograph on one instrument.

We next take up a curious old affair, dated somewhere in England, in 1662, and addressed to the Mr. John Pynchon already noticed. It purports to be a letter, partly of religious consolation, and partly of business ; and both consolation and business, as was the custom in those earnest old times, are discussed with all the writer's heart. The hand-writing is beautiful, but peculiar, and not to be decyphered by many modern eyes. It displays a laudable attention to economy of paper. There is nothing in it, however, sufficiently striking to demand an extract.

Then follows a note from E. H. Barker, Esq. one of the book-worms of England, and editor of Webster's Dictionary in that country. It is an apology to a friend for not being able to find some volume or other belonging to him, but promises that " to-morrow the fox shall be *unearthed* " from a very large box of books and papers where it lies.

The next is a truly precious memorial—a note of Alexander Cunningham from Dr. Hugh Blair, author of the "Sermons" and "Lectures on Rhetoric." Both the authorship and the subject-matter induce us to extract it entire, although it has already been printed in Currie's Life of Burns.

"*Dear Sir*,—As you told me that you had in view in the new Edition of Mr. Burn's works to publish some of his Letters, I now send you enclosed (as I promised you,) his Letter of thanks to me upon his leaving Edinburgh. It is so much marked by the stroke of his Genius, that I thought it worth while to present it, among letters from some other persons. If you think it proper to be published with other Letters of his, I have no objection. You will please take a copy of it, and send me back the Original, which I mean to keep. I would have called with it, but I am still confined by some remains of the Gout, and by a Cold which I contracted on coming to town.

"Yours, most faithfully,   HUGH BLAIR.
"*Argyle Square, Friday, 2d December.*"

It will be seen here that Dr. Blair in a few instances retains the antique fashion of beginning his noun-substantives with capital letters. Another peculiarity, and identical with Sir Walter Scott's, which we formerly noticed, is, that he rarely ever dots an i or crosses a t, and is much too sparing of his punctuation. Out of the thirty-eight small i's occurring in the note, to say nothing of several neglected j's, only five are dotted. What could have been the secret cause of this distinction? Was it mere caprice, or was it everlasting principle? Perhaps a few dots were conscientiously sprinkled here and there to preserve the justs rights of this excellent little letter from utter prostration. The t's fare a great deal worse, for they have not the sign of a cross from the beginning to the end of the note. There is nothing, not even a difference in length, to distinguish them from the lofty l's. The entire note, however, is written in a large, bold, legible hand; wonderful almost, in fact, for a man of about eighty years of age, which Dr. B. must have been at the time of writing it. Do we then see before us the actual chirography in which were penned those beautiful and admirable sermons that have charmed so many thousand readers of taste and pious sensibility, as well as those far-famed lectures, which, in spite of some defects, have formed and guided the taste of the last and present generations of English and American scholars? Emotions, at once classical and sacred, may well be excused for overflowing at the sight of a relic like this. Nor can we be induced to dismiss it without fondly lingering over it a little longer, and detecting even the slightest peculiarity, which may transport us in imagination into the familiar presence of the much honored dead. Behold, then, the highly decorated flourish of the initial H in the signature of Hugh Blair! See the long and graceful dash which the hand of the octogenarian struck forth upon the superscription of the note! Who can fail to perceive

even in these minute characteristics, the external
traces of that elegant mind which had so long been
employed in the fervent contemplation of beauty in
all its forms and manifestations?

We must also notice the large thick black wafer,
which mutely tells the story of some recent bereave-
ment in the family of the venerable sage. The irregular folds, which considerably differ from a perfect parallelogram, shall be charitably ascribed to
the trembling hand of age, or to the unavoidable
hurry of the moment. Doubtless the writer had
many billets to answer, and many attentions to
respond to, on his occasional visits to town. Nor
shall criticism be severe on the slight mistake at the
beginning of the note, where, in the expression
" Mr. Burn's works," by a wrong location of the
apostrophe, the poet's name is written as if it were
Burn instead of Burns. We remember that some
enemy of the Doctor during his lifetime, goaded by
the fact that ten editions of the first volume of his
sermons were called for in one year after their publication, malignantly sent forth to the world an appalling list of all sorts of errors discovered in that single volume of a Professor of Rhetoric and Belles
Letters in the University of Edinburgh. A far different feeling, even a sacred and revering curiosity,
has actuated us in thus examining, as it were, the
very shreds and dust of this hallowed instrument,
which we now reluctantly dismiss.

We have next a sensible, fatherly letter, dated
Edinburgh, 1786, from the Earl of Dalhousie to

some teacher in Colmar on the Continent, to whom he had consigned his two sons for their education. He wishes their preceptor to pay particular attention to their Latin, but leaves every thing else to his experience and discretion.

Following this, we take up what must be allowed on all hands to be quite an autographical gem. It is the superscription of a note, addressed by Frederic the Great to his confidential friend and correspondent, the distinguished Baron de la Motte Fouqué. The paper employed by his Majesty was a thick, coarse, bluish white. But what had the greatest warrior of the age, when writing to one of his ablest generals, to do with pink-colored, hot-pressed, wire-wove, gilt-edge, billet-doux fabrics? The superscription is written in a noble and beautiful style—bold, grand, flowing, as if executed by a hand accustomed to the victories of the seven years' war—at the same time, however, perfectly distinct and legible, as if characteristic of a monarch who was equally inclined to the pursuits of literature and taste. The leading address is in French, after this fashion :

> "To my General of Infantry,
> The Baron de la Motte Fouquè,
> at
> Brandenburg."

At one corner of the superscription is written in the German language this announcement :—"Accompanied by a box of cherries, and two melons."

On another fold of the paper is written in French, in Fouque's hand-writing, which confers on it a highly additional value, the following notice :—

> " Sans-Souci, July 5, 1766.
>   Invitation to come to Sans-Souci,
>   together with the reply."

Sans-Souci, it will be remembered, was the well-known name of the palace near Potsdam, where Frederic the Great was fond of residing. He is sometimes called the philosophe of *Sans-Souci.*

The autograph is still farther enriched by a distinct and finely preserved seal of the royal coat of arms. The device is gorgeously beautiful.

Two intelligent Germans, to whom we have shown the whole specimen, much doubt whether, after all, it contains the veritable hand-writing of the renowned monarch. They assert that Frederic having only had a French education, was incapable of writing such correct German as the inscription in the corner of the note. They think it probable that the whole direction proceeded from the pen of the Royal secretary. If these suggestions should prove correct, of course the delightful visions of our imagination respecting the correspondency of the hand-writing with Frederic's character must be dispelled into air, unless we suppose that the secretary himself, by long and intimate acquaintance with his master, had imbibed some of his lofty qualities.

The votaries of legal literature may next enjoy a

rare treat from inspecting a business-letter written by William Murray, afterwards Earl of Mansfield, to the Marchioness of Annandale. It is dated Lincoln's Inn, 1st June, 1742, the year in which he was appointed Solicitor General at the age of thirty-seven. Accompanying, though unconnected with this letter, is the endorsement of a pecuniary draft by Lord Stormont, father of Lord Mansfield.

Adjoining this, we have a ticket of admission into Professor Dalziel's highest Greek class, with the name of Alexander Murray written upon it by the Professor himself. The sight of it may refresh many an eye that owes the deepest obligations to those lucid notes in the Collectanea Majora and Minora.

There is next a very curious historical document, penned by the Earl of Annandale in the year 1707, in the midst of the troubles which distracted Scotland at that period. Many a letter has been printed far less interesting than this. It transports us to the very field of battle, where we are told of prisoners coming in and Highlanders threatening attacks, and the Duke of Argyle having returned to the camp, and eight score of the enemy having just been seen climbing the hills, &c. &c., and all written on a piece of paper so small as to show the extreme scarcity of that article even in the government camp.

Lo! another precious relic! A leaf from the Diary of Henry Kirke White, the poet. We all remember that poor Henry passed some time in an attorney's office before he was assisted by Mr Wil-

berforce to prepare for an University education.
While breathing that ungenial atmosphere, he committed to paper this brief skeleton-record of a few of
his unhappy days. The very sight of it is dreary
and melancholy like the writer's heart. All that we
here learn of his occupations, is, that on Saturday,
the 8th of some month or other, he was engaged in
" entering up the Hall books ; on Monday the 10th,
copying all the morning certain letters for Mr. En-
field ; on Wednesday, fair copying a schedule of
fines and amercements ; on Thursday, do. do.,
another copy on unstamped parchment ; on Friday
the 14th, drawing advertisement of two heifers, the
property of Edward Musson, being stolen or strayed
out of his close in the parish of Radford. Attending the printer therewith," &c. &c.

One blessed blank appears amidst these worldly
details. It is that of Sunday the 9th. Nothing is
recorded under this date, except the simple day.
And one cannot but vividly sympathise with such
a being as Kirke White for this short though happy respite from labours which he must have loath-
ed. Henry Kirke White's Sabbath ! It is almost
a subject for a poem. Imagination follows him to
his closet, to his church, to his lonely evening
walk, to the long portion of his night spent over
his Bible, his Milton, or some of England's noblest
divines. The hand-writing of this specimen is manly, and elegantly plain.

This is succeeded by another rarity ; a letter from
the celebrated George Whitefield, dated London,

June 13, 1755, then in the 41st year of his age, to his nephew James Whitefield at Savannah in Georgia. It is so characteristic, that it must here be inserted entire :

" *My Dear Jemmy*—I wrote to you a few days ago by a Carolina ship, and since that have received your two letters, which convinced me that you was not ungrateful. May this crime of crimes in respect either to God or man, be never justly laid to your charge ! Remember your present as well future and eternal all in a great measure depends on the improvement of a few growing years. Be steady and diligent and pious *now*, and you will find that God will do wonders for you. The Captain is mightily pleased ; and your father, notwithstanding his affection to see you, is glad you are provided for. Your sister Fanny will soon be married, and Fanny Greville is already disposed of. Her husband (a young attorney of Bath,) hath sent me a very obliging letter. Oh that my relations were born of God ! I hope you will not rest without it. To encourage you in outward matters, I have sent you, in *part of payment*, some loaf sugar, which I thought would be a good commodity. Your father also hath sent you some buckles, knit breeches, and a dolphin cheese, with a letter. All which I hope will come to hand. Write often ; work hard, and pray much, and believe me to be, my dear Jemmy,

" Your affectionate uncle and assured friend,

"G. W."

We next come to a little note of thanks from Frederic William, the present King of Prussia, to a German author, from whom he had received the present of a Biography of Calvin. The signature alone is in the hand-writing of Frederic, the rest of the note by some private secretary. There is nothing else remarkable about it, except perhaps the royal munificence with which a whole sheet of superfine letter paper is devoted to the writing of three close lines. The circumstance marks perhaps an advance in refinement from the whitey-brown paper employed in the note of Frederick's warlike predecessor, which has already been remarked upon.

Following this, is a curious affair, which appears to be enveloped in a little mystery. It is something like a mourning card, containing an inscription by the celebrated Lavater. It was lately given to Dr. Sprague of Albany by Lavater's son-in-law at Zurich, in Switzerland, the birth-place and residence of the great physiognomist. The following is an exact translation of the whole inscription :

" To a Friend after my Death.
Let every thing be a sin to thee, and that
alone, which separates thee from the
Lord.   18th November, 1794. L."

The sentiment is so excellent, that we will attempt to give it here a metrical clothing :

Detest as sinful, and detest alone
Whate'er removes thee from th' Eternal One.

Another card succeeds, of a different kind, but of
still more value, probably, as an Autograph. It is from
the celebrated Goethe, who asks of Professor Riemer
the loan, for a short time, of the Bohemian Gram-
mar. This, by the way, is an excellent method of
borrowing books. The card is a kind of substantial
acknowledgment, which leads at once to the re-
covery of a missing volume often of more value to
its owner than money. When will the borrowers
of books exercise consciences void of offence in this
matter, and be as scrupulous in restoring to the proprietor some cherished author, or the fragment of
some precious set of twelve or twenty volumes, as
they are in renewing a note at the Bank or discharg-
ing the bill of a flourishing tradesman? Until a
more scrupulous punctuality on this subject shall prevail, the morality and the civilization of lit rature
will be far from perfect. To return to Goethe's
card, we have only further to observe, that the *signature* alone appears to be the hand-writing of the great
magician-poet, while the rest of the manuscript probably proceeded from his amanuensis.

It was intimated on a former occasion that one
of the strongest passions of Autograph-collectors is
to procure a complete list of the Signers of the Declaration of Independence. Mr. Tefft has recently
received from his friend, Dr. Sprague of Albany,
among numerous other invaluable specimens, the autograph of *Richard Stockton*, one of the Signers of
the Declaration. It has been for years upon his
list of desiderata, and was almost despaired of, as be-

ing probably no longer extant. Accompanying it was an autograph of *Mrs.* Richard Stockton, the poetess, who received from Gen. Washington the highest compliment he ever paid.

Among the less important documents of this collection, we have—

First, A Note, dated Strasbourg, 1785, from Charles, Prince of Soleure, who appears to be a very dutiful young prince, and is anxious to make arrangements for a visit from his two brothers.

Next, A Note from Constable, the great Edinburgh publisher, enclosing Two Guineas to Alexander Murray, who has sketched on the back of it the outlines of a sermon.

Next, one from Sophie de la Roche, a celebrated authoress of the last century, who appears in this note to address some English friends who had placed a daughter under her care at Spire.

Next, a superscription in the hand-writing of Spring Rice, one of the ablest of the present ministry of Great Britain.

Next, a Note of two lines from Benjamin Constant, informing Monsieur Monod where some individual resides. This is a valuable autograph.

Next, one from Napier, the present editor of the Edinburgh Review, who almost rivals his predecessor Lord Jeffrey for the illegibility and obliquity of his manuscript.

Next, a precious scrap from Alexander Humboldt, informing some publisher of the height of the city

of Hague, to be noticed in the margin of a forth-
coming volume.

Next, a Manuscript Leaf from the original copy
of the celebrated "Words of a a Believer," by the
Abbé de la Mennais.   Wild as the work is, he appears to have adopted much pains and method in the
transcription of it.

Next, a sweet little Quaker Note from Amelia Opio
to some bookseller, ordering a number of works,
which she wishes to present to a friend.

Next, a billet from George Combe, the celebrated
phrenologist, on the subject of an overcharged letter in the Post-Office.

Next, a scrap from Dr. Bowring, soliciting interest to obtain certain subscriptions.

We then come to a mass of billets, memoranda,
and letters—from Schlosser, an admired German
poet ; from Grand Pierre, head of the Mission School
in Paris, a very eloquent and able man ; from D'
Aubigné Professor at Geneva, author of the History
of the Reformation, and various other works ; from
Gaussen, another distinguished professor at Geneva ;
from Steffens, the great natural philosopher ; from
Raumer, author of Travels in England, &c. &c. ;
from Gesenius, the Biblical critic ; from Cheneviere,
author of many works ; from Philip Buttman, the
great Greek scholar ; from Francis Bopp, the best
Sanscrit scholar of the age ; from Freytag, the Ori-
entalist ; from Frederic de Schleiermacher, the greatest theologian of his time ; from A. Pfeffel, the
diplomatist, and brother of the blind poet ; from

John Henry Pestalozzi, distinguished for his efforts in the cause of education, &c. ; from Boettiger, the celebrated Antiquarian ; from Twester, author of many works ; from Professor Hengstenberg, the great Biblical critic, &c. ; from Coquard, the poet, preacher, &c. &c. ; from Malan, the reformer ; from the Bishop of Exeter ; from the Bishop of Quebec ; from G. De Felece, one of the most learned theologians in France ; a leaf from Busler's Church History, &c. &c. &c. ; Notes or letters from George Bennett, Esq. the excellent missionary circumnavigator ; from William Youngman, author of various theological and other works, a man of great talent ; from George Payne, Tutor at the Western Academy, and author of the Elements of Mental Philosophy ; from Felix of Bolbec, one of the ablest theological writers in France ; from Principal Baird of Edinburgh, who applauds and criticises a literary work recently presented him by a friend ; from the Rev. Dr. Lee, the greatest ecclesiastical historian in Scotland ; from J. S. Buckingham, the indefatigable and enterprising Member of the House of Commons ; from John Wilks, the celebrated living champion of the Dissenting interest in Great Britain ; from the Duchess de Broglie, daughter of Madame De Stael ; from the late Dr. Robert Winter, the revered patriarch of the Baptist denomination ; from Pfeffel, nephew of the German poet, and ambassador to Bavaria ; from David Irving of Edinburgh, a distinguished author ; from the Rev. Dr. Arundel, Secretary of the London Missionary Society, to George

Bennett, Esq.—an interesting letter ; from the Rev. Greville Ewing of Glasgow, author of a Greek Lexicon and other works, a letter evincing great delicacy of sentiment; from Oberlin, a celebrated Professor at Strasburg ; from the German poet Knebel, translator of Lucretius, &c. ; from Mullner, one of the greatest tragedians of Germany, whose merits have been made known in England by translations of several of his tragedies in Blackwood's Magazine ; from the Rev. Dr. Burnet, one of the ablest extempore speakers in Great Britain ; and from the Marchioness of Annandale, dated 1725, acknowledging the receipt of £1500, arrears of jointure, due her from her husband.

The admirers of German sacred literature will be gratified by the inspection of a manuscript leaf from the original of Neander's Church History. He is the most popular ecclesiastical historian of the present day. The sheet before us appears to be the conclusion of the explanatory notes, and inculcates the spirit in which true Christianity can alone be received and cultivated, viz: the spirit of a little child. This manuscript was presented by the author himself to the Rev. Dr. Sprague of Albany, who again generously transferred it to Mr. Tefft.

Allusion has already been once or twice made to Dr. Alexander Murray. This gentleman was Professor in the University of Edinburgh, and the greatest Oriental scholar of his day. He died about the year 1813. He was author of a " History of the European Languages," " Life of Bruce the Traveller,'

and other works. We have before us a few extremely interesting memorials of his genius and pursuits.
One of them is a sheet of paper, crowded in every
part with some of the exercises of the great linguist
in acquiring a foreign tongue. Among his other accomplishments, he was an elegant poet ; and accordingly, we have here a few rough but very curious
sketches from his muse. The following unfinished
stanza, which appears to be the commencement of
a song intended for some festive club, will strongly remind us of the daring, reckless tone of Robert
Burns :—

> " Though whingean' carles should vex their hearts,
>   And ca' our social meetings sin,
> Awa! we ken their halie arts !
>   An honest man defies their din.
> When brithers twelve in Session sat,
>   And HE was HEAD that ken'd them a',
> The Deil came ben, and claim'd his debt,
>   The *sourest* man————."

Probably he was here about to write *amang them a'*.
But perceiving that it would make a false rhyme, he
threw by the whole affair, which has thus remained
incomplete.

On another scrap of paper, we find a few elegiac
stanzas, quite unfinished, and full of interlineary cor-
rections and erasures, but intermingled with beautiful
touches of poetry.

A gentleman of Charleston, S. C. has recently
presented Mr. Tefft with a letter addressed to him

seventeen years ago, by the celebrated Macauley, late a distinguished member of Parliament, and now a Judge in Bombay, and one of the most brilliant contributors to the Edinburgh Review. It was written when both himself and his correspondent were members of the University of Cambridge in England, and bears evident marks of that resplendent talent which has since so frequently dazzled and delighted the public of Great Britain. Some characteristics of Macauley as a writer may be found in the Pruning Knife of Southern Rose, Vol. 4, No. 8.

Another gentleman of Charleston has contributed a signature of Gen. Moultrie, attached to some public instrument, and accidentally found in the street. Moultrie had a curious device or flourish with which he ornamented his signature. It resembled more than any thing else a *fortification,* with its bastions, its salient angles, its retreating angles, its squares, compartments, &c. Might there not have been always about him a kind of unconscious memory of the most important crisis of his life, and which outwardly expressed itself in this very characteristic manner?

In a former article on Autographs, we mentioned the collection of the Rev. Dr. Raffles of Liverpool. We are now permitted to present the following extract of a letter from that gentleman to Mr. Tefft respecting some portion of his collection, and we must confess that the extraordinary value and magnificence of its contents far surpass our utmost previous conceptions.

" You ask me about my collection of Autographs,
36

my method of arrangement, &c. &c. I have several series. The first and principal series consists
of the autographs, chiefly letters, of eminent and
remarkable persons of all classes and countries from
the time of Henry VII. of England to the present
day. These are put upon tinted paper of folio size ;
one leaf of the paper containing the autograph, and
the other the portrait, or something else illustrative
of the history of the individual :—for instance, with
Addison's autograph you will find his portrait after
Sir Godfrey Kneller, and an original number of the
Spectator. With Dr. Johnson's, you will find a
view of the house in which he was born, at Litchfield, and the house in which he died, &c. This
collection I hope soon to bind, and expect it will
amount to twenty volumes. To this I intend adding
a supplementary volume of Biographical Notices.
This volume is alphabetically arranged.

2d—My *American collection.* This is not yet arranged. It contains the signers of the Declaration
of Independence—one of which alone is wanting*
—all the Presidents, with many of the Vice-Presidents and Governors of States ; Divines, and other
public characters,—civil, naval, military and miscellaneous. I have not yet determined as to the
way in which I shall arrange these ; but if on folio
tinted paper like the others, I should think that it
would amount to eight or ten volumes.

3d—*Authors.* I have a large collection of letters

* George Taylor.

of authors of all kinds, which I intend to bind up alphabetically, with portraits in quarto, leaving a blank leaf between each letter for biographical no-tices. This will contain many duplicates of such as are in the first-mentioned series, and to these I may perhaps add Artists.

4th—*Nobility.* Containing duplicates of such as are in the first collection by reason of their celebri-ty, or in the third in consequence of their being authors; or such as, having nothing but their *rank* to distinguish them, are already in neither of the above series.

5th—To the above classes I may add several distinct and separate volumes, which are complete in themselves;—e. g.

A volume containing one hundred and twenty au-tographs, letters of the late Rev. Andrew Fuller—quarto.

A volume containing letters of Fuller, Ryland, Fawcett, Pearce (of Birmingham,) &c.—folio.

A volume of letters to George Whitefield, all en-dorsed by himself—folio.

Do.   Do.   —quarto.

The entire MS. of James Montgomery's *Pelican Isle,* with other poems, composing his last published volume—quarto.

The entire MS. of Wiffen's translation of Tasso —2 vols. quarto.

The Church Book of Oliver Heywood, the reject-ed Minister.—An invaluable little book, written wholly with his own hand, containing his covenant, and that of the church, and biographical notices of the members.

A Thesis, by **Dr. Watts.**

A Manuscript (Algebra,) by Abraham Sharp of Bradford, the friend and correspondent of Sir Isaac Newton,—a 4to. vol.

A considerable collection of foreigners, not included in the first series.

A collection of Notes, which will form several volumes octavo.

A folio volume of documents on vellum.

A folio volume of *franks* of the Peers at the coronation of George IV, &c. &c. &c.

I am, sir, &c.   THOS. RAFFLES."

In a letter recently received, Dr. Raffles says: " Pray, are your *Signers complete?* I look with mingled emotions of sorrow and hope upon the only *hiatus* I have in mine."

We formerly inquired why so considerable a proportion of Autograph-collectors appear to be *clergymen.* Might not a phrenologist account for it by the faculty of *reverence,* which may be supposed to be common between both descriptions of persons? The same sentiment which conducts the mind to the venerable records of Scripture, and to the Ancient of Days, may guide them also to other relics of antiquity, and every surviving memorial of greatness. The following paragraph from the newspapers exhibits this taste in rather a curious form :—

" The Rev. Dr. Cotton, ordinary of Newgate,

has, far a long series of years, been devoting his attention to the collection of dying speeches, trials, &c. of celebrated criminals, as well as their autographs ; and whenever they could possibly be obtained, of their portraits also. The Rev. Ordinary likewise possesses an extraordinary collection of Chinese drawings, representing the torments in after-life upon evil-doers, according to Chinese belief."

In our first essay on Autographs, we complained that the English Cyclopedias contained very scanty and miserable notices of the subject. A friend has since kindly conveyed to us a volume of the " Dictionnaire de la Conversation et de la Lecture," from which we translate the following article, as an appropriate conclusion to our autographic lucubrations.

"AUTOGRAPH, from the Greek *autos*, self, and *grapho*, to write, signifies a writing from an author's own hand. If the men of former generations had attached the same value as we do to autograph manuscripts of great writers, to letters, and to the signatures of celebrated personages, we should neither be compelled to regret the loss of so many Greek, Latin, and French productions, of which there remain scarcely the titles or even a melancholy remembrance, nor the destruction of so many letters, memoirs, and diplomatic documents, which might have assisted in dissipating the darkness and the contradictions that envelope the history of ancient times and the middle ages, and in filling up the chasms with which it abounds. In countries

36*

where elementary instruction is as yet but little dif-
fused, in ages when it was unknown, and even at
very recent epochs, when it was too much neglected, avaricious, ignorant, or superstitious heirs
sold by weight, or delivered to the flames, without
scruple and without examination, all papers which
had been transmitted them by deceased relatives.
This is no longer the case at the present day, especially at Paris. The preservation of papers and of
autograph writings has become the object of a special anxiety, of a sort of idolatry, which among some
individuals has degenerated into a mania, a folly.
From this state of things has resulted a new kind of
commerce, which traffickers and speculators openly
undertake for the sake of profit. Letters, autographic documents, signatures affixed to diplomas, to
public acts, or to receipts, upon paper or parchment,
are taken clandestinely from public libraries, from
various archives, and from other literary and political depositories, by unfaithful officers or unscru-
pulous amateurs. They are sought for, they are
discovered, among grocers and dealers in goods.
Purchased for a mere trifle, they are resold to the
curious at a very high price. The search for these
kinds of manuscripts has also produced a new
branch of industry. As comparatively but few persons are wealthy enough to form expensive collections of autographs, the defect is supplied by engravings, and by the still more economic processes
of lithography. *Fac-similes*, traced after the originals, have been published, either separately, or in

new editions of our best classic authors, Corneille,
Racine, Boileau, Bossuet, Fénélon, Lafontaine, Madame de Sévigné, Voltaire, J. J. Rousseau, &c.
They have been inserted in picturesque travels and
other works. But it is principally in collections
devoted to the purpose that they are found in the
greatest number. One of the most prominent is the
work-entitled " L'Iconographie Universelle," (Universal Likeness-Magazine,) where the *fac-simile* of each
illustrious personage is subjoined to a biographical
notice of him, accompanied by his portrait. It is
especially in *L'Isographie des hommes célèbres,*
(*Hand-writings of celebrated Men Imitated,*) published in thirty-one numbers in quarto, from 1827 to
1830, that we find the most curious and the most
numerous collection of fac-similes of autograph letters and signatures. It contains not less than seven
hundred, of which the originals were borrowed from
the library of the King, from those of Vienna,
Prague, Munich, &c., from the archives of the
kingdom and of the different bureaus of administration, and from private cabinets. Lithographic collections of autographs have likewise appeared in
England and in Germany; but they are neither so
complete, nor so well arranged, nor so well executed.
The Royal Library of Paris possesses an immense
collection of manuscripts, autograph letters, and
signatures of kings, princes, ministers, warriors,
scholars, and illustrious persons of both sexes, whether French or foreigners, from the 13th century to
the present time. Conspicuous among them are the

voluminous correspondences of Marguerite of Va-
lois, Queen of Navarre; of the Dukes of Guise,
the constable de Montmorency, the mareschal de
Saulx-Tavannes, the cardinals du Bellay, de Richelieu, de Retz and de Noailles, de Peiresc, and de
Bouillaud; collections of letters from Francis I.
Henry IV. Louis XIV ; the original manuscript of
the Telemachus of Fenelon.   There also is a choice
selection of signatures by men of every kind of celebrity, affixed to receipts and other instruments on
parchment, among which are three or four signed
by Molière, and discovered a few years ago.   This
is all that remains of the hand-writing of our most
illustrious comic author.   Several thousand pounds'
weight of parchments of a similar description have
been sold at different times for very insignificant prices
to tradesmen, who, after selecting out the rarest and
most interesting specimens, have sold them again to
different amateurs.   The rest has been passed off
to bookbinders and to glue-makers.*   Autographs
also abound in the archives of the *Palais de Justice*,
and the different departments of administration, still
more in the archives of the kingdom, where, among
rare and curious documents, there is preserved a
charter of St. Louis, together with the original of
the instrument containing the famous oath pronounced, in the tennis-court at Versailles, in 1789,
and subscribed by the great majority of deputies to
the States General.   In the same place, also, are

* *Glue*, it may be remembered, is made from skins, and of
course from parchments.—*S. Rose.*

preserved the signatures of all the members of the National Convention, and of several other legisla. tive assemblies. However rich France may be in autographs, she is surpassed, not in number, but in antiquity and rarity, by Italy and Spain, if it is true that the library of Florence contains the Gospel of St. John, written by his own hand, and that several autograph manuscripts of St. Augustine exist in the library of the Escurial. The most important collections of autograph letters and signatures in the possession of amateurs in Paris, are those of M. Le Courte de Château-Giron ; the late Marquis de Dolomieu ; Mons. de Monmerqué, counsellor of the royal court ; Mons. Guilbert-Pixérécourt, a professor of literature ; Mons. Bérard, a Deputy and Counsellor of State ; Mons. Berthevin, formerly keeper of the Royal Printing Establishment. That of Mons. Villenave, more numerous perhaps than the others, contains, it is said, twenty-two thousand signatures or different writings ; but the greatest part of them were inscribed by persons more remarkable by their rank, their titles, and their offices, than for their actions or productions. For instance, all the French generals of the Revolution, even the most obscure, figure in this collection. We will also refer to the collections of M. de Saint-Gervais, the Marquis Aligre, M. Anatole de Montesquiou, and Mons. Perié, director of the Museum at Nimes, and husband of Madame Simons-Candeille."

NOTE.—It may be mentioned, as an instance of

the extreme difficulty of procuring a complete set of the signatures to the Declaration of Independence, that Mr. Tefft, although an American, and enjoying for many years great facilities in the pursuit of autographs, has been able, with the utmost exertions, to procure no more than *thirty-nine* out of the original *fifty-six* signatures. It is remarkable that Dr. Raffles of Liverpool should have been so much more successful in this branch of the pursuit. Mr. Tefft's present list of *desiderata* is as follows :—Braxton, Floyd, Hart, Lynch, jun., L. Morris, Middleton, Morton, Nelson, jun., Penn, Ross, Read, Rodney, Stone, Smith, Taylor, Thornton, Wilson. Should the present notices ever meet the eye of some *happy* possessor of any of these lacking signatures, perchance he may be still *happier* by generously transmitting them to the address of I. K. Tefft, Esq. Savannah, who, we feel assured, would in that instance complete the degrees of comparison, and become in very deed *the happiest*.

THE END.